Parliament and international relations

Parliament and international relations

Edited by
Charles Carstairs
and Richard Ware

Open University Press
Milton Keynes • Philadelphia

Open University Press
Celtic Court
22 Ballmoor
Buckingham
MK18 1XW

and
1900 Frost Road, Suite 101
Bristol, PA 19007, USA

First Published 1991

British Library Cataloguing in Publication Data

Parliament and international relations.
  1. Foreign relations
  I. Carstairs, Charles.   II. Ware, Richard
  327.41

  ISBN 0–335–09699–9
  ISBN 0–335–09698–0 (pbk)

Library of Congress Cataloging in Publication Data Available

Typeset by Scarborough Typesetting Services
Printed in Great Britain by St Edmundsbury Press Ltd
Bury St Edmunds, Suffolk

Contents

List of figures and tables

Abbreviations

ABM	Anti-ballistic missile
AIDS	Acquired immune deficiency syndrome
BAG	British–American Group
BBC	British Broadcasting Corporation
CAABU	Council for the Advancement of Arab–British Understanding
CAB	Commonwealth Agricultural Bureaux
CAFOD	Catholic Fund for Overseas Development
CCHR	Chile Campaign for Human Rights
CIA	(US) Central Intelligence Agency
CIIR	Catholic Institute for International Relations
COE	Council of Europe
CPA	Commonwealth Parliamentary Association
CPRS	Central Policy Review Staff
CPSU	Communist Party of the Soviet Union
CRO	Commonwealth Relations Office
CSCE	Conference on Security and Co-operation in Europe
DES	Department of Education and Science
DTI	Department of Trade and Industry
EC	European Community
ECC	European Communities Committee
EDM	Early Day Motion
EEC	European Economic Community
EP	European Parliament
EPC	European Political Co-operation
ESU	English-Speaking Union
FAC	Foreign Affairs Committee

FCO	Foreign and Commonwealth Office
FO	Foreign Office
FRG	Federal Republic of Germany
GCHQ	Government Communications Headquarters
GLCM	Ground-launched cruise missile
HC	House of Commons
HL	House of Lords
HMG	Her Majesty's Government
IMF	International Monetary Fund
INF	Intermediate-range nuclear forces
IPU	Inter-Parliamentary Union
IRA	Irish Republican Army
KGB	(USSR Committee of State Security)
LRINF	Longer-range intermediate nuclear forces
MEP	Member of the European Parliament
MoD	Ministry of Defence
MORI	Market and Opinion Research International
MP	Member of Parliament
NAA	North Atlantic Assembly
NAO	National Audit Office
NATO	North Atlantic Treaty Organization
ODA	Overseas Development Administration
ODM	Ministry of Overseas Development
PAC	Public Accounts Committee
PESC	Public Expenditure Survey Committee
PLO	Palestine Liberation Organization
PNQ	Private Notice Question
PQ	Parliamentary Question
PRCA	Public Relations Consultants Association
SAS	Special Air Service
SDI	Strategic Defense Initiative
SDP	Social Democratic Party
SLD	Social and Liberal Democrats
SNP	Scottish National Party
SO	Standing Order
SRINF	Shorter-range intermediate nuclear forces
TASS	Telegraphic Agency of the Soviet Union
Unesco	United Nations Educational, Scientific and Cultural Organisation
Unicef	United Nations (International) Children's (Emergency) Fund
UPUP	Ulster Popular Unionist Party
USIS	United States Information Service
UUP	Ulster Unionist Party
WEU	Western European Union

Foreword

The Study of Parliament Group was formed in 1964, and consists of academics interested in parliamentary studies, together with an approximately equal number of present and past officers of both Houses of Parliament. One of the aims of the Group is to

> advance and further the study of and reseach into methods of Government through Parliament (including the working of Parliament and Parliamentary Institutions) or other branches of political science in, and for the benefit of, the community as a whole, and to publish the results of such study and research.

Under the auspices of the Study of Parliament Group a wide range of books and articles has been published since 1964 and evidence has been presented to parliamentary committees.

In January 1987 the Group decided that it would be appropriate to conduct a study of 'Parliament and Foreign Affairs' and established a working group for this purpose with the following membership: Carole Andrews (House of Commons Library), Charles Carstairs (retired civil servant and House of Commons Clerk; joint convenor), Christopher Hill (London School of Economics; co-opted), Michael Lee (Bristol University), David Millar (retired official of European Parliament), Crispin Poyser (House of Commons Clerk), Michael Ryle (retired House of Commons Clerk), Donald Shell (Bristol University), Paul Silk (House of Commons Clerk), Philippa Tudor (House of Lords Clerk) and Richard Ware (House of Commons Library; joint convenor). The late David Watt, who joined the working group at the beginning, unhappily did not live to take a part in its work.

The working group benefited greatly from a series of frank, informal discussions with Members of both Houses of Parliament. These included two former Foreign Secretaries, several past and serving ministers in the Foreign and Commonwealth Office, Opposition spokesmen and prominent back-benchers from the Government and Opposition sides. Since all of these conversations took place under Chatham House rules we do not identify our chief witnesses here, but we are indebted to them for their time, comments and ideas.

We would also like to express our appreciation to the Nuffield Foundation for financial support of the project and to the following who assisted us at various stages: Hazel Armstrong, Dr Pamela Beshoff, Henry Bogsch, Jean Butler, Dermot Englefield, Richard Feasey, Professor Roger Morgan, Robert Rogers and Robert Twigger.

The Study of Parliament Group has no collective view on the matters discussed in this book and responsibility for the chapters which follow lies with the authors. We are conscious that events are moving fast and that some of the matters discussed in this book may soon be seen in a different light. For example a major review of the Select Committee system is being undertaken by the House of Commons Procedure Committee and new moves towards European Political Union are on the horizon. As this book goes to press war has broken out in the Middle East. We cannot anticipate events, but it is hoped that the book may help to clarify some of the problems which will confront Parliament in the years to come.

CC
RW

ONE

Introduction

■■■■■■■

'The record of Parliament on foreign affairs is unimpressive.' Such was
the conclusion of Professor Peter Richards in 1967.[1] More recently a
Chatham House paper, entitled *Options for British Foreign Policy in the
1990s* by Christopher Tugendhat and William Wallace, found that
Parliament was often left uninformed about the thinking behind foreign
policy decisions. The authors conclude, 'Quiet diplomacy – the attempt to
avoid public discontinuities by not admitting, even to the government's
parliamentary supporters, the longer-term implications of the policies
pursued – has, as we have argued, characterised the conduct of British
foreign policy.'[2] The members of the Study of Parliament Group who
initiated and carried out the present study did not begin with any
assumptions about the adequacy of current practices but they considered
that there was a need to examine how Parliament deals with foreign
affairs toward the end of the twentieth century and to ask whether, in this
particular sphere, Parliament has been as fully informed as it should be if
it is to exercise effective criticism or scrutiny over ministers' conduct of
their wide responsibilities. They wondered in particular how the British
Parliament would maintain an influence over British foreign policy as the
process of European Political Co-operation gathers pace. Can Westminster contribute to the monitoring of a common European foreign policy or
should it leave the job entirely to the European Parliament?

In this study we are not concerned only with the role of Parliament in
monitoring and scrutinizing the foreign policy of the executive. In certain
circumstances Parliament can itself become an actor, or rather a company
of actors, on the world stage. It may not be the habit of the British

Parliament to adopt resounding appeals to other parliaments and to world opinion, but British parliamentarians do actively participate in international relations. For example in the 1980s British MPs kept open a dialogue with representatives of Argentina through the Inter-Parliamentary Union (IPU) for several years while there were no diplomatic relations between the Governments of Britain and Argentina because of the Falkland Islands conflict. Small numbers of MPs also visited Syria, Libya and Iran and met senior political figures in those countries without the blessing of the British Government and sometimes against its advice. In the autumn of 1990 several prominent MPs paid similar visits to Iraq in the hope of negotiating the release of British citizens held there after the invasion and occupation of Kuwait. It also became common for British MPs to serve as official or unofficial observers of foreign elections, usually in countries attempting a return to democracy such as Panama, Namibia (both in 1989), Nicaragua, Hungary, Czechoslovakia, Bulgaria, the former German Democratic Republic and Romania (all in 1990). In a different sense Parliament plays a part in international relations every time that ministers or officials invoke the attitude of Parliament as a factor limiting their freedom to make concessions to other governments.

We have chosen our title with this wider role in mind, despite the fact that 'international relations' is not a term normally used in Parliament. The more usual parliamentary term is 'foreign affairs': there are foreign affairs debates, foreign affairs spokesmen and foreign affairs committees. The definition of foreign affairs tends to be very broad and may embrace aspects of trade, defence, economics and overseas aid. For the purposes of measuring parliamentary activity we have taken the term to refer to those matters which are primarily the responsibility of the Foreign and Commonwealth Office (FCO). By this definition overseas aid is included, because the Overseas Development Administration (ODA) is a specialized branch of the FCO, and so are arms control negotiations, but trade and most aspects of defence are excluded.

There has been little direct academic study of parliamentary handling of foreign affairs. Occasional shafts of light have been thrown on this subject incidentally to studies of Parliament (or the House of Commons) in general or of British foreign policy. Arthur Ponsonby published *Democracy and Diplomacy* in 1915 as part of his campaign against secret treaties and for 'democratic control'.[3] In the 1920s Francis Flournoy made a detailed study of the behaviour of the British Parliament in connection with the initiation of wars,[4] but failed to complete the additional studies which he planned on treaty-making and crisis management. More recently, but still over twenty years ago, came the already cited *Parliament and Foreign Affairs* by Peter Richards. William Wallace's *The Foreign Policy Process in Britain* of 1976 is much more concerned with Government than Parliament.[5]

The seeming neglect of the subject is surprising, since there can be few countries whose welfare, even whose identity, are more deeply involved in its relations with the outside world than Britain. It is difficult to escape the conclusion that this relative neglect reflects to some degree an inhibition on the part of Parliament itself. While the direct influence of the House of Commons over British foreign policy has fluctuated considerably since the mid-nineteenth century, there have always been parliamentarians (in Government and in Opposition) who felt that questions of foreign policy were altogether too difficult and too sensitive to be subjected to the same rough handling in Parliament as matters of domestic policy and legislation. This view appears to have been particularly prevalent since the Second World War, a reflection, perhaps, of the new sensitivities created by nuclear weapons and the risks involved in the long 'cold war'.

'Foreign affairs' were historically a prerogative matter, reserved to the sovereign, and by extension to the Cabinet which, in its early days, was known as 'the committee for foreign affairs'.[6] This view persisted long after parliaments had made good their place, even primacy, in the control of matters more obviously and continuously touching the immediate interests and the pockets of the electors. Domestic affairs were, and to a large extent continue to be, the daily bread of parliaments. The British Parliament after all came into being to approve 'supply' which then enabled it to exact concessions or actions from the Crown and these concessions or actions were in the main in the area of domestic policy. Several of the parliamentarians interviewed for this study commented on the lack of political and electoral mileage in foreign affairs most of the time. Foreign affairs may be of the greatest, even overwhelming, consequence for the welfare of the nation, but problems of foreign policy seldom present themselves so clearly or continuously to the electorate as do domestic issues.

Even after Parliament had effectively asserted its practical day-to-day control of domestic policy, by its determination of the complexion of the Government, the belief lingered on that the conduct of foreign affairs was a thing apart, something of an esoteric mystery, not appropriate for detailed intervention or constant scrutiny. In the course of numerous skirmishes in the nineteenth century Parliament won a precarious right to carry out retrospective investigations into obvious fiascos such as the conduct of the Crimean War, the Jameson Raid and the Dardanelles campaign but the option was only rarely exercised. The closest parallel in recent years – Lord Franks's investigation into the events preceding the Argentine invasion of the Falkland Islands in 1982 – was the work of Privy Councillors who were also parliamentarians rather than of Parliament itself, although both Houses debated the resulting report.[7]

Another reason for the distancing of Parliament from foreign affairs in recent years may lie in the fact that the direct calls of foreign policy and the Foreign and Commonwealth Office as an institution on the public purse are very limited. The contrast with military expenditure is instructive. In theory the use of force (or preparation for the possible use of force) in self-defence or in deterrence of aggression by another party is and should be subordinated to foreign policy. Clausewitz laid down that 'war is not a mere act of policy, but a true political instrument, a continuation of political activity by other means'.[8] From the parliamentary point of view, however, defence is directly expensive in a way which foreign policy usually is not. Consequently it is not surprising that FCO expenditure (including expenditure on overseas aid) is rarely debated in the House of Commons (even although the Foreign Affairs Committee conscientiously works its way through the Estimates and reports accordingly), whereas the Defence Estimates give rise to the annual ritual of a two-volume Government statement, a full-scale Defence Committee inquiry, a two-day debate on the floor of the House and several detailed reports each session by the Public Accounts Committee. It is worth noting that the predecessor of the Foreign Affairs Committee, namely the Defence and Foreign Affairs sub-committee of the Expenditure Committee, concentrated overwhelmingly on defence matters. This no doubt reflected the composition and interests of the sub-committee, but these in turn were not unrepresentative of the interests of the House at large.

Finance and the absence of legislation apart, is it still the case that foreign affairs must be regarded as inherently different in their parliamentary treatment from domestic affairs? There may be very good reasons to avoid negotiating with foreign governments over the dispatch boxes of the House of Commons, but Britain acts on the international stage as a partner in two major international organizations governed by treaty – the European Community and NATO – and seeks wherever possible to co-ordinate policies with the other members of these alliances. Britain is also, still, a permanent member of the United Nations Security Council. Much of the dialogue is conducted in private, but much also is conducted in public. Moreover, with fifteen partners in NATO and eleven in the European Community, some of them with quite different traditions in respect of parliamentary accountability in foreign policy, the British Government may not be in a position to determine how much information about negotiations within the alliance is made public. For example on the question of negotiations with the USSR to remove short-range nuclear weapons from Europe in the spring of 1989 and again a year later, the British Government tried to keep all of its public pronouncements in line with agreed NATO policy, but other allied governments, especially those of Belgium, the Netherlands and the Federal Republic of Germany, were prepared to be much more forthcoming about their national stance, partly because the issue had to be resolved within their governing coalition of political parties.[9]

The foreign affairs agenda has also changed in nature over the last twenty years. The British Parliament no longer legislates for those parts of the world which were formerly the Crown's territories overseas, and the British Government has reduced its commitments to the management of international affairs. British membership of the European Community (EC) has tended to occupy a major part of the parliamentary agenda since 1972. Other questions of foreign policy have been set largely by changes in the international system itself, particularly the proliferation of negotiations on economic and social matters. The Study Group took evidence from a number of back-benchers and ex-ministers who regretted that the 'end of empire' had made MPs more parochial, less skilled in foreign languages, and less directly involved in the affairs of other countries. Some went as far as to say that Britain has no real foreign policy beyond Europe and NATO.

The evolution of European Political Co-operation, that is the harmonization of the foreign policies of the twelve EC member states, also poses a challenge to traditional British attitudes towards parliamentary scrutiny of foreign affairs. Both Houses of Parliament have mechanisms for scrutinizing EC draft legislation and contributing thereby to the complex process of harmonization in which all twelve governments and parliaments are involved together with the European Commission and the European Parliament. These mechanisms have been severely tested by the legislation associated with the achievement of the single internal market at the end of 1992 and new procedures may have to be devised – a matter beyond the scope of this study.[10] However, what procedures exist for Parliament to monitor European Political Co-operation?

The executive began to make a series of adjustments to the structure of the overseas departments in the 1960s. The Duncan Committee developed the concept of 'the areas of concentration' and began thinking about the harmonization of domestic policies with what was happening overseas.[11] At the same time the executive inaugurated forms of policy planning in foreign affairs, the judgement of priorities and the calculation of costs. The FCO also began to think more about its relations with Parliament. After the Sachsenhausen affair it established a liaison unit and then after the Falklands conflict an expanded parliamentary office.[12] There was some FCO interest in creating a separate Select Committee on foreign affairs even before the system of departmentally related Select Committees was established in 1979.

The adaptation of the structure of the executive to meet the needs of the international agenda cannot be replicated exactly in the formal institutions of parliamentary procedure. The procedures are governed by rules and usages, but these are the creations of the two Houses themselves. No doubt the views of the Government of the day carry considerable weight and will usually prevail in the short term, but the complexion of the Government is in itself a reflection of Parliament and

Parliament is able to respond to changing requirements. The changes in rules (e.g. Standing Orders) may be slow, but they will always be determined by Parliament. Moreover, Parliament, like other living organisms, is able to adapt existing institutions and usages for purposes other than those for which they were originally intended.

This book explores the responses of the British Parliament to recent changes in the climate of international affairs and to Britain's place in the world. It reviews what has been made in recent years of existing usages whether quasi-statutory, as in Standing Orders, or consensual, as in the much greater body of usages described in Erskine May.[13] However, it would be a mistake to explain parliamentary practice solely in terms of procedure. Neither is it sufficient to rely only on the record of *Hansard*. Some of the main responses to international changes may have taken place 'behind the scenes', particularly in the informal consultations between ministers, back-benchers, and the representatives of overseas governments or other lobbies.

The structure of the book therefore follows a distinction between the formal and the informal. It begins with an account of proceedings on the record in the House of Commons and attempts to measure changes in this area. It examines the various opportunities which arise for debating and asking Questions on matters of foreign policy and looks for underlying trends in the way that the Commons allocates its time between foreign and domestic issues. It also considers how the activities of the Foreign Affairs Committee established in 1979 relate to business in the Commons Chamber.

Rather than devote a separate chapter to the activities of the Select Committee (which have been analysed elsewhere),[14] we have attempted to place them in the context of parliamentary consideration of foreign affairs as a whole. Further references to the Foreign Affairs Committee will be found in the case studies (Chapters 6–9) and in the concluding chapter.

Chapter 3 is devoted to the parliamentary handling of treaties and the working of the Ponsonby Rule, a topic rarely discussed in the context of the UK but one which in some other countries with written constitutions is central to parliamentary influence over foreign policy.

In Chapter 4 attention turns to the less formal 'off-the-record' activities relating to foreign affairs, such as back-bench committees, the participation of back-bench Members in international assemblies, the significance of outgoing and incoming parliamentary delegations and overseas contacts in general, and the nature and extent of the influences, by lobbying and otherwise, sought or actually brought to bear on Members. Changes in this area are by definition difficult to quantify or even to identify. It is naturally the case that much of the activity on the record which is charted in Chapter 2 reflects the informal contacts and networks described in Chapter 4. The connections are not always obvious, but some patterns do emerge from the juxtaposition and an attempt is made to identify the characteristics of those MPs who form the core of the parliamentary foreign affairs community and those who make more occasional contributions limited to particular subjects or regions.

Chapter 5 considers the relevant procedures of the House of Lords and the extent to which it may be said to have a role distinct from that of the House of Commons. Again, the formal and the informal are contrasted.

Chapters 6–9 represent a series of case studies which cut across the evidence presented in the earlier chapters. These case studies were selected to reflect the ways in which both Chambers have used their procedures to deal with specific matters in very different circumstances. Two of the studies, on the status of Gibraltar and relations with Chile, are concerned with the ways in which external interests and pressures interact with parliamentary procedures over a period of years. Gibraltar exemplifies an issue of direct British responsibility overseas, whereas the question of relations with Chile involves no direct British responsibility but carries a strong ideological and party-political overlay. The second study, on the US bombing raid on Libya in 1986, looks at the immediate parliamentary response to a short-term emergency. The third study, on the negotiations leading to the INF Treaty of 1987, considers the difficulties experienced by Parliament in attempting to monitor and come to grips with a complex and sensitive arms control issue stretching over three parliaments.

Chapter 10 looks at a development which has far-reaching implications for the role of Parliament in foreign affairs, namely European Political Co-operation (EPC), the working out, at ministerial level, of a progressively closer and more unified foreign policy by the member states of the European Community. This is discussed under the general headings of the evolution of EPC, the Single European Act of 1986 (and its constitutional consequences), the European Parliament and EPC, and the impact of the EPC on Westminster.

The final chapter brings together some tentative conclusions. At this stage it is not possible to do more than identify issues and problems. We feel that the attempt is worthwhile because, apart from anything else, the developments in Europe raise problems for Parliament of a kind not so far encountered in its long history. The response of Parliament to the new international climate is part of the task of determining what British interests might be in a world where there is talk of increasing multi-polarity and increasing interdependence.

TWO

Proceedings on the record: the floor of the House, the Foreign Affairs Committee and other committees

■■■■■■■

Introduction

The objective of this chapter is to provide an overview of the way the House of Commons considers foreign affairs in its formal proceedings, and to give some indication of the ways in which this has changed since the end of the Second World War. The data available on the time spent and the subjects covered by Parliament are therefore examined, so that changes in parliamentary behaviour can be explained: it is important to have clear evidence of what the record says in order to be able to speculate about what it may be disguising. This requires examination of what the House of Commons has considered and of the rules of procedure by which such consideration has come about. Parliamentary procedure consists of a set of rules which have evolved over many centuries and which have now arrived at a state of complexity which is bound to bewilder the casual observer. Most of the procedures in regular use today do have a logical basis and, even when they retain certain archaic features, serve a contemporary purpose. However, few procedures, outside of the realm of finance, are specific to a particular subject or department and therefore in order to describe the practice of the House of Commons in relation to foreign affairs it is necessary to look, if only briefly in some cases, at almost every significant procedural device.

The years since 1945 have seen great changes in the United Kingdom's position in the world, in its interests and in its policies. These changes are reflected in the foreign affairs subjects which the House of Commons has considered, and there appears to have been a slight reduction in the priority attached by the Commons to foreign affairs over this period, as measured by the proportion of time devoted to them. Yet the procedures which the House has employed to examine foreign affairs in the Chamber have not significantly changed. Outside the Chamber, a major development has been the introduction of a Select Committee on Foreign Affairs in 1979.

The observations made in this chapter are drawn principally from study of four post-war sessions at ten-year intervals (1946–47, 1956–57, 1966–67, 1976–77) and the six recent sessions 1983–84 to 1988–89, together with the information on 1962–63 provided in Peter Richards's *Parliament and Foreign Affairs* (1967).[1]

Overall time devoted to foreign affairs

It is of interest first of all to consider how much time is devoted by the House of Commons to foreign affairs and how this has changed. Table 1 gives details of the amounts of time spent by the House over the years, distinguishing between the different departments concerned and distinguishing so far as possible since 1972 between FCO time spent on European Community and non-European Community issues. (Where Prime Ministerial time is included, it has been allocated to the most appropriate department or subject.)

The FCO has a number of predecessor departments. In 1946 the relevant offices were the Foreign Office, the Colonial Office, the India Office, the Burma Office and the Dominions Office. There was also the task of the administration of occupied Germany and Austria, which was the responsibility of the Chancellor of the Duchy of Lancaster. In 1947 the India and Burma Offices were wound up and the Dominions Office was succeeded by the Commonwealth Relations Office (CRO). For a period (including the 1962–63 session), the posts of Commonwealth Secretary and Colonial Secretary were held by one person, while responsibility for Central Africa rested with the First Secretary of State. In 1967 the Colonial Office was merged with the CRO to become the Commonwealth Office and in 1968 this then merged with the Foreign Office to become the Foreign and Commonwealth Office. Overseas development functions rested with appropriate parts of the above departments until 1961 when the Department for Technical Co-operation was established. This was then included in a new Ministry of Overseas Development (ODM) in 1964, which has continued either as a separate ministry, or as a distinct agency within the responsibility of the Foreign Secretary, until the present.

Table 1 Time spent by the House of Commons on foreign affairs 1946–89[a]

	1946–47 (hours)	1956–57 (hours)	1962–63 (hours)	1966–67 (hours)	1976–77 (hours)	1983–87[b] (hours)	1987–89[c] (hours)
Foreign Office/FCO	90[d]	101	78	125	39	223½	121
FCO (EC)					29½	135½	51
Colonial and Commonwealth Offices[e]	30½	71	57½	72½			
India & Burma Offices	48½						
Overseas Development Ministry/ Administration			9[f]	12	11	57	18½
Total	169	172	144½	209½	79½	416	190½
Total hrs in sessions	1 418	1 220	1 336½	2 423	1 370½	5 941	3 560½
Foreign affairs as % of total hours	11.9	14.1	10.8	8.6	5.8	7.0[g]	5.4[f]

Notes:
a The definitions used in adding up the time spent in each session on consideration of foreign affairs are not watertight. Broadly speaking, any debate or other proceeding in which a minister from the FCO or one of its predecessors has taken a significant part has been included. Where, therefore, a debate has been a joint one with another department the whole proceedings have been included. This method excludes debates on most European Community Documents, which are the responsibility of the relevant subject department such as Agriculture, Environment or Transport. Debates, statements, etc., by the Prime Minister have been included where these clearly relate to foreign affairs issues even where no FCO Minister has taken part, though Oral Questions to the Prime Minister have been excluded.
b Total of four sessions in the 1983–87 Parliament.
c Total of first two sessions of 1987 Parliament.
d Including 24 hours in respect of matters within the responsibility of the Chancellor of the Duchy of Lancaster for the administration of occupied Germany.
e Including Dominions Office, Colonial Office, Commonwealth Relations Office and Commonwealth Office.
f Technical Co-operation Department.
g 6.7% (1983–84); 7.2% (1984–85); 8.0% (1985–86); 4.0% (1986–87); 5.5% (1987–88); 5.2% (1988–89).

It would be wrong to try to draw very specific conclusions from these figures – a survey of a much greater number of years would be needed. Nevertheless, it is reasonable to suggest that there has been a slight decline in the time spent by the House of Commons on foreign affairs, from a figure of a little over 10 per cent in the early post-war decades to a figure somewhat over 5 per cent in more recent times. (It may be, however, that the 1989–90 session, which saw a number of debates on events in Eastern Europe, will belie this trend.)

This proportion of overall Commons time is consistent with the Foreign and Commonwealth Office's position as one of sixteen major Government departments. This basic consistency is not entirely surprising. There are forces within Government and Parliament which directly encourage a certain consistency in the allocation of time on the floor of the

House to different departmental interests – e.g. the rota for Question Time, the general practice of the Opposition of covering most departments at least once in their use of their Opposition (formerly Supply) days, the rationing of legislative time, etc. Nevertheless, foreign affairs might be thought to be less susceptible to this process than other departmental interests: first because the relevant departments have, as is discussed later in this chapter, only a limited legislative programme (which tends to form such a regular part of some other departments' Commons activity) and, second, because foreign affairs issues, when they *do* reach the floor of the House, are often major crises which quite suddenly pre-empt major stretches of House of Commons time.

The fact that a certain consistency is maintained despite this arises in part because while the precise timing and impact of a crisis is of its very nature unpredictable, nevertheless one or two such major issues tend to crop up each session on a surprisingly regular basis. Thus in 1946–47 a quarter of the total time spent on foreign affairs was devoted to the issue of Indian independence; a similar proportion of time in 1956–57 was spent on the Suez crisis. Just over thirty hours were spent on discussing the UK's application for membership of the European Community and on Rhodesia respectively in the 1962–63 and 1966–67 sessions. Major issues in the early sessions of the 1983–87 Parliament included Grenada, the Hong Kong Treaty and the European Communities (Finance) and European Communities (Amendment) Bills. Indeed the relatively little time devoted to foreign affairs in 1976–77 and in the three sessions 1986–89 can in large measure be accounted for by the absence in those sessions of a major issue to cause lengthy special debates. There have been calls from MPs for more time to be available for debating foreign affairs, but it is difficult to assess how far such calls are quantitatively or qualitatively different from calls for more time to be spent on other subjects. There is little evidence that debates on foreign affairs are substantially better attended than those on other subjects.

Yet within the relatively consistent overall trend significant changes have taken place in the subject matter considered by the House. Up to the mid-1960s, and before entry into the European Community, much of the focus of overseas issues was towards Britain's imperial and Commonwealth responsibilities and commitments. Since 1972 a somewhat equivalent focus has been towards issues and commitments arising out of membership of the European Community. An additional focus since the 1960s has been overseas development, which was previously largely subsumed within the tasks of colonial administration. Table 2 gives an indication of how this is reflected in the way in which the House of Commons has spent its time.

The proportion of the time taken up by purely Foreign Office affairs (later Foreign and Commonwealth Office affairs), as opposed to imperial,

Table 2 Division of Commons foreign affairs time pre-1972 and post-1972

	Percentage of time spent							
	Pre-1972				*Post-1972*			
	1946– 47	*1956– 57*	*1962– 63*	*1966– 67*	*1976– 77*	*1983– 87*	*1987– 89*	
Foreign Affairs (Foreign Office)	53	59	54	60	49	54	63	FCO (non-EC business)
Colonial/Aid Commonwealth	47	41	46	40	37	32	27	FCO (EC business)
					14	14	10	Aid
Total	100	100	100	100	100	100	100	Total

post-imperial and developmental issues (pre-1972) and as opposed to European Community and developmental issues (post-1972), has been very constant at between half and two-thirds of the total. The time previously devoted to colonial and Commonwealth affairs has been broadly replaced by time spent on overseas development and European Community issues. This is not meant to indicate of course that colonial and Commonwealth issues have not been significantly discussed since 1972, nor that consideration was not given to the European Community before 1972. Neither proposition would be true: a great deal of time was spent before 1972 debating applications to join the European Community and the terms of accession, and much time has been spent since then on such colonial and Commonwealth issues as the Falkland Islands, Hong Kong, etc. However, Table 2 does indicate the way in which use of House of Commons time has reflected the changed role and position of the UK in world affairs.

Proceedings on foreign affairs on the floor of the House

Foreign affairs issues may arise on the floor of the House of Commons under a variety of procedures, as for other subject areas, though the balance between the different types of proceedings may be somewhat different for foreign affairs. It is worth considering the different procedures if any qualitative assessment of the time the House devotes to foreign affairs is to be attempted. This is because different types of debates or proceedings can have a very different character and significance. For example it is the procedure involved which will generally

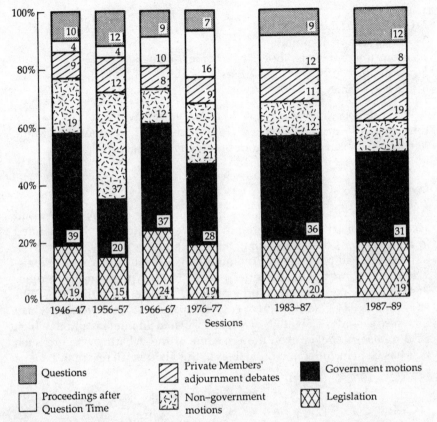

Figure 1 Division of foreign affairs discussion between different types of proceedings

determine the time of day – and thus, very often, the degree of attendance and the amount of interest and media coverage – at which an issue is raised. Again, different procedures come into play according to whether the discussion is precipitated by the Government or by the Opposition or by a Private Member. Although the variety of procedures available to the House may seem confusing, one of the essential justifications of the variety is that it prevents the attention of the House from being monopolized by any particular interest. Hence the existence of certain procedures and time-slots dedicated to the Opposition parties (in practice to their parliamentary leadership), of some dedicated to back-benchers (allocated usually by ballot), of some in the gift of Select Committee chairmen and of some (the greatest part) at the disposal of the Government of the day.

It is instructive to consider the consideration given to foreign affairs in six categories:

1 legislation
2 Government motions
3 non-government motions
4 adjournment debates chosen by Private Members
5 proceedings after Question Time
6 Question Time

A final category consisting of various procedures which do not take up time on the floor of the House is also discussed. The proportion of time devoted to these various categories is illustrated in Figure 1.

Legislation

Although the FCO is responsible for a programme of both primary and secondary legislation, the programme is a very limited one. It has tended to represent less than one-fifth of all foreign affairs discussion. By comparison over 40 per cent of Commons time overall is devoted to legislation, reflecting the much larger part legislation plays in many other departments' parliamentary programmes. The actual number of Bills sponsored by FCO and its predecessor departments (a definition which therefore excludes a few Bills in which FCO had an interest and to which FCO ministers spoke, even though some of the debating time for such Bills has been included in other tables in this chapter) in recent years is as follows:

	1966–67	76–77	83–84	84–85	85–86	86–87	87–88	88–89
No. of Bills	12	0	0	2	6	3	2	3

There was, in addition, just one Bill introduced by a back-bencher in the period covered which became law. This was the International Parliamentary Organisations Bill of session 1988–89.

The subject matter of FCO-sponsored legislation tends to fall into three broad categories. In the post-war period up to the 1970s, a high proportion of the Bills were concerned with the granting of independence to former colonies. Eight of the twelve Bills in 1966–67 were of this nature. By contrast there have been no pure independence Bills since 1983 (though the Hong Kong Bill of 1984–85 can be regarded as such).

In more recent years the FCO has found itself proposing a second kind of legislation, relating to Britain's membership of a network of treaties and international organizations – particularly the European Community. In the 1983–87 Parliament for example the House devoted over thirty-three hours to the European Communities (Amendment) Bill of session 1985–86, which gave force to the Treaty known as the Single European Act (see Chapter 10). The large amount of time is accounted for by the fact that the committee stage was taken on the floor of the House, as is normal with legislation of constitutional significance. Substantial further time before that was devoted to the European Communities (Finance) Bill of session 1984–85 (the principal responsibility for which rested with HM Treasury). Further examples include the Arms Control and Disarmament (Privileges and Immunities) Bill of 1987–88, which conferred diplomatic immunities on the arms control inspectors and observers created by the Stockholm Agreement of 1986, and the Multilateral Investment Guarantee Agency Bill of 1987–88. It is worth noting that legislation giving effect to treaty obligations of this sort is frequently the only means by which treaties get debated in the House of Commons. (This point is considered further in Chapter 3.)

The third – less significant – category of FCO primary legislation comprises those Bills concerned with the statutory basis and operation of the Government's instruments of foreign policy administration, such as the Commonwealth Development Corporation Bill of 1985–86.

It is worth stressing that most of the FCO's Bills give rise to very little controversy or debate. Of the sixteen Bills in the period 1983–84 to 1988–89, only five – the Hong Kong Bill, the European Communities (Spanish and Portuguese Accession) Bill, the European Communities (Amendment) Bill, the Arms Control and Disarmament (Privileges and Immunities) Bill and the Antarctic Minerals Bill – gave rise to more than three hours of debate on the floor of the House. Similarly little time is spent on such Bills in Standing Committees. Five of the sixteen were referred to a Second Reading Committee and thus received only a formal second reading on the floor of the House. It is also worth noting that because almost all Bills either are so insignificant as to arouse no controversy, or are the subject of preceding negotiations which make alteration of the terms politically impossible, very few FCO Bills receive any significant amendment in their passage through the House of Commons. Of the sixteen FCO Bills in the 1983–89 period, only one received more than one amendment.

As for secondary legislation, the FCO, like other departments, is responsible for a steady flow of statutory instruments which have to be laid before Parliament. These are mostly either 'affirmative' orders, requiring resolutions in both Houses giving approval to the orders, or 'negative' instruments, for which a debate will take place only if a 'prayer' against the order is tabled within forty days of the instrument being laid. In either case, debate will generally be limited to one and a half hours taken after ten o'clock at night unless the instrument is referred instead to a Standing Committee.

In practice, although the FCO is responsible for about forty statutory instruments each session very few are debated on the floor of the House.[2] One exception to this is the series of orders introduced by the Overseas Development Administration (ODA) providing for Britain's contributions to the various multilateral development agencies. A number of others, including in particular many of the orders applying statutory immunities and privileges to new international agencies, are debated briefly in Standing Committee. No debates were held on negative instruments relating to foreign affairs in the 1983–89 sessions. Overall, between 1983 and 1989 nine debates on FCO or ODA statutory instruments were held on the floor of the House, covering eleven instruments, and a further three debates took place on relevant European Community Documents. Twenty-eight instruments, and one European Community Document, were debated in Standing Committee.

Government motions

Perhaps the most important proceedings in the Commons on foreign affairs are the various Government motions on foreign affairs. To some extent such motions, which enable the House to discuss various topical issues, take the place held by legislation in other departments' programmes. Procedurally such debates can be regarded as falling into three categories: the debate on the Address (i.e. on the Queen's Speech opening each session of Parliament), debates on a motion for the adjournment of the House, and debates with substantive motions. In practice it is more instructive to consider such motions under two headings: those which form a regular part of the sessional timetable of the Commons, and those which do not.

In general, three or four regular debates related to foreign affairs take place in a normal session. They are usually full-day debates, that is they run the whole length of the main part of the Commons day, beginning between 3.30 pm and 4 pm and ending at 10 pm. The first such debate is held on one of the five or six days during which the House debates the Queen's Speech. After the opening day of that debate, which is of a wide-ranging nature, each day is allocated by negotiation between the parties to different topics: one day is almost always allocated to foreign affairs or, more normally, to foreign affairs together with defence or some other related subject (though in 1976–77, exceptionally, no day was so provided). The day's debate allows members to discuss the broad range of international issues and the Government's policy towards them. Such debates tend not to be very closely focused. One indication of this is that although during the debate on the Queen's Speech a number of divisions on amendments tabled by Opposition parties take place on specific issues it is relatively unusual for an amendment on a foreign affairs matter to be tabled and voted upon. (Such a vote has taken place on five occasions since 1945.) In years where the Queen's Speech coincides with a major foreign policy issue – such as 1956–57 when the Queen's Speech followed very closely on the military operations around the Suez canal – then more of the debate on the Speech might in practice be related to that issue.

The second type of regular foreign affairs motion is the semi-annual or annual debate on developments in the European Community. Although these debates take place on the basis of a substantive motion to take note of a (usually somewhat outdated) six-monthly Government Report on 'Developments in the European Community', it is in practice a very wide-ranging debate on EC issues. The debates are generally opened and wound up by FCO ministers. They are not a vehicle for Members to examine in detail particular pieces of EC legislation or activity which may be the responsibility of other departments, but general points about them, or the rate of progress on them, can be raised. The House of Commons Procedure Committee in November 1989 recommended that the value of these debates should be enhanced by holding them shortly before each European Council meeting, with the focus of discussion being more overtly on future, rather than past, developments.[3] This recommendation was accepted by the Government in May 1990.[4]

The third regular fixture is the annual debate on foreign affairs which takes place on a motion 'That this House do now adjourn'. The 'adjournment debate' is a device much used for enabling wide exchanges of views with no substantive motion before the House which would limit debate. There are very few theoretical constraints to what is in order on such a motion and it is only the announcement in advance (and on the Order Paper) of the proposed subject for debate, and the practice of the House and of the occupant of the Chair, which keeps the debate within the confines of the subject intended to be debated. Although the debate provides an opportunity for members to raise topics which they might otherwise find difficult to raise, the breadth of foreign affairs as a topic means that the debate tends to have very little of a common thread or focus and to be somewhat superficial. A number of back-bench contributions are likely to be of the character of special pleadings for their particular interests and to have little relevance to the flow of the debate as a whole. It is difficult for opponents of the Government to pin the Foreign Secretary down on any point, unless there is a major issue of the day which naturally predominates in the discussions.

The weakness of using this device – long-standing though it may be – for an annual discussion on foreign affairs has been noted by a number of Commons Members interested in these matters, including the Foreign Affairs Committee, and has led to calls for the replacement of the annual foreign affairs adjournment debate by more targeted debates, for example on East–West relations or the Commonwealth. The following exchanges between back-benchers and the then Leader of the House, Mr John Wakeham, illustrate this. On 12 January 1989[5]

Mr Ivan Lawrence (Burton): Is my right hon. Friend aware that many hon. Members believe that the provision usually made for foreign affairs debates is completely inadequate? Instead of having occasional debates over the whole *tour d'horizon* of British interests, would it not be better to have more debates on regional issues so that most of us might have an opportunity to speak on important matters?

Mr Wakeham: I recognise my hon. and learned Friend's concern which is shared by a number of our colleagues. I recently wrote to my right hon. Friend the Chairman of the Select Committee on Foreign Affairs setting out my views on the matter. I shall try to meet the spirit of what my hon. and learned Friend says, but, looking at past debates, considerably more hon. Members would have been able to take part if some of the speeches had been a little shorter.

and, on 27 April 1989[6]

Mr Michael Latham (Rutland and Melton): Does my right hon. Friend recall that more than once he has said that he sympathises with the idea of half-day debates on specific foreign affairs subjects? However, nothing has happened. All we get is late-night orders on Euro-rubbish. Will he think again about the matter and make arrangements for specific foreign affairs debates?

Mr Wakeham: I tried, but it was not possible to meet my hon. Friend's demands in the immediate past. I was unable to get it tied up in the way that I wanted. My hon. Friend knows that the Select Committee is looking into European matters . . .

While this campaign did not enjoy much success in the 1988–89 session, the following session of 1989–90 has witnessed a distinct though perhaps only temporary change. Not long after the usual one day devoted to foreign affairs and defence in the debate on the Queen's Speech, the House of Commons proceeded to debate 'Eastern Europe' on a Government motion for the adjournment on 1 December 1989 and 'East–West Relations' on a similar motion on 22 February 1990. These debates on specific themes may have been more a response to the great interest aroused by the revolutions in Eastern Europe and their implications for Western Europe, including the UK, rather than a concession to the earlier pressure in this direction. The fact that the new Leader of the House, Sir Geoffrey Howe, had previously been Foreign Secretary may have played a part. Certainly the twice-yearly 'tour d'horizon' foreign affairs debates – i.e. the Queen's Speech debate and the annual adjournment debate – had acquired a poor reputation in the eyes of foreign affairs specialists. While many recognized that they were still necessary, because no other format would allow Members the freedom to refer to problems in any part of the globe, it was also obvious that the result was nothing like a debate in the proper sense of the word. In order for a debate to acquire a political significance (or, in the phrase favoured by many MPs, 'to send a message') it has to have some focus and coherence.

The strength of a debate which does have a focus is illustrated well by the debate held on 22 February 1990. Although formally the debate was again on the motion 'That this House do now adjourn', in Government time, the Government had also announced a specific subject for the debate, namely 'East–West Relations'. Such a wide theme could have allowed for debate on many regions of the world, but the House, with a few exceptions, took it to refer to the momentous changes underway in Europe. The Foreign Secretary set the scene:

> We are debating the future shape of our continent: the impetus towards democracy in eastern Europe and in the Soviet Union; the emergence in central Europe of a united Germany; and the reduction, on an unprecedented scale, of the armed forces that for decades have opposed one another across a divided Europe.[7]

The majority of speakers concentrated on the theme of a future political and security 'architecture' for Europe, that is the future of NATO given the imminent unification of Germany, the prospects for pan-European institutional development based on the Conference on Security and Co-operation in Europe (CSCE: 'the Helsinki process'), the possible relevance of the Western European Union and the Council of Europe and the implications of political change in Eastern Europe for the existing plans to accelerate the integration of the European Community. Some contributors took side-swipes at domestic political targets, some widened the debate to take in regions such as the Horn of Africa which were also being affected by East–West change, some reported on their visits to Eastern Europe or on meetings held under the auspices of the Inter-Parliamentary Union (IPU) or the North Atlantic Assembly (NAA). Whereas in the traditional unfocused foreign affairs debate these points might have interrupted the flow of argument, here they fitted in to the central theme. The FCO Minister who replied to the debate, William Waldegrave MP, declared himself 'surprised and fascinated' by the consensus which he detected in the House in favour of 'widening' rather than 'deepening' European unity and he expresses his own preference for 'a wider and slightly looser Europe'.[8]

Such targeted debates are not, of course, a new development of session 1989–90, but they do not occur on a regular basis. They arise in the same way as time is provided for debate on any other issue in the House, that is to say, from a mixture of factors including the priority given to the issue by the Government, pressure from the Opposition and other sources within the House, and the intrinsic significance of the subject. The debates may take place on substantive motions or (as in the example of 22 February 1990 just discussed) as adjournment debates. The topics

Table 3 Debates on Government motions 1976–89

	1976–77	83–84[a]	84–85	85–86	86–87[b]	87–88[a]	88–89
Regular debates							
On the Address	0	1	1	1	1	1	1
Adjournment	1	2	1	1	1	1	1
EC developments	1	2	2	1	1	2	3
Other Govt debates							
Adjournment	2	3	1	2	0	1	2
Substantive	0	3	2	2	0	1	0

Notes: a Long session   b Short session

covered have been fairly wide-ranging and have included most of the major issues of the 1983–89 period: Grenada, INF (intermediate-range nuclear forces) discussions, Hong Kong, GCHQ (Government Communications Headquarters), the EC budget, Falkland Islands, the Anglo-Irish Agreement, Libya and Unesco. They have frequently been on issues for which there has been joint responsibility between the FCO and another department.

The time available is, however, always limited and the demand from other interests for debates is every bit as great as that from foreign affairs interests. Thus (more frequently at least than in the House of Lords, as is pointed out in Chapter 5) major developments can go by without being the subject of a set-piece debate on the floor of the House in Government time. One example of this is perhaps the Israel/Palestine question, which has not been the subject of a Government debate in the House of Commons, despite its continuing significance as a foreign affairs issue, in the 1983–89 period, although it has been debated in the House of Lords. Sometimes in such cases debate will take place none the less, but precipitated by back-benchers or by the Opposition.

Table 3 indicates the frequency of the various types of debate on Government motions.

Non-government motions

Motions can be brought before the House other than by the Government in a variety of ways: as Opposition motions, as Private Members' motions, as emergency debates and as motions on Estimates. There is little pattern to their occurrence, though (as can be seen from Figure 1) between them they take up fairly consistently about one-fifth of foreign affairs time. Table 4 indicates their frequency in recent years.

The Opposition parties have twenty days at their disposal during a normal session on which they may choose the subject of debate, three of which are in the hands of minor parties. A number of the Opposition days

Table 4 Full or half-day debates on non-government motions 1976–89

	1976–77	83–84[a]	84–85	85–86	86–87[b]	87–88[a]	88–89
Opposition (formerly Supply) Days	1	1	3	2	1	1	2
Private Members' motions	1	2	1	0	0	2	1
Emergency debates	1	1	0	0	0	0	0
Estimates debates	1[c]	1	0	1	0	0	0

Notes: a Long session   b Short session   c Supply Day on a motion on a Select Committee report

are divided up into two half days. In the 1983–87 Parliament, there were a total of 104 Opposition debates under this system, of which, as can be seen from Table 4, only seven were devoted to foreign, European and development issues; three of these were on South Africa, and three were on development issues.

Opportunities for Private Members to table a motion for debate are limited to between fifteen and twenty occasions a session. Such debates are half-day debates generally on a Monday or Friday, when the attendance in the House is usually low. The right to choose and table a motion is subject to ballot. Most Members choose a topic involving domestic policy (often including a constituency interest), and only three such debates in the 1983–87 Parliament covered foreign affairs issues (on the USSR, on Europe and on development) out of sixty-four such debates overall.

Emergency debates, which are three-hour debates taking place under what is now Standing Order No 20 on occasions when the Speaker is satisfied that the subject matter should be given priority over other matter set down for debate, are infrequent. They take place following an application to the Speaker by a back-bencher or Opposition front-bencher, but most successful applications are by members of the Official Opposition front bench. A total of seven such debates took place in the 1983–87 Parliament, of which one (on Grenada) was on a foreign affairs issue.

Estimates day debates take place on a motion for the approval of a Vote for public funds to carry out a particular service which technically is a Government motion. However, the days are at the disposal of the Liaison Committee, a committee which is composed of the chairmen of all the Select Committees in the House. In theory, any Member can request the Liaison Committee to appoint a particular Vote for debate. In practice applications come from other Select Committees of the House and relate to reports those committees have made or are working on. Both of the debates which took place on foreign affairs in the 1983–87 Parliament (on Grenada and on Famine in Africa) took place at the instigation of the Foreign Affairs Committee and followed from reports of that committee.

Adjournment debates chosen by Private Members

The procedures of the House of Commons provide a number of means by which Private Members can raise issues of their choice for a limited debate on a motion for the adjournment (i.e. at a time when there is no substantive motion before the House). These debates differ from the major adjournment debates discussed on pp. 17–18 principally in that they are much briefer, they take place at less convenient times, and the subjects are chosen by back-benchers.

The most familiar of these is the daily half-hour adjournment debate which takes place at the conclusion of the rest of the day's business. It thus usually happens very late at night or in the early hours of the next morning and can take longer than half an hour only if the previous business of the House has been concluded early. Not surprisingly very few Members of the House tend to be present other than the Member who (generally by ballot) has won the opportunity to introduce the topic of his or her choice, the minister who is to reply, and a Government Whip. The procedure is very much geared to enabling Members to raise small issues, often local constituency issues. Foreign affairs topics – unless they have a constituency interest – are chosen only infrequently. Nevertheless, some daily adjournment debates do involve FCO ministers each session, as Table 5 indicates. Subjects which were chosen more than once in the 1983–87 Parliament included Cyprus, the Law of the Sea Convention, BBC External Services, Soviet Jewry, aid to Ethiopia, and South East Asian refugees.

Opportunities for slightly longer debates on a motion for the adjournment can arise under two further procedures. First, about eight short debates take place on the last sitting day before each recess, and second, about ten or eleven short debates (of about one and a half hours each) take place under Standing Order No 54 on each of three all-night sittings which occur each session following the passing of a Consolidated Fund Bill. Table 5 indicates the frequency of foreign affairs debates of these types. Those on foreign affairs represented about one-tenth of all such debates in the 1983–87 Parliament. Subjects which were raised more than once in this way included Afghanistan, Central America, Sri Lanka and aid to Africa.

In all these types of adjournment debates the back-bencher who has chosen the topic will often have picked a subject in which the Member has some specific involvement. This might be in one of the forms discussed in

Table 5 Private Members' adjournment debates on foreign affairs 1976–89

	1976–77	83–84[a]	84–85	85–86	86–87[b]	87–88[a]	88–89
Daily	4	10	14	5	6	10	6
Recess debates	1	5	4	3	1	5	6
SO No. 54	4	6	1	2	2	10	4

Notes: a Long session   b Short session

Chapter 4, such as active participation in an all-party group, membership of a parliamentary delegation (such as that to the Council of Europe Parliamentary Assembly) or contact with an outside pressure group. For example two of the back-bench speakers in the debate on Latin America under Standing Order No 54 on 27 July 1989 had recently returned from representing the All-Party British–Latin America Group on a visit to Chile two months earlier, including the instigator of the debate, Mr Calum Macdonald, Labour Member for the Western Isles. Similarly the debate on Romania which was the subject of the daily adjournment debate for 23 February 1990 was precipitated by a member of a recently returned Inter-Parliamentary Union delegation to that country, Mr Neil Thorne, Conservative Member for Ilford (South).

Proceedings after Question Time

The period between the conclusion of Oral Questions at 3.30 pm and the point at which the main business of the day commences has long been the time at which, in a variety of ways, the House's attention can turn briefly (and occasionally not so briefly) to highly topical issues. These include statements by ministers, Private Notice Questions (PNQs) and applications for emergency debates under Standing Order No 20. (The moving by Private Members of motions giving leave to bring in Bills – so-called 'Ten Minute Rule' Bills – also occurs at this time, but it is only on very rare occasions that Members seek to introduce such a Bill on a foreign affairs topic.)

Statements by ministers may relate to announcements on new policy proposals which have been under consideration for some time, or on the Government's reaction to some development or event elsewhere. Occasionally the issue is of such importance that the statement will be made by the Prime Minister. Of over seventy-five statements made on foreign affairs issues in the 1983–87 Parliament, nearly one-third were made by the Prime Minister. These mostly followed heads of government meetings in which she had taken part, including European Council meetings. This ratio is consistent with the figures from other years examined, except for 1962–63, where the then Prime Minister (Mr Macmillan) made no foreign affairs statements at all.

Statements will usually be made at the choice of the Government, though in practice a major event involving British interests will nearly always lead to a statement. Private Members, including the Opposition front bench, can raise urgent issues which the Government would not otherwise bring to the floor of the House by tabling a Private Notice Question, which can be asked at the conclusion of Oral Questions if allowed by the Speaker, or by applying for an emergency debate. In the latter case, applications are frequently made not in the serious expectation that the request will be granted – as was pointed out above, only 7 such debates were held on any subject in the 1983–87 Parliament, out of 280 applications[9] – but as a means of giving a Member two or three minutes to speak to the House on why the issue is important. Around five PNQs and perhaps three or four emergency debate applications relating to foreign affairs might be made each session, though the figures can be somewhat erratic. Griffith and Ryle [10] noted that about one-fifth of PNQs asked by front-bench Opposition spokesmen between 1977 and 1987 referred to foreign affairs or events outside the UK.

Additionally each Thursday afternoon Members have the opportunity to raise issues with the Leader of the House as supplementary questions to the Leader's statement outlining the proposed business of the House for the forthcoming week. Under the guise of a supplementary question asking for a debate to be held on a particular issue, a Member can briefly raise the issue directly and draw the attention of the Government, and other Members, to it.

Although all these proceedings after Question Time do not between them make up a great deal of time they do play an important part in the quality of that coverage. It is the time at which, for a variety of reasons, more Members will be present than for the more formal proceedings on legislation or motions and it is the period of the House's proceedings which attracts most press and broadcasting coverage. It is often the time at which major issues – which may come to take up large parts of House time in the coming weeks – are first brought to the attention of the House. Together with Question Time, proceedings at 3.30 pm after Questions are concluded are a mechanism which in general makes it very difficult for the Government to escape all accountability for a given course of action, in those instances where other procedures – in particular substantive motions – have not been brought into play.

Question Time

Oral Questions to ministers take place in the House of Commons from 2.30 to 3.30 pm each Monday to Thursday, with time allotted to particular departments or ministers on a rota basis. The amount of time taken up by Questions on foreign affairs has reduced from a little over 1 per cent of overall House time in the period up to the 1960s to somewhat under 1 per cent since then. During this time there has been a continuing reshuffle in the exact allocation of time as the various ministries have changed and merged.[11] Since 1979 the basic pattern has been for FCO questions other than on aid to come up for a full session of Questions (about fifty-five minutes) once every four weeks and for Questions to the Minister for Overseas Development to come up for ten minutes once every three weeks. Until 1986 the last twenty minutes of FCO questions were allocated to EC matters, leading to a position in which, typically, about ten FCO questions out of fifty to sixty which had been tabled, and five EC questions out of about ten, were answered in the available time. This led to complaints by some members that EC questions were getting disproportionate attention, at the expense of other issues. A revised system was introduced in March 1986, whereby separate questions on EC issues were abolished and were incorporated into the general list of FCO questions. This revision in turn led to complaints by other Members that EC issues did not get the attention they deserved.

In practice, about fifteen Questions altogether are covered in a typical FCO Question Time, of which one or two are EC Questions (out of about ninety tabled Questions, of which about ten are EC Questions). Many EC Questions are about European Political Co-operation rather than about the Community as such, and supplementary questions often cover specifically UK foreign policy. Although, as just noted, only about fifteen out of ninety tabled Questions on FCO issues (and about five out of about fifteen on ODA issues) are answered orally, about forty-five Members (ten on ODA issues) altogether get the chance to take part either by asking their tabled Question or during the supplementary exchanges.

The choice of who has the opportunity to ask supplementary questions rests with the Speaker. Among the grounds on which the Speaker will choose amongst those trying to get in are the degree to which the Member has shown interest or knowledge in the subject in hand and the extent to which the Member has been a regular attender at Question Time. At the same time the Speaker will seek to balance the foreign affairs 'regulars' with a fair opportunity to other Members to contribute. By way of example, in the 1987–88 session (a longer than average session) a grand total of 624 Oral Questions and supplementaries were asked during FCO Question Time (including ODA Questions), involving in all 227 Members of the House (excluding the ministers replying). Most of the Opposition front bench spokesmen for the Labour party and the Liberal party were called in every session of Question Time, but otherwise only forty-three Members were called more than three times in the eleven sessions each of

FCO and ODA Questions. These Members were mostly from amongst those who might be classified – by examination of their activity on the floor of the House, or in asking Written Questions, or in membership of relevant all-party groups, etc. – as amongst the eighty or so most committed foreign affairs specialists. A number, however, were principally interested in particular issues rather than foreign affairs in general. For example Mr Tom Clarke, Labour Member for Monklands, asked twelve Questions, but eight of those were on development matters, and Sir Dennis Walters, Conservative Member for Westbury, asked seven Questions, all of which were related to Middle East issues. Sir Peter Blaker on the other hand, an ex-Foreign Office minister, was called on nine occasions, each Question being on a different topic.

One feature of Question Time worth noting is the proportion of Prime Minister's Question Time which is devoted to foreign issues. This is difficult to measure because (particularly in more recent years) the Questions tabled give little indication of the intended subject matter of the supplementary question, and the various supplementaries to one Question may cover a variety of different topics. However, examination of Prime Minister's Questions over the years suggests that foreign affairs issues took up about one-eighth of Prime Minister's Questions in the 1983–87 Parliament (compared to about one-third in 1956–57 and 1966–67).

Other procedures

This is perhaps a convenient point at which to note those foreign affairs interests and activities of which Members give notice in the same way as for Oral Questions, but which do not feature on the floor of the House, namely Written Questions and Early Day Motions (EDMs).

Questions tabled on the Order Paper for oral answer which are not reached during the time available are given a Written Answer. But Members can also table Questions expressly for Written Answer for the purpose of eliciting information about activities and policies or for calling for changes in policy. The numbers of such Questions have risen over the years (though not by as much as the numbers of Questions tabled for Oral Answer). In recent years, the number of Written Answers given by the Foreign and Commonwealth Office (including the Overseas Development Administration) has been about 2,500 per session, a figure which is not far from the average for other departments.

Early Day Motions are motions put down on the Order Paper which generally have no serious expectation of being debated, but act as a means of calling attention to an event or publicizing a point of view or (since other Members may then sign their names to the EDM) of gathering support for a course of action. There is no exact way of measuring how many of these are on foreign policy and on international events but the proportion is around 15 per cent.[12]

Study of Written Questions asked and of Early Day Motions tabled is revealing as a means of identifying individual Members' interests in specific subjects. For example forty-four out of fifty-three Written Questions to the FCO by Mr Michael Latham, Conservative Member for Rutland, between 1987 and 1989 concerned the Middle East dispute and matters relating to the Jewish people, and the same Member also tabled more Early Day Motions on these topics than any other Member. There is thus little correlation between the frequency with which a Member asks Written FCO Questions and the breadth of his or her interests in foreign affairs as a whole. In both of the two sessions 1987–88 and 1988–89 the two highest 'scorers' were Dr Dafydd Elis Thomas (Plaid Cymru) and Mr Tony Banks (Labour), but over half their questions concerned just one subject. In Dr Thomas's case, this was nuclear proliferation and disarmament; in Mr Banks's case the subject was the protection of endangered species of animals. The frequency with which a Member asks Written Questions can be a misleading indicator in another way also: an outside person, acting as a Member's researcher, can, through a Member, ask a large number of Questions on a topic which reflects the researcher's interests more than the Member's.

For the sake of completeness a brief mention should also be given to petitions. Petitions may be presented to the House by a Member on behalf of outside individuals or groups on almost any issue, calling for action from the House. Such petitions may be introduced briefly by the Member on the floor of the House, though most are presented 'formally', that is to say without being spoken to at all. Very few such petitions relate to foreign affairs issues, though in 1986 a spate of such petitions were presented calling for action in the case of the dissident Soviet poet, Irina Ratushinskaya.

Proceedings on foreign affairs in committee

The floor of the House is of course only part – albeit the major part – of the picture of House activity in foreign affairs, as in any other field. Work is going on at the same time in both Standing Committees and Select Committees (particularly, since 1979, in the Foreign Affairs Committee).

Proceedings in Standing Committees

Proceedings in Standing Committee on Bills do not feature significantly in the House's consideration of foreign affairs. This is because, as noted earlier, relatively few Bills are concerned with foreign affairs or development issues. Those which are tend to have their committee stage (where Bills may be considered and amended in detail) on the floor of the House rather than in a Standing Committee either because they are of major (often constitutional) importance – such as the European Community (Amendment) Bill of 1985–86 – or because they are so uncontroversial that they will take up no time on the floor, such as the Diplomatic and Consular Premises Bill of 1986–87. Of the sixteen relevant Bills introduced in the period 1983–84 to 1988–89, ten had their committee stages on the floor of the House. Of the six which went to Standing Committee, four took only one meeting to complete. Five of the sixteen Bills were so uncontroversial as to have their second readings take place in committee rather than on the floor of the House, with the longest of those meetings taking 1 hour 40 minutes.

Secondary legislation gives rise to more Standing Committee activity than primary legislation, in that a number of instruments – mostly orders for capital grants to international development funds or orders giving certain diplomatic or legal status to representatives of international organizations – require House of Commons approval but are not sufficiently controversial to require time on the floor of the House. However, of twenty-two Standing Committee meetings on twenty-nine instruments and EC documents (more than one instrument can be considered at one meeting) in the sessions 1983–89 only two took longer than one hour, with several taking less than five minutes. No debates on negative instruments ('prayers') on foreign affairs matters were held in Standing Committee.

The Foreign Affairs Committee

The establishment of the Foreign Affairs Committee (FAC) in 1979, as part of a much wider reform of the structure of Select Committees, has been the biggest single change in the organization of the scrutiny of foreign affairs issues by the House of Commons. The effect of the 1979 reforms overall must not of course be exaggerated: foreign affairs were covered before 1979 as part of the remit of the Defence and External Affairs Sub-committee of the Expenditure Committee established in 1970 and development was covered by the Select Committee on Overseas Development, established in 1972, and by earlier committees. Nevertheless, as has been discussed in commentaries on the 1979 reforms elsewhere,[13] they were something of a quantum leap in the role of Select Committees in the life of the House of Commons.

Like the other departmentally related Select Committees established under what is now Standing Order No. 130, the FAC is charged with examining the 'expenditure, administration and policy' of the department to which it is related and its 'associated public bodies'. This gives the FAC an interest in the Foreign and Commonwealth Office, the Overseas Development Administration, the British Council and the BBC External Services, together with a number of much smaller bodies. The Expenditure Committee of 1970–79 had had narrower terms of reference, confined in theory to expenditure, so that the FAC has greater freedom to inquire into purely policy areas than had its predecessor. The FAC has from time to time considered issues which involve the responsibility of other departments – e.g. overseas student fees (Department of Education and Science), trade with the USSR and trade with South East Asia (Department of Trade and Industry) – just as other departmentally related committees have from time to time considered issues of interest to the FCO.

The FAC has eleven members, with a quorum of three. A certain continuity of membership has been maintained after each General Election: seven of the members nominated in 1983 had been members of the 1979–83 committee, and six of the members nominated in 1987 had been members of the 1983–87 committee. In addition, four of the members first nominated in 1979 had been members of the former Defence and External Affairs Sub-committee of the Expenditure Committee or of the former Select Committee on Overseas Development. These included Sir Anthony Kershaw, the Conservative Member for Stroud and former Foreign Office minister, who became the FAC's first chairman and remained chairman until his retirement from the House in 1987. Out of a total of twenty-nine members who have served on the FAC at some time since 1979, fourteen have been former front-benchers, of whom six have been FCO ministers or foreign affairs spokesmen. The FAC has thus generally had a certain expertise among its membership. This expertise has been augmented by the specialist advisers employed by the FAC (under the general rules for such advisers, under which a Select Committee may appoint outside experts, on a *per diem* remuneration, to assist it). These have included former diplomats, academics, and staff of independent research institutes such as the Royal Institute of International Affairs. The precise role of advisers can differ from adviser to adviser, from inquiry to inquiry, and from year to year. In some inquiries, such as that on the patriation of the Canadian Constitution, advisers have been heavily involved in drafting the report and in others, notably in the majority of inquiries in the 1983–87 Parliament, their role has been slight.

Compared to the role and powers of committees in certain other parliaments the powers of the Commons' departmentally related Select Committees, including the Foreign Affairs Committee, are limited. Although the terms of reference are wide-ranging in subject matter, the

FAC's role is limited to inquiry and monitoring. Thus legislation and treaties are excluded in the sense that the FAC has no power to amend or veto or delay legislation or treaties. This is not to say that the committee cannot examine legislation or treaties – they can and do, as in the case of the inquiries into the British North America Acts in 1981 (mentioned above) or the Single European Act in 1986 – but that the committee's recommendations have no direct effect and that the extent to which they may be acted upon depends upon the degree to which the committee can affect the general debate on the issues by force of argument and publicity. Likewise, the FAC has no executive power over aspects of the FCO administration, such as expenditure or senior and ambassadorial appointments, as some foreign committees have. Calls for the Foreign Affairs Committee – and other committees – to have much wider powers of investigation and legislation, akin to the powers held by committees in Washington, arise from time to time, but these raise much wider questions affecting all Commons Select Committees and the whole Parliament–Government relationship.

The FAC has tended to hold between thirty-five and forty formal meetings during a full session. Most of these are meetings at which evidence is taken from ministers or other witnesses from Government, or from outside, such as academics and, on occasion, from foreign politicians and ambassadors. Many meetings are, however, private deliberative sessions at which the FAC considers its choice of topic, its mode of proceeding, and the content of its reports. Subjects for inquiry may be, and are, suggested by outside sources, including other Members, pressure groups, aid organizations and (informally) the Government. The decision as to what to examine rests, however, entirely with the members of the committee, and in practice the subjects chosen reflect the interests of the members of the committee, led by the chairman, at the time. In general, the FAC attempts to avoid subjects which are too likely to be unamenable to a cross-party approach. The inquiry into the sinking of the *General Belgrano* and the surrounding diplomatic events, in which there was a total party split on the text of the report, is an example of what can happen if the topic is too controversial in party political terms.[14]

The range of topics formally considered can be seen from the full list of published reports listed in Table 6 (pp. 35–6). Some are very brief, reflecting either a small topic or an interim report, while others are substantial. Many concern aspects of FCO administration or expenditure, and the basic expenditure plans of the FCO have led to a report in each year not interrupted by a General Election since the FAC was established (except the very first). Most of the reports, however, concern some current topic of importance, whether broad-brush and unrelated to a particular event (such as UK–Soviet relations) or directed at a specific issue (such as the introduction of 'full cost' fees for overseas students in

1980). Several such reports have been in part inquests on recent events, for example the reports on Grenada in 1984 and on Diplomatic Immunities and Privileges in 1984/5 (which reviewed the Libyan Embassy shooting and the attempted kidnap of Mr Umaru Dikko). The committee is free to return to subjects it has considered in the past, either issuing a separate report (as in the case of the Turks and Caicos Islands development) or covering the topic as part of its annual expenditure monitoring inquiry. Indeed the committee's effectiveness is enhanced by this type of harrying role.

A number of the reports are concerned primarily with development issues. Before 1983 development issues were considered by a distinct sub-committee. The FAC, along with only two other of the departmentally related committees, had been given the power under the 1979 reforms to set up a sub-committee. This was partly with a view to enabling the work of the former Select Committee on Overseas Development to be continued. The Foreign Affairs Committee was, however, not required to nominate overseas development as the subject for the sub-committee, or indeed to set up the sub-committee at all, and since 1983 the FAC has chosen not to appoint a sub-committee. This has meant that development issues have received less formalized attention in the FAC's programme than previously. At the same time it has meant that they are brought properly before the whole membership of the committee, rather than just the sub-committee members, and that the issues are considered in a more integrated way with the accompanying political questions.

But the work of the committee in considering foreign affairs on behalf of the House is not limited to the formal process of a specific inquiry and report. Some hearings are held unrelated to particular inquiries. Of significance in this category are the various meetings (about twice a year) held with the Foreign Secretary to discuss a range of topical issues. This practice was begun in the 1979–83 Parliament when the then Foreign Secretary (Lord Carrington) was in the House of Lords and was thus not subject to the normal accountability of Commons Question Time, but was continued after Lord Carrington ceased to be Foreign Secretary in 1982. As an example, at one such meeting in July 1986 the committee questioned the then Foreign Secretary, Sir Geoffrey Howe, on disarmament and UK–USA relations, and, briefly, on the US bombing raid on Libya (this latter being a subject to which the committee otherwise devoted no time, as noted in the case study in Chapter 7).[15] A recent development has been to take evidence from the Foreign Secretary shortly before each EC summit meeting. Additionally much work is done by the FAC outside the confines of the formally recorded meetings. The committee travel abroad in connection with inquiries (a total of fifty-two different countries and three dependent territories had been visited by the FAC, though rarely by all its members, up to the end of the 1988–89 session) and holds numerous informal meetings between members of the committee and political leaders and representatives of other states and organizations both at Westminster and elsewhere.[16] As an example, a number of meetings were held with Chilean politicians visiting London, often at the invitation of the British Government, in the years immediately prior to the end of the Pinochet regime.

What effect has the work, or the existence, of the Foreign Affairs Committee had on the House of Commons's consideration of foreign affairs? In terms of quantity of work done, it is certainly highly significant: the FCO and the Government have been held to account on far more issues, and in respect of some issues in far greater depth, than would have been the case without the existence of the committee. How far Government policy, or implementation of policy, has been affected by the committee's work and recommendations is more difficult to assess. Outright acceptance of recommendations which the Government were not otherwise inclined to follow anyway is rare, but, as with other Select Committees, this is not a full measure of the many indirect ways in which the FAC may have contributed to shifts in policy or to the climate of opinion from which policy arises.

Equally the effect of the committee's work on the Chamber is difficult to assess. Certainly, as with other departmentally related Select Committees, the Foreign Affairs Committee has found it difficult to bring its work systematically to the attention of the House as a whole. The principal direct contribution has perhaps been to provide a number of better-informed members for the existing debates. But a number of FAC reports have been debated in the House, either directly or as integral parts of wider debates and it is clear that other Members of the House interested in foreign affairs, such as Opposition front-bench spokesmen, keep themselves reasonably informed about its work. Arguably the committee's most significant work was in respect of the debate on the patriation of the power to amend the Canadian Constitution in the early 1980s, in which the FAC's greatest influence was perhaps in Canada rather than in the UK. This may reflect the way in which a Select Committee (not just the Foreign Affairs Committee) can have maximum effect when it reaches a cross-party accord on a highly topical, but relatively narrow, issue. It also illustrates one of the ways in which Parliament can play a direct role in international affairs, without the mediation of the Government.

Other Select Committees

The Foreign Affairs Committee is not the only Select Committee forum in which foreign affairs are considered. Two other committees must be noted in particular: the Select Committee on European Legislation and the Committee of Public Accounts. It should also be remembered that the House can at any time set up an *ad hoc* committee to consider a specific issue. This was not infrequently done before the establishment in 1979 of a committee system which allowed a comprehensive coverage of Government activity, though only one such committee was established on a foreign affairs issue (on Cyprus in 1975) since 1945. None has been established on foreign affairs since 1979.

The Select Committee on European Legislation was established in 1974 to scrutinize draft legislative proposals from the Commission to the Council of Ministers and some non-legislative documents submitted to the Council of Ministers or European Council. A major function is to establish which are of sufficient importance to be considered by the House, either on the floor of the House or in a Standing Committee on European Community Documents. It publishes relevant evidence and representations submitted from interested parties. Although the FCO is formally the lead department on European Community matters, the lead on particular proposals is taken by the department responsible for policy in the area concerned. Thus, very few such proposals – mostly those concerned with overseas development or general issues – are the direct concern of the FCO and most of the committee's work does not therefore directly affect the House of Commons' consideration of foreign affairs. However, its role and activity give it a close interest in the institutional structure of the European Community, in the relationship between those institutions and the British Government and Parliament, and the broad direction of policy on the European Community. It has taken a lead in current moves to enhance the quality of House of Commons consideration of European Community issues, principally with the Single European Market in mind. The Commons' Procedure Committee has since reported a number of recommendations on procedures for considering European legislation[17] and it remains to be seen what effect the subsequent changes may have.

The terms of reference and programme of the Committee of Public Accounts (PAC) bring all Government departments within its field of interest. It operates on the basis of reports prepared by the National Audit Office (NAO) and generally takes further written and oral evidence from the Government department or agency involved before issuing a report. Recent studies by PAC in the foreign affairs field have included reports on management of the overseas estate (1984–85), the financial control and accountability to Parliament of the BBC External Services (1987–88), and manpower aid to developing countries (1987–8). Altogether seven PAC reports between 1983 and 1988 concerned the FCO or ODA, which should be compared to the forty or so reports that PAC agrees each year. Its remit goes beyond questions of financial probity to questions of value for money in expenditure and administration, and this is reflected in the reports noted above. The limits of what amounts to value for money inquiries are not always easy to determine and PAC has been accused by other committees from time to time of straying into areas of policy. This has happened in the field of foreign affairs where the issue of the appropriate nature and quality of embassy buildings in certain capitals was approached differently by the PAC and by the Foreign Affairs Committee, with the former stressing the need for financial efficiency and the latter the possible diplomatic disadvantages of being seen to withdraw from prestigious buildings. In general, the PAC does not exert a significant influence on any issues of policy in the diplomatic field, though the potential for its involvement could be higher in the area of overseas development where 'policy' and 'administration of policy' are more closely linked.

Conclusion

The foregoing analysis has shown that, despite the small quantity of legislation associated with foreign affairs and the FCO, foreign affairs business holds the floor of the House of Commons to much the same extent as the business of other major departments, including those which do regularly bring forward legislation. A variety of political and procedural considerations constrain the amount of time actually devoted to foreign affairs to an amount which is reasonably consistent taking one year with another and in relation to other departments' interests. If the amount of time devoted to foreign affairs none the less may seem to some to be unsatisfactory, this is probably because of the vast range of topics which fall into the category of 'foreign affairs' by comparison with which the affairs of a home department might seem narrowly focused and parochial. Nevertheless, the procedures available are flexible, and since the dates of recesses are not rigidly fixed and the House can and does often sit late into the night, the Government of the day does have some freedom to accommodate extra debates and statements on foreign affairs if there is a pressing need, often following consultation with Opposition parties through the 'usual channels'. Indeed, in extreme cases, such as the Falklands conflict, the House can choose to sit at a weekend or in the middle of what would normally be a recess, although such events have been rare. Few foreign affairs developments will go by with no reaction by the House or its Members of some kind, whether it is just a Written Question or Early Day Motion, or a full-scale debate.

If the primary purpose of Parliament is to give vent to the interplay of arguments and interests which determine public policy, then the proceedings on the record, on the floor of the House and in committee, which are described in this chapter, constitute the main manifestation of Commons's activity in foreign affairs. However, that they are not the sole part of that activity is readily apparent. The 'behind the scenes' activities described in Chapter 4 complement and help to explain much of what takes place on the record. Though less visible and more difficult to describe they may be no less important.

Table 6 Reports of the Foreign Affairs Committee 1979–90

The most substantial reports of the Committee, in terms of length, are indicated in **bold type**. Relatively brief reports are in *italic type*. The letters after the title of each report indicate the principal field(s) covered by the report: foreign policy and FCO administration, excluding the EC (F), European Community issues (E), and aid and development (A).

Session	*Report*	*Ref.*	*Title*
1979–80	1st	HC 490	Moscow Olympic Games (F)
	2nd	HC 511	*FCO Organisation* (F)
	3rd	HC 553	Overseas Students' Fees (A)
	4th	HC 718	ODA's Development Divisions (A)
	5th	HC 745	Afghanistan (F)
1980–81	1st & 2nd	HC 42; HC 295	**British North America Acts** (F)
	3rd	HC 26	Turks and Caicos Islands (A)
	4th	HC 343	FCO/ODA Expenditure for FY 1981–82 (F/A)
	5th	HC 211	Mexico Summit (Brandt Report) (A)
	6th	HC 117	Zimbabwe (British Aid) (A)
	7th	HC 166	Gibraltar (F)
1981–82	1st	HC 128	*British North America Acts* (F)
	2nd & 3rd	HC 330; HC 406	FCO/ODA Expenditure for FY 1982–83 (F/A)
	4th	HC 71	Commonwealth Development Corporation (A)
	5th	HC 47	**Caribbean and Central America** (F)
1982–83	1st & 3rd	HC 117; HC 250	*Wiston House International Conference Centre* (F)
	2nd	HC 112	*Turks and Caicos Islands* (A)
	4th	HC 25	ODA's Scientific and Special Units (A)
1983–84	1st	HC 280	*FCO/ODA Supplementary Expenditure FY 1983–84* (F/A)
	2nd	HC 226	Grenada
	3rd	HC 480	The Fontainebleau Summit (E)
	4th	HC 421	FCO/ODA Expenditure for FY 1984–85 (F/A)
	5th	HC 268	**Falkland Islands** (F)

Table 6—continued

Session	Report	Ref.	Title
1984–85	1st	HC 127	Diplomatic Immunities and Privileges (F)
	2nd	HC 56	Famine in Africa (A)
	3rd	HC 11	**Events of 1–2 May 1982 (Belgrano)** (F)
	4th	HC 295	FCO/ODA Expenditure for FY 1985–86 (F/A)
	5th	HC 461	Unesco (F/A)
1985–86	1st	HC 123	*Famine in Africa/Supplementary expenditure FY 1985–86* (A)
	2nd	HC 28	**UK–Soviet relations** (F)
	3rd	HC 442	Single European Act (E)
	4th	HC 255	FCO/ODA Expenditure for FY 1986–87 (F/A)
	5th	HC 368	The Philippines (F/A)
	6th	HC 61	South Africa (F)
1986–87	1st	HC 114	**S E Asia and Indo-China** (F/A)
	2nd	HC 32	Bilateral Aid: Country Programmes (A)
	3rd	HC 23	Cyprus (F)
	4th	HC 24	*Cultural Diplomacy* (F)
1987–88	1st	HC 297	Famine in the Horn of Africa (A)
	2nd	HC 279	Iran/Iraq Conflict (F)
	3rd	HC 280	Arms Control and Disarmament (F)
	4th	HC 429	*FCO/ODA Expenditure for FY 1988–89* (F/A)
1988–89	1st	HC 16	**Eastern Europe and the Soviet Union** (F)
	2nd	HC 281	Hong Kong (F)
	3rd	HC 264	*FCO/ODA Expenditure for FY 1989–90* (F/A)
1989–90	1st	HC 255	Unesco (F/A)
	2nd	HC 82	Operation of the Single European Act (E)
	3rd	HC 264	*FCO/ODA Expenditure for FY 1990–91* (F/A)
	4th	HC 335	German Unification (F/E)

▮▮▮▮ THREE

Parliament and treaties

▮▮▮▮▮

In many countries parliaments have a constitutionally defined part to play in the ratification of treaties. The significance of parliamentary powers in respect of treaties varies a good deal and depends on the standing of the parliaments themselves. In some cases, such as the USA, the powers conferred on the Senate are of fundamental importance in defining the influence of the legislature in the field of foreign policy. In the absence of a written constitution the part played by the British Parliament in the ratification of treaties rests on convention and practice. This chapter explores the rules which govern treaty procedure in the UK and looks at some ways in which they might be improved.

The subject has rarely been tackled in this way before and the details are not widely understood outside of the Foreign and Commonwealth Office. The reader is warned in advance that there are many complications along the way. I have tried to explain these as clearly as possible and to provide helpful examples. Most, if not all, of the complications do have a rational explanation and reflect the complexity of a modern world order which relies heavily on bilateral and multilateral agreements.

Treaties and the treaty-making power

The Vienna Convention on the Law of Treaties (in force since 1980) defines a treaty as 'an international agreement concluded between States in written form and governed by international law, whether embodied in a single instrument or in two or more related instruments and whatever its particular designation'. Only a minority of such agreements are in fact designated as 'treaties'. In general that name is reserved for agreements of particular significance. Other common designations are 'convention', 'protocol', 'agreement' or 'exchange of notes', but there may be agreements described as 'act' or 'final act', 'concordat' or 'agreed minute'. The use of the various terms is explained in *Satow's Guide to Diplomatic Practice*.[1]

The definition quoted above includes the phrase 'governed by international law'. Under Article 102 of the Charter of the United Nations, 'every treaty and every international agreement entered into by any Member of the United Nations' must be registered with the UN Secretariat and published. Agreements which are not registered in this way may not be invoked before any organ of the United Nations. Since the latter include the International Court of Justice this means in effect that unpublished agreements are not governed by international law. This, of course, does not prevent governments from concluding confidential agreements, but such agreements are not enforceable in international law.

According to constitutional practice in the UK, Parliament has no formal role in treaty-making, the power for which is vested in the executive, acting on behalf of the Crown. Where a treaty requires a change in UK legislation or the grant of public money, then Parliament may vote in the normal way to make or deny the required provision, but otherwise it can overcome the will of the executive to conclude a particular treaty only by expressing disapproval and relying on political pressure to change the mind of ministers, or, in the extreme case, by withdrawing its confidence from them. The lack of formal parliamentary involvement in treaty-making distinguishes the British Parliament from most other national legislatures. With few exceptions, most written constitutions stipulate that parliamentary approval of treaties is required before ratification for at least some categories of treaty. For example the constitution of the USA provides that treaties shall be made by 'the President by and with the advice and consent of two-thirds of the Senators present and voting'.[2]

The difference between UK and foreign practice is actually less than it appears. Early in the twentieth century a practice was established whereby any treaty *subject to ratification* is laid before Parliament for at least twenty-one days before ratification is carried out (ratification being by executive instrument under the prerogative – in effect merely a written confirmation of willingness to be bound and the attachment of the Great Seal to a facsimile of the treaty). This practice began as an undertaking given in 1924 by Arthur Ponsonby, the Under-Secretary of State for Foreign Affairs in the first Government of Ramsay MacDonald. As a back-bencher, Ponsonby had been an avid campaigner for more open government in the field of foreign affairs (e.g. in *Democracy and Diplomacy*, 1915). Ponsonby's undertaking, given in the course of the Second Reading of the Treaty of Peace (Turkey) Bill on the afternoon of 1 April 1924, was actually in two parts: to lay every treaty, when signed, for a period of twenty-one days before ratification and publication in the Treaty Series, and to *inform* the House of all other 'agreements, commitments and understandings which may in any way bind the nation to specific action in certain circumstances'.[3] The 'Ponsonby Rule' was withdrawn during the subsequent Baldwin Government, but it was reinstated in 1929 and gradually hardened into a constitutional practice, observed in principle by all Governments, except in cases of emergency.[4]

The practice is recorded in the current (twenty-first) edition of Erskine May's *Parliamentary Practice* in the following terms:

> When a treaty requires ratification, the Government does not usually proceed with the ratification until a period of twenty-one days has elapsed from the date on which the text of such a treaty was laid before Parliament by Her Majesty's command. This practice is subject to modification, if necessary, when urgent or other important considerations arise.[5]

The FCO interprets the rule as applying to accession as well as ratification. Accession arises when the British Government *accedes* to a treaty of which it was not an original signatory while the treaty was open for signature.

There is no presumption that Parliament will debate every treaty laid under the Ponsonby Rule, but once Parliament has been presented with the text of an important or controversial treaty it is difficult in practice for the Leader of the House to resist a debate on it. Indeed Ponsonby's original announcement included the promise that 'if there is a formal demand for discussion forwarded through the usual channels from the opposition or any other party, time will be found for the discussion of the treaty in question'.[6] Consequently it may be said that any controversial treaty *which requires ratification* is as likely to be debated in the House of Commons as in other comparable parliaments. In practice such treaties are rare: the Hong Kong treaty, which is discussed in more detail on pp. 44–5, offers a recent example.

In addition, the British Government, like other governments, frequently concludes agreements with other governments which are not subject to ratification. Ratification was the norm in treaty-making when it was necessary to ensure that the ministers or diplomats who had negotiated the treaty had not exceeded their instructions and that the Government in question was prepared to be bound by the text which they had signed. Modern communications have made it possible for negotiators to remain constantly in touch with their governments. As a result the modern view of international law is that treaties need ratification only if a specific requirement for it is written into the treaty.[7] This would still normally be the case where national legislation is needed to implement the treaty or where there is a strong political content.

By contrast, in financial and technical matters governments often find it expedient to agree that a particular arrangement will enter into force immediately upon signature or upon mutual notification shortly after signature, without any process of ratification. Agreements of this nature would not normally be designated as 'treaties', but they are no less enforceable in international law for lack of ratification. In the USA they are known as executive agreements and are presented to Congress within sixty days of conclusion under the Case-Zablocki Act 1972, but in most countries the requirement to inform Parliament is absolute only where the agreement requires ratification or specifies that there should be parliamentary approval. In the UK agreements not subject to ratification are normally laid before Parliament, as Command Papers in the Treaty Series, only after they have entered into force. However, when a substantial delay is anticipated between signature and entry into force, the text is often printed in the 'Country' Series of Command Papers after signature in order to meet the demand for copies from interested parties. Like all Command Papers these are laid before Parliament, but not for it to express any opinion: the Government is already fully bound by the agreement.

A third category of international agreements consists of those which are not published at all. These are most commonly known as Memoranda of Understanding and may or may not be classified as confidential. As noted above, they are not strictly treaties and are not governed by international law. None the less, such non-binding agreements are quite common between allied governments, for example, in respect of detailed defence arrangements. In the USA even these agreements are communicated to Congress, but the President may determine that only the Foreign Affairs Committees of the two Houses should be informed, and then in conditions of secrecy. British Governments have not normally felt under any obligation to submit agreements of this nature to Parliament. A recent example of limited disclosure after entry into force was that of the UK–US Memorandum of Understanding on British participation in the Strategic Defense Initiative (SDI). The fact that the memorandum had been signed was announced to Parliament by the Secretary of State for Defence,[8] but its contents were not revealed except, at a later date and in confidence, to the Defence Select Committee.[9]

Treaties which come before the House of Commons

Treaties and other agreements not yet in force may be debated by the House of Commons for a variety of reasons and under a variety of procedures. In addition to the small number which are debated, there are others which are laid under the Ponsonby Rule and thereby receive tacit approval. In the following discussion the common element is that all of the agreements are submitted before entry into force, though this does not in all cases imply that Parliament has the power to set them aside.

Treaties which require legislation

The most important of these in recent times has been the Treaty of Rome, which was given effect in the UK by the European Communities Act 1972. Any amendment has also to be by UK legislation. Thus, for example, the enlargements of the EC to include Greece, Spain and Portugal required legislation. More recently, the agreement by the 'Twelve' to amend the Treaty of Rome by means of the Single European Act (a treaty, not an Act of Parliament) was given effect in the UK by means of the European Communities (Amendment) Act 1986 and was debated at some length in both Houses of Parliament.

However, one of the effects of the Treaty of Rome and the European Communities Act was to confer certain treaty-making powers on EC bodies, enabling them to negotiate economic agreements with non-EC states and international organizations on behalf of the Community as a whole. Such agreements are not subject to the Ponsonby Rule and are officially published in the UK only after entry into force. Proposals for EC external agreements are sent in draft to the House of Commons Select Committee on European legislation along with other EC Commission Drafts. The Select Committee is required by its terms of reference to report 'whether such proposals or other documents raise questions of legal or political importance . . . and to make recommendations for the further consideration of such proposals and other documents by the House'. In practice, the Committee very rarely comments on draft external agreements and they are almost invariably listed at the back of its reports among the documents which 'do not raise questions of legal or political importance'. The House of Lords Select Committee on the European Communities does occasionally examine the issues arising from the external relations and agreements of the EC. For example in the 1988/89 session it delivered a substantial report on *Relations between the European Community and Japan* (HL 65).

Treaties with direct financial implications

These require the assent of the House of Commons because they affect revenue. The most common type are bilateral agreements to avoid double taxation. The texts are laid in the form of draft Orders in Council and are occasionally debated. For example the draft UK–Sweden double taxation agreement was debated on 22 February 1984,[10] and similar agreements with France and Mauritius were debated together and approved on 15 January 1987.[11]

Treaties which stipulate parliamentary approval

Where an agreement is of political nature and is known to be controversial, one or both of the governments involved may wish to safeguard its position by writing an express requirement for parliamentary approval into the text.

Such was the case with the Anglo-Irish Agreement on Northern Ireland of 1985. The Agreement was signed by the Prime Ministers of the UK and the Irish Republic at Hillsborough on 15 November 1985 and the text was presented to Parliament on the same day as Cmnd 9657. The text referred to the condition of parliamentary approval being obtained in both countries before entry in force, but did not refer to ratification. There were two days of heated debate in the House of Commons on 26–27 November 1985 before a vote in which the Agreement was approved by 473 votes to 46. On 29 November the two governments exchanged notifications and the Agreement entered into force. On 11 December 1985 the text was presented to Parliament once again (Cmnd 9690), but this time as no 62 (1985) of the Treaty Series.

It will be noted that in this example only fourteen days elapsed between signature and entry into force, but (1) the Ponsonby Rule did not, strictly speaking, apply because this was not a treaty requiring ratification, and (2) the Government had in any case taken the initiative in seeking parliamentary approval and providing time for the debate.

Treaties which require ratification

Treaties and other agreements which do require ratification are laid as Command Papers and are notionally classed in the 'Miscellaneous' series or in a 'Country' series. For example, an agreement with Mauritius signed in 1986 appeared as 'Mauritius no 1 (1986)' when it was laid under the Ponsonby Rule and reappeared after ratification as 'Treaty Series no 6 (1987)'. The fact that a treaty has been laid is brought to the attention of Members of Parliament by means of its inclusion in the list of papers laid each day, which is appended to the daily *Votes and Proceedings*. Treaties fall into the category of 'other papers' which follows 'papers subject to affirmative resolution' and 'papers subject to negative resolution'. The description of the document in its long title gives little indication of its contents or significance and to discover these a Member has to request a copy of the Command Paper from the Vote Office.

Strictly speaking, the Ponsonby procedure applies only to agreements

Table 7 Agreements requiring ratification 1986–88 (some titles abbreviated)

1986–87
1 Agreement on the Reconstruction of the Commonwealth Agricultural Bureaux as CAB International (Cm 17)
2 Protocol amending the Convention for the Prevention of Marine Pollution (Cm 87)
3 Agreement with Jamaica for promotion and protection of investments (Cm 99)

1987–88
1 Convention establishing the Multilateral Investment Guarantee Agency (Cm 150)
2 Agreement on an International Trust Fund for Tuvalu (Cm 160)
3 Convention on Social Security between Sweden and the UK (Cm 245)
4 Convention on the Law of Treaties between States and International Organisations (Cm 244)
5 Montreal Protocol on Substances that deplete the Ozone Layer (Cm 283)
6 Protocol on Privileges and Immunities of Eutelsat (Cm 305)
7 Agreement among USA, Belgium, West Germany, Italy, Netherlands and UK on INF Treaty inspections (Cm 312)*
8 European Convention for the Prevention of Torture (Cm 339)
9 Protocol for the suppression of unlawful acts of violence at airports (Cm 378)
10 Final Act of the Conference on Privileges and Immunities of Eumetsat (Cm 397)
11 Convention between member states of the EEC on Double Jeopardy (Cm 438)
12 International Natural Rubber Agreement (Cm 468)

Note: * It is not entirely clear that this Agreement was laid under the Ponsonby Rule. It was laid ahead of entry into force, but the text does not refer to ratification. It says that the Agreement 'shall be subject to approval in accordance with the constitutional procedures of each Party'.

which require ratification, but in practice it seems to be applied also in other cases where a two-stage process occurs. For example in certain international organizations, such as the World Health Organization, it is possible for a member state to propose amendments to the constitution which other member states may or may not accept. If the British Government is inclined to accept, it lays the text first as a Command Paper in the Miscellaneous series, though the second stage is to be acceptance rather than ratification. Another analogous case arises with resolutions to extend existing agreements.[12]

How many texts are currently laid under the Ponsonby Rule? The FCO does not keep statistics of the flow of such texts, but totals and lists may be compiled by examining the Command Papers of any given period. In the session 1986–87 (a short session, running from November 1986 to the dissolution of May 1987) there were only three texts laid which required ratification and a further two of the kind described in the previous paragraph. In the session 1987–88 (a long session running from June 1987 to November 1988) there were twelve requiring ratification and three of the second kind. Table 7 lists the agreements which required ratification and were presented to Parliament in the course of these two sessions and gives some indication of the wide range of subjects covered by the UK's bilateral and multilateral agreements with other countries.

Of the fifteen texts listed in Table 7, three were debated before ratification: Cm 150 and Cm 339 because they involved primary and secondary legislation respectively and Cm 283 because related EC documents were recommended for debate by the European Legislation Committee. The low proportion of treaties and similar agreements actually debated is not a new phenomenon. In 1953 Viscount Hinching-brooke asked Mr Selwyn Lloyd how many major treaties ratified since 1939 had been subject to an appropriate resolution by both Houses of Parliament. By way of reply Mr Selwyn Lloyd listed seventeen major political treaties of which only two (those setting up the United Nations and NATO) had been the subject of motions before ratification, though others had been dealt with under 'Treaties of Peace' legislation.[13]

An example of the Ponsonby mechanism being applied to a major political treaty is the Sino-British Agreement on Hong Kong, which came before Parliament during the 1984–85 session.

Negotiations between Britain and China on the future of Hong Kong had taken place between September 1982 and September 1984. The status of Hong Kong rested (at least in official British eyes) on a series of nineteenth-century Sino-British treaties, the last of which gave Britain a ninety-nine-year lease on the 'New Territories'. This lease is due to expire in 1997 and applies to 92 per cent of the Colony. Rather than attempt to hold on to the remaining 8 per cent under a treaty not recognized as valid by China, the British Government decided to negotiate an agreement for the orderly return of the whole territory to Chinese sovereignty in 1997 with agreed safeguards for the Hong Kong population.

A Draft Agreement was reached in September 1984 and laid before Parliament along with some explanatory material as Cmnd 9352. A debate in Government time was arranged for 5 December 1984 and the Draft Agreement was approved. On 19 December 1984 the Prime Minister signed the Agreement in Beijing. The Agreement required ratification and this in turn required UK legislation because it involved the cession of territory and special arrangements for nationality. The Hong Kong Bill was published on 10 January 1985, received a full-day debate on second reading in the House of Commons (21 January 1985) and a shorter second reading debate in the House of Lords (19 February 1985). Only after it had passed all stages and received the Royal Assent was the Agreement ratified by means of an exchange of instruments. Thus it entered into force on 27 May 1985. In June 1985 it was published again (Cmnd 9543) as Treaty Series no 26 (1985).

It may be seen from this account that the Hong Kong Agreement was published and debated in draft before signature – a procedure not required by the Ponsonby Rule, but explained by the peculiar importance and sensitivity of the Agreement. Because of this there was no need to lay the text again after signature and it was available to the House throughout the 159 days between signature and ratification, during which the Hong Kong Bill was debated and passed in all its stages.

Agreements which are politically but not legally binding

These are strictly not treaties at all (see the definition on p. 37) but share many characteristics with treaties. The thirty-five-nation Conference on Security and Co-operation in Europe (CSCE) produced a Final Act on 1 August 1975, usually known as the Helsinki Final Act. The Final Act imposed a wide range of obligations upon the signatories and the latter declared 'their determination to act in accordance with the provisions'. Nevertheless, the text stated quite explicitly that the Final Act was not eligible for registration under Article 102 of the UN Charter, that is it was not to be governed by international law.

The CSCE has given rise to a number of follow-up conferences and agreements, including the Stockholm Conference of 1984–86 which resulted in the signature of a 'Document' on Confidence-and-Security-Building Measures on 19 September 1986. Like the Helsinki Final Act, the Stockholm Document was to be 'politically binding' (para 101) but not legally binding. The Document was to enter into force on 1 January 1987 and there was no provision for parliamentary approval or ratification. Indeed if any of the signatories had attempted to withdraw from the agreement between signature and entry into force the long hard work needed to achieve a thirty-five-nation consensus would have been wasted. None the less the British Government presented the Document to the House of Commons as Cm 26 in November 1986, before entry into force, though not classed in any series.

Possible changes to current practice

The treaty procedures described in this chapter may appear so complicated and untidy as to encourage the view that the system is in need of a complete overhaul. In practice it is difficult to identify a set of simplifying changes which would cover all the cases and not cause new difficulties. The complexity partly reflects the reality that international agreements come in all shapes and sizes. It is also undeniable that many of these agreements are of a technical and uncontroversial nature and contain little of political interest which would reward increased attention on the part of Parliament. It is interesting to note, by way of comparison, that in the mid-1980s the Foreign Affairs Committee of the French National Assembly was given little to do other than to scrutinize draft treaties and as a result it acquired a reputation as 'a refuge for lazy deputies'.[14] These considerations should not, however, discourage us from examining some possible changes to current practice.

These could include giving Parliament a formal role in approving treaties, as in many other countries, or could be limited to improving the present arrangements for scrutiny of those treaties already routinely presented to Parliament. The first would mark a significant constitutional change, but would not in all probability lead to major difficulties between legislature and executive since it has long been the practice of governments to seek parliamentary approval for controversial treaties (e.g. the Anglo-Irish Agreement of 1985, discussed on p. 42). If new procedures were used by oppositions to pre-empt parliamentary time for the debate of less controversial treaties or in order to draw attention to issues of principle (e.g. on overseas aid) reflected in routine co-operation agreements, this could cause difficulties for governments and their legislative programmes. It is arguable that parliamentary interest in foreign affairs would be increased if Parliament had a formal role in treaty-making, but a change in the formal position would not necessarily make for more effective scrutiny.

With or without a change in the formal position, more effective scrutiny of the Government's activities in the field of international agreements would almost certainly involve the establishment of some kind of specialist committee. In many parliaments treaties would fall within the remit of the Foreign Affairs Committee or equivalent. The House of Commons FAC has devoted considerable attention to the operation of the Single European Act (see Chapters 10 and 11) and made an excursion into the field of arms control negotiations and treaties in 1987–88 but it is unlikely that it would want to devote much time to the routine scrutiny of the more technical conventions. The task could, perhaps, be taken on by a special sub-committee of the Foreign Affairs Committee, but in that case it would require more members and resources. Some treaties and agreements would no doubt be of greater interest to other departmental Select Committees such as Transport or Environment, but at present they would take an interest only if the treaty or agreement in question related to one of their current inquiries.

One possible solution might be a small Select Committee on treaties similar to the existing Select Committee on European Legislation. Such a committee would examine all of the treaties laid under the Ponsonby Rule and make recommendations as to whether they should be considered by the whole House, by one of the departmental Select Committees (which would then report to the whole House) or not at all. As with the negative procedure for statutory instruments it would not be necessary for Parliament to give formal approval to all treaties. Difficulties could arise, however, if the new committee found substantially more agreements to be worthy of attention than are currently debated. The accumulation of even a small backlog could delay the ratification of international agreements.

There might also be a case for reviewing the terms of the Ponsonby Rule in view of the fact that treaties requiring ratification are now fairly rare. It is probably still true that the more momentous treaties are subject to ratification, but some quite significant agreements fall through the net. For example the Single European Act of 1986 was extensively debated because it required UK legislation, but the 'Decision' on the implementation of European Political Co-operation which accompanied it was published in the UK only in Minutes of Evidence to the Foreign Affairs Committee and this was after the second reading in the House of Commons of the European Communities (Amendment) Bill.[15] Thus a political agreement of considerable significance was not debated at all.

Another anomaly arose out of the INF Treaty of 1987 (see Chapter 8). The treaty itself was between the USA and USSR, but the UK, as one of the countries from which missiles were to be removed, was party to agreements on verification procedures with both sides. One agreement involved the USA and all of the NATO-basing countries and was 'subject to approval in accordance with the constitutional procedures of each party' (Cm 312). It was therefore arguably subject to the Ponsonby Rule. The other agreement, between the UK and USSR, was in the form of an Exchange of Notes (Cm 311) with no provision for ratification before entry into force. The Exchange of Notes was actually published as a Command Paper before entry into force, but not for parliamentary approval. While they were debated at length in the US Senate and in the USSR Supreme Soviet, none of these treaties was formally debated in the House of Commons. They were referred to in debates on legislation to confer diplomatic privileges and immunities on arms control inspectors, but the fact that this legislation did not refer to the INF Treaty led to some difficulties between participants in the debates and the occupants of the Chair over what it was in order to discuss. (The episode is treated in greater detail in Chapter 8.)

The problem with the Ponsonby Rule is that it makes parliamentary scrutiny depend on a rather arbitrary consideration – i.e. whether or not ratification is stipulated in the text. At present it can easily happen that an Agreement with Country A stipulates ratification because ratification is required by the constitutional law and practice of Country A; whereas an almost identical agreement with Country B omits reference to ratification because the law and practice of Country B (which may not have a Parliament at all) does not require it. The first agreement would be subject to scrutiny by the House of Commons under the Ponsonby Rule; the second would not.

Similar problems have arisen for the US Congress with the inexorable rise of the 'executive agreement', but procedures were devised under the Case-Zablocki Act 1972 whereby the legislature is formally consulted by the executive on whether particular international agreements should be concluded as treaties (subject to Senate ratification) or as executive agreements.[16]

The procedures currently governing parliamentary scrutiny of treaties in the UK are complex. The really significant treaties – the Hong Kong Agreement, the Anglo-Irish Agreement, the Single European Act – are debated, albeit under a variety of procedures. The complexity of the procedures partly reflects the complexity of international law and practice in treaty-making, but it also stems from the lack of formal treaty-making powers conferred on Parliament under the British constitution and the resulting resort to indirect methods of scrutiny. It may be that the treaties of major importance are scrutinized and that those of minor importance do not require detailed scrutiny. If there is a problem, it is probably that treaties and agreements of middling importance to the UK receive inconsistent and haphazard attention under the present system and it is in this area that improvements might be sought.

FOUR

Behind the scenes in the House of Commons

The impact of international events and of changes in British power is felt more obviously in those activities of parliamentarians which do not stand on the formal record of proceedings. MPs conduct themselves within circumstances which reflect recent changes in the international system.

This chapter explores the principal features of what might be construed as informal activity. It covers a wide range of phenomena. At one end are the elaborate procedures and formalities of bodies such as the Inter-Parliamentary Union (IPU) and the Commonwealth Parliamentary Association (CPA); at the other are private conversations between MPs who act as consultants and their clients. Apart from business interests declared in the Register or overseas visits described in annual reports, few activities can be quantified. It is impossible to provide a comprehensive picture of so many relevant consultations, discussions and private briefings.

There are two main features worth investigating. First, MPs seem less likely to have a direct knowledge of overseas matters from their own business and private contacts, and to be more dependent on special arrangements designed to provide them with the facts and arguments used by interested parties. MPs develop an instinct for identifying information that will have political value; their daily post-bags contain unsolicited mail from all kinds of groups; they are regularly making choices between which events to attend, which invitations to accept, and which to ignore. They have to judge where they stand in the face of the blandishments of public relations firms and of the clients in their

consultancies. Overseas affairs are subject to the same professionalization of the media as the domestic.

Second, governments and other official and unofficial bodies take more
direct interest in the public opinion of other countries and other
parliaments. MPs are one of the key target audiences in any campaign
designed to feed opinion leaders; they enjoy a status that can be used for
political purposes by their own and foreign governments. The Foreign
and Commonwealth Office sometimes wishes to use overseas the
argument that the House of Commons will insist on certain conditions;
foreign governments find it convenient to report the reactions in
Westminster to their own or to their opponents' moves. Even the KGB
has been accused of furthering its own position in Soviet affairs by
'feeding a line' to be picked up in Western parliaments. Overseas affairs
in the House of Commons are part of the wider fields of international
competition.[1]

This chapter follows the impact of international affairs and of changes
in British power on the House of Commons within a framework of
understanding suggested by these two main features of political communications. It describes both changes in the international climate and
the forms of adjustment to them which the British Parliament has
experienced. It explores the hypothesis that both the Government and
the Opposition front benches are constrained in what they can consider
about overseas affairs by the ways in which back-benchers can be made
more receptive to overseas interests. Ministers and Opposition leaders
hesitate to pursue options which will clearly attract animosity in
Parliament.

Context of learning

The impact of external events on the House of Commons can be seen both
in the organizations to which MPs are exposed and in the range of issues
which they are obliged to consider. They are awash with information
from many different sources. Those who deplore the quality of parliamentary interest in foreign affairs are commenting as much on the
difficulty of making sense of British interests as on the inadequacy of
contemporary judgements.

The conditions with which parliamentarians have had to come to terms
fall into a number of different phases, each marked by shifts in the
technology and style of communication. The first phase in Britain was a
combination of the issues of decolonization in the Commonwealth and
immigration from the Commonwealth, and it was quickly followed by the
British application to join the European Economic Community (EEC). All
these questions between 1955 and 1965 prompted the creation of pressure

groups and promotional public relations agencies which improved lobbying techniques and the tactics of securing media coverage. The next phases are tied to the cultivation of *détente* by the superpowers and to the flotation of the world's principal currencies. They coincide with the development of television through satellites in orbit, and with the sending of words and pictures by digital means. Remote sensing began to make more traditional forms of spying redundant. Important messages remain disguised by surrounding 'noise'; there are just more messages and more 'noise' to process. The Helsinki Accord of 1975 has gradually changed the frequency and method of East–West communication. More recent phases have been dominated by round-the-clock stock-trading in Tokyo, London and New York, and by the greater internationalization of finance for industry. In Britain the prospect of open trading within the EC after 1992 has brought extensive preparations. Firms need to be familiar with the different regimes in public affairs, especially in tax and labour law. Parliamentarians are deemed appropriate candidates for the consultancies which industrialists and contractors wish to employ.

Changes in the context of managing information can also be measured by the activities of international organizations which work for special causes. The *Year Book of International Organizations* notes the arrival since the early 1970s of international secretariats which co-ordinate the propaganda activities of parliamentarians across the world. For example, the Parliamentary Association for Euro-Arab Co-operation was founded in 1974, Parliamentarians for World Order in 1977, the European Committee for the Defence of Refugees and Immigrants in 1982, and the Association of Western European Parliamentarians against Apartheid in 1984. The international affairs sections of directories of pressure groups have grown apace, particularly because of the proliferation of civil rights cases which attract the attention of the media.

The impact of the decline of British power on the House of Commons was felt in a parallel set of changing circumstances. Both the major political parties were split by the question of entry into the European Community, but in different ways and with different effects. The Conservative party suffered initially from the loss of Empire but then gained confidence with the prospect of joining Europe. The Labour party was divided both by the dependence of the UK on the USA for the continued possession of a nuclear deterrent and by the prescriptions available for counteracting the UK's declining competitiveness in production and trade. As deindustrialization took place and as inward foreign investment in the British economy seemed to offer the best hopes of continued prosperity, the parties were also unable to create an agreed set of bipartisan policies. The Labour party was split with the creation of the Social Democrats in 1981. The latter resisted greater state intervention in the economy. The New Right did not carry the whole of the Conservative party into support for monetarism, and remained divided between loyalties to an open international economy and pressures to assist local British enterprise. More than anything else, the decline of British power simply created different kinds of parliamentary constituencies on the ground, such as the inner-city multi-ethnic community, the area with traditional industrial skills overtaken by new technology, and the science park with Japanese investment. MPs found themselves representing a new range of interests with their characteristic problems.

All these changes also coincided with the arrival of a new kind of candidate into parliamentary politics, particularly after Mrs Thatcher's electoral success in 1979. The Conservative party had fewer traditional public servants and more 'self-made men'. The Labour party relied more for its parliamentary candidates on 'knowledge and service industries' and less on the representatives of manual workers' trade unions. The MPs of the 1980s could not be expected to develop the judgement of statesmen with experience of using British power in the world to substantial effect.

During the same period, although the press, radio and television gave extensive coverage to overseas affairs, and reporters provided regular analyses of the foreign policies of other governments, the middle classes came to rely more and more on 'sound bites' for their understanding of the world and less and less on editorials and informed comment in quality newspapers. The latter employed fewer and fewer staff correspondents stationed overseas, and relied more and more on a limited number of international agencies.

The forms of adjustment

At the heart of the adjustment of the House of Commons to the changes in the international climate lie the attitudes of MPs to the generation, distribution and use of political information. By the late 1980s 180 MPs declared that they acted in some way as political consultants. There were well over 1,000 secretaries and research assistants with privileged access to the Palace of Westminster, all of whom might be tempted to capitalize on their knowledge of Parliament and to move into consultancy work. MPs and their research assistants know where they can secure appropriate briefing material, and which networks of influential people they can engage. Information can be bought, sold and exchanged. Parliamentarians can be hired for specific forms of advocacy and for advice on the most effective methods for securing the co-operation of governments, firms and other interested parties.[2]

Briefing can be acquired by back-benchers very quickly from a wide range of suppliers. There is a spectrum of sources, from the House of

Commons Library research staff at one end to the special pleadings of a private client at the other. The Library has a regular clientele of back-benchers and often flurries of activity as Members prepare for foreign visits or conferences. The Opposition front bench has the additional resource of analysis provided by the party headquarters.

The most obvious adjustment to the new climate of information is in the Foreign and Commonwealth Office itself. That department used to be regarded in Westminster as a home of misunderstandings, simply because it rarely required a knowledge of parliamentary procedure in order to pass legislation and its staff served for so long abroad that they lost touch with the niceties of British politics. The importance of securing a better understanding in Parliament of British positions in foreign policy became apparent, first when the parliamentary commissioner for administration (the Ombudsman) showed his interest in the fairness of departmental procedures after the Sachsenhausen affair in 1968, and second when the Falkland Islands lobby succeeded in blocking discussion of the proposal to lease the sovereignty of the territory to Argentina in 1980. By that date the FCO was prepared to welcome the proposal that a Select Committee should be established to consider foreign affairs. After Sachsenhausen it had created a parliamentary liaison unit; after the Falklands War this was extended to include a broader service of monitoring parliamentary committees and of providing hospitality and briefing for MPs. The Parliamentary Relations Unit keeps a computer data base on Members' interests and activities in foreign affairs. Such professionalism is a characteristic expression of the need to supplement traditional channels of influence in order to counteract the alternative sources of briefing which MPs can use.

Junior ministers in the FCO remain mediators between the department and back-bench opinion. The Secretary of State for Foreign Affairs will on occasion see the back-bench committee members of his own party. The FCO takes 'straw polls' from trusted MPs who are thought to be representative of parliamentary opinion. During the 1980s Conservative ministers chose such back-benchers as Sir Anthony Kershaw, then chairman of the Foreign Affairs Committee, and Sir Peter Blaker. The Opposition front bench is also sometimes given hints about the policy lines to be pursued. The FCO has the advantage of being able to brief MPs when they are abroad through its ambassadors. Some former Labour ministers may stay in British embassies serving a Conservative Government (e.g. Lord Callaghan). Select Committees travelling abroad and delegations from the British branches of the Inter-Parliamentary and Commonwealth Association are also entertained and briefed by British Ambassadors and High Commissioners. The Foreign Office often includes classified information in these briefing sessions which take place abroad, and provides Members of all parties and persuasions with the full hospitality accorded to embassy guests. Embassies also arrange for MPs to meet foreign politicians, journalists and experts.

But the briefing given by the British Government is not always the first to be considered. There are so many alternative sources. After a General Election there can be in Westminster almost the feel of a recruitment fair, as different networks test the orientations of new Members and bring them into the appropriate groupings. Some new Members may of course have strong connections before they enter the House. For example the various 'solidarity' groups on the hard Left of the Labour party may supply candidates for election. Some Conservative candidates may already have close ties with South African business. But for those Members who are elected before they have acquired any specific connections, there may be choices of identity to be made. The Council for the Advancement of Arab–British Understanding (CAABU) and the South Atlantic Council which seeks lasting solution to Anglo-Argentine differences like to look for recruits. Similarly the Cyprus CPA group is eager to strengthen British support for the cause of Greek Cypriots; Turkish Cypriots have their own group. The British–American Group (BAG) in 1988 received financial support from the House Administration Committee in order to send up to five newly elected MPs to the course run at Harvard University for newly elected Congressmen.[3]

Entry into a group concerned with overseas affairs may carry connotations of party identity or party reputation. The majority of groups contain Members who have a natural affinity with one of the major parties, and in some cases the group leadership is provided by MPs who seem unlikely to reach the front benches. Networking on behalf of different overseas causes can provide an alternative political career. The ambitious MP chooses his or her associates with care.

Denis Healey in his memoirs describes the mechanisms which 'assist impecunious socialists to learn something of the outside world'.[4] He stresses the value of the Konigswinter and Bilderberg conferences and of the proliferation of cultural congresses which used to be funded by the Ford and Rockefeller Foundations for the Congress of Cultural Freedom. He sees no shame in being funded by sources close to the CIA if the effects are beneficial to future socialist ministers. For example Healey attended many conferences on defence where he met Paul Nitze – an excellent apprenticeship for a future Secretary of State for Defence. Susan Crosland in her biography of her husband makes a traditional distinction in describing the apprenticeship of Tony Crosland, a future Secretary of State for Foreign Affairs: 'Tony didn't know anything about foreign affairs; he knew about international socialism'.[5]

MPs have the option of finding their own niche within established international institutions, such as the North Atlantic Assembly, the Inter-Parliamentary Union or the Commonwealth Parliamentary Association, or of creating their own vehicles for the aggregation of information and influence. The established institutions receive public money through regular Treasury grants-in-aid; other bodies have to raise subscriptions or find sponsors. The amount of foreign money going towards back-bench activity, either directly or indirectly, is difficult to quantify. For example the Bruges Group has its own funds and the Heritage Foundation is also occasionally active in Britain.

The established international institutions are cross-party, but follow different principles. There are three overseas parliamentary assemblies for which British delegations are chosen through the party managers. All three have been affected since 1979 by the direct elections from Britain to the European Parliament. First, the North Atlantic Assembly (NAA: previously known as the Conference of NATO Parliamentarians), which began at the instigation of back-benchers, not governments, has been attended by MPs since 1955. Second, the consultative assembly of the Council of Europe was set up in 1949. Third, the assembly of the Western European Union (WEU), which followed the signature of the Paris agreement of 1954, first met in 1955. The delegates, eighteen representatives and eighteen substitutes, chosen to attend the Council of Europe (COE), also attend the WEU assembly; they are formally nominated by the Prime Minister after negotiations between the Whips. None of these assemblies has lived up to the expectations of its founders, and there is some evidence to suggest that young and more ambitious MPs decline invitations to become delegates.

The Inter-Parliamentary Union and the Commonwealth Parliamentary Association recruit members who pay a token subscription, but choose those who will represent them through the all-party Whip. Their respective executive committees then select those who will travel on their behalf. The Speaker, technically the presiding officer of the British branches, takes an active interest in their work. Each executive committee tries to bring in a broad range of members from all parties and persuasions. This approach means that the party managers tend to dismiss the value of activities promoted by these bodies. 'Members' travel agents!' is a common off-the-cuff judgement. In 1982 the chairman of the British IPU group said that he did not wish it to be debased into some kind of travel club.[6]

The mechanisms of the self-funded groups are more personal and idiosyncratic. Some groups respect the wishes of 'founding members'. For instance Dennis Walters, whose constituents in Gloucestershire complained about his devotion to Arab affairs,[7] remains a strong figure in CAABU, which he founded with Christopher Mayhew in 1967. Cyril Townsend had a close personal involvement in founding the South Atlantic Council. A major step in the development of such groups is securing funds for a full-time secretariat. CAABU has a full-time director;

the Rowntree Trust has financed the South Atlantic Council. It is quite common for meetings and conferences sponsored by back-bench groups to be organized and financed through the clients of political consultants.

The all-party back-bench country groups vary in the extent of their activities. Back-benchers have for a long time sponsored what were originally called bipartisan groups in order to provide a point in Westminster for welcoming and entertaining visitors from the country concerned, and an organization which can sponsor travel abroad for themselves. But there has always been a problem of finance. A great deal of the entertainment and travel may have to be met through some association with the hospitality allowances of the British Government and of the country's embassy.

The affiliation of back-bench country groups with the Inter-Parliamentary Union seems to have been developed in a systematic manner during the late 1950s. Alfred Bossom (1881–1965), the Member for Maidstone (1931–59) who became a life peer in 1960, was an architect with an international practice who cultivated 'friendship societies'. He was chairman of three country groups in 1958 (Belgium, Luxembourg and Iran) which then affiliated with the IPU. By 1965 there were twenty-five such affiliated groups; by 1980 there were fifty-seven. A special resolution reduced the number to forty in 1988. These formal links between the IPU and the back-benchers reflect the changing character of parliamentary interest in foreign affairs. But affiliation does not carry access to the Treasury grant-in-aid which the IPU British group receives, although the IPU may from time to time make some small subventions.[8]

The vitality and value of an all-party group is partly a function of the determination of the foreign government concerned and of its Embassy or High Commission in London. Ambassadors may differ in the degree to which they have a personal interest in cultivating back-bench opinion. For example an Australian High Commissioner, who had served in his own Senate, was interested in developing CPA links even though his officials were more interested in informal groups of academics and civil servants. Ambassadors may also vary in the degree to which they wish to support certain causes in Westminster.

The US Embassy in Grosvenor Square has a built-in advantage. The British–American Group is the only all-party group to enjoy its own Treasury grant-in-aid which its executive negotiates before each budget. The BAG's annual conferences also provide the USA with regular opportunities to select the MPs which it would like to invite and to influence.

Other embassies may be constrained to express their government's points of view because of the persistence of long-term rivalries among different factions in Westminster. The case study in Chapter 9 explains the role of the Chilean Embassy. The FRG Embassy for a long time encouraged and paid for MPs to visit Germany, sometimes through the auspices of specially created foundations. For Labour members the Friedrich-Ebert-Stiftung has provided links with Social Democrats; for Conservative members the Konrad-Adenauer-Stiftung has provided links with the German right-of-centre. The German Embassy is very close to the activities of the British–German all-party country group, the only one in the House to have designed a tie for its members combining the motifs of the German eagle and the Westminster portcullis. The division of Cyprus into Greek and Turkish sections has corresponding boundaries in the back-bench activity. The diplomatic representatives of the two parts of the island provide rival briefings and sponsor visits for those MPs who wish to see their side of the cease-fire line. In all such cases the all-party country groups provide access to back-bench opinion.

The international meetings of the IPU have in recent years become more carefully structured by the Western powers.[9] Since 1975 (the year of the Helsinki Accord and of the IPU conference in London) each meeting has been preceded by a 'caucus' of Western representatives exploring the possibilities of developing a common line and explaining the issues which are sensitive for their public opinion at home. These preparations and consultations have been known by the original number of participants, '10 PLUS and 12 PLUS', although they now attract the representatives of more than twenty nations. There is no formal report to Parliament from British IPU representatives, although the small steering committee of the British group has considerable scope to plan its interventions. This committee may well acquire advance intelligence of what is happening overseas, but it can channel knowledge into the appropriate circles in Britain only very informally.

Similarly the British delegates to the NAA and COE/WEU assemblies bring information to Westminster from the many meetings within the different frameworks of Europe. Those who followed events before 1970 tended to include some of the strongest advocates in favour of Britain joining the EEC.

Outside the framework of established institutions and grants-in-aid, it is hard to distinguish between those groups which began with a British initiative and those which are at the British end of a set of world operations. There is a wide spectrum of different inputs. At one end are Church charities; at the other are private firms established perhaps with help from abroad in order to pay the expenses of foreign visits. The Catholic Institute for International Relations (CIIR) has a wide-ranging education and information programme on issues of justice and development in the Third World. It occasionally pays for an MP to travel abroad, usually with the help of another sponsor, so that he or she can gain first-hand knowledge of a particular issue. Denis Healey on South Africa and George Foulkes on Latin America have been associated with CIIR in

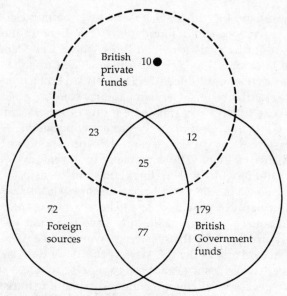

Figure 2 Known sources of funding for individual MPs

Note: ● MPs in this category may be under-recorded

this way.[10] Rindalbourne Ltd is an export-import company specializing in East European trade. Lord Wilson of Rievaulx is one of its paid non-executive directors. It was directly concerned with the arrangements of visits by parliamentarians to Romania during the Ceauşescu regime.[11] The FCO itself looks favourably on some sponsoring bodies; an ex-diplomat, Alan Brooke Turner, runs the Great Britain–East Europe Centre.

Where foreign funding seems to be the most apparent is for causes sponsored either by the 'hard Left' or the 'hard Right', or by different sides in the Arab–Israeli dispute. There are some MPs who take an interest in Latin America. The arrangements to secure a visit to Nicaragua by the Labour leader Neil Kinnock began with a delegation sponsored by CIIR in 1982. Jeremy Corbyn went there with sponsorship from the Scottish Medical Aid Group, but he occasionally funds his own travel or secures funds from his constituents such as the Islington Muslim Association. He even briefed himself on the claims of 'Kurdistan' by inviting Kurds from his constituency. Jeremy Corbyn is married to a Chilean and shares an office with Chilean Solidarity.[12] Some MPs become closely identified with civil rights causes.

Overseas governments and overseas organizations are the most reliable sources of funding for travel of MPs who wish to support particular interests. The IPU and CPA executives using the all-party Whip

Table 8 Known foreign visits by MPs 1983–87

	Members	Visits
With private funding	70	84
With the IPU, CPA and BAG	237	498
With NAA/COE/WEU	56	650 (est)
With foreign support	197	470
Total visits		1 702 (est)

Sources: Registers of Members' Interests, Annual Reports of IPU, CPA and BAG, *Hansard*, interviews.

distribute their favours in ways which cut across parties and interests. Funding from British firms and interests seems to be the least forthcoming, in so far as evidence can be gleaned from the Register of Interests and group annual reports.

The four years covered by the Parliament elected in 1983 can be used to illustrate characteristic patterns of funding and travel.[13] There is no reason to believe that the years since 1987 have been different. In round figures between 1983 and 1987 about 400 MPs were funded to travel abroad in order to get first-hand experience, some making several trips under different auspices. These Members made well over 1,700 visits during this period. There are no published figures for NAA/COE/WEU visits. Those in Figure 2 and Table 8 are estimates. The evidence suggests that the 200 who accepted foreign money were more likely to make several trips and more likely to make use of the knowledge they had acquired by intervening on the floor of the House, asking Questions or signing Early Day Motions.

It is impossible to determine how much more travel is funded by British firms and British interests other than that already declared in the Register of Interests. The rules of the Register add to the difficulty, because they state that Members are not obliged to declare payments made to their firms, but are obliged to record simply those payments made to their own accounts. The speculations that surrounded the case of John Browne, the Member for Winchester, in February–March 1990 suggested that many Members went overseas for their firms or were the directors of overseas companies.[14] For example the debates on Hong Kong have been enhanced by the presence of members who hold Hong Kong directorships. Some pressure groups believe that they can 'win friends' without making payments and getting their supporters identified on the Register of Interests.

Among the declared interests the most conspicuous support for MPs to undertake foreign travel came from the tourist lobby, particularly British

Airways, and from groups in favour of improving British roads, such as the Roads Campaign Council. When he became chairman, Lord King made it a policy that British Airways should spend a regular proportion of its income on public relations. Singapore Airways also entertained the MPs who were invited to see its facilities. It succeeded in securing landing rights at Manchester through a campaign organized by the political consultants who had been hired, Political Communications Ltd.

The clearest connections between travel, briefing and parliamentary debate are those campaigns mounted on behalf of overseas interests in order to capture parliamentary attention at Westminster. For example the government of the South African homeland of Bophuthatswana has made a concerted attempt to mobilize support for its cause in the House of Commons. Shenley Trust Services, a company owned by the Member for Honiton, Sir Peter Emery, was hired in 1981–84 to co-ordinate the diplomatic acceptance of the Republic of Bophuthatswana. It advised the government of that homeland to set up the Bophuthatswana National Commercial Corporation to act as an embassy in London. Ian Findlay[15] became the director of Bophuthatswana National Affairs and Andrew Hunter MP chairman of the British–Bophuthatswana Parliamentary Group. MPs were invited to visit the homeland, and to enjoy the facilities of its entertainment complex called Sun City. The formation of the British–Bophuthatswana Parliamentary Group led to two debates and considerable support for an Early Day Motion. Such a group could not, however, get all-party support and affiliation to the IPU.

Campaigns of this kind usually indicate that the promoters are having difficulty in gaining access to the British Government or are uncertain about the reception of their cause in British society. The most significant sponsors of MPs' visits abroad during the 1983–87 parliament were the colonial governments of Hong Kong and Gibraltar, the governments which had been subject to economic sanctions such as South Africa and the Namibian administration, and the governments with intractable difficulties in their domestic affairs which receive the attention of the international press. Countries with such difficulties included Sri Lanka and Turkey.

The most constant connections which pass almost unnoticed and unrecorded are those between MPs and the USA. The officially recorded visits of the British–American Group and of those invited by different US official agencies, such as USIS (United States Information Service), are likely to be a small proportion of the trans-Atlantic travel which MPs undertake. There are so many levels of historic contact in which MPs are not surprisingly involved, particularly through such bodies as the Ditchley Foundation and the English-Speaking Union (ESU), as well as through university and college exchanges. British MPs take a close interest in the election campaigns conducted by US parties. For example the Labour party has several members who join Democratic party campaign trails in order to study techniques of presentation and draw lessons on tactics. Many Conservative MPs go to the USA on private business.

Party and partisanship

The process of adjustment to new forms of communication has brought the major political parties into some common modes of behaviour and judgement. Back-benchers on each side of the House understand both how to generate briefing material on overseas affairs and how to recognize what sources their opponents are using. There are occasional 'leaks' of the briefing material provided by London embassies. The Government itself may from time to time find that its 'planting' of Oral Parliamentary Questions and supplementaries among trusted MPs of its own party has been exposed to Opposition ridicule.

What the front benches have in common is the difficulty of controlling the agenda of debate in the face of the freedom which back-benchers enjoy. Members have opportunities to use their overseas contacts in systematic ways. There are a number of minor manoeuvres among the supporters of different positions in the all-party committees and in the party committees. For example the South Africa all-party group underwent an internal reconstruction as a result of anti-apartheid Conservatives approaching their Labour colleagues in order to 'dethrone' John Carlisle,[16] who was considered by some to be a South African Government apologist. The Conservative back-bench group on the EC experienced another 'palace revolution' to remove from office those who were considered too 'soft' on EC affairs.

Mavericks are always hard to control. Some Members can be engaged by overseas interests without the Whips of their own parties being informed. The Labour Whips in 1966 introduced rules designed to compel their members to reveal overseas activities, but the rules were hard to enforce. Ron Brown, the Labour Member for Leith, accepted invitations in 1986 from the Governments of Afghanistan and of Libya, much to his party's embarrassment.

An analysis of those who intervene in foreign affairs debates, organize Early Day Motions and put down Questions on foreign affairs suggests that there are a number of different categories of 'activist'.[17] During the 1983–87 Parliament there were forty-nine Members who displayed constant interest in foreign affairs: twenty-six Conservative, nineteen labour and four Liberal/Social Democrat (see Table 9). The Conservative Members contained a high proportion who had either worked overseas or been overseas with the armed forces. The Labour Members seem to have been drawn into overseas affairs through civil rights groups or through academic contacts. Some represented such bodies as the World Peace Council. Perhaps the most striking feature of the activists from all parties was the set of issues on which they concentrated their attention. They focused almost exclusively on Europe, Israel, South Africa and China or China's relationships with Hong Kong. These countries commanded the most attention, not the issues which cut across national boundaries such as pollution, migration, drugs or disease.

Table 9 Sources of funding for overseas visits 1983–87*

Party groups	Visits
Labour Party	1
Labour Committee for Transatlantic Understanding	1
Labour Group for Human Rights in Sri Lanka	1
Parliamentary Labour Party defence and services	1
Total	4
Political organizations and charities	
Airlie House Conference	1
American Enterprise Institute	1
Arab League	6
Aspen Institute	3
Association of W. Euro Parliamentarians against Apartheid	1
Austrian Socialist Party	1
British Christian Charity	1
British Peace Council	1
British–American Chamber of Commerce	1
Chicago Committee for Foreign Affairs	2
Council for Arab–British Understanding	2
Cyprus EDEK	1
Czech Peace Committee	1
Deutsche-Strategie Forum	4
Druze in Lebanon	1
El Salvador Solidarity	1
English-Speaking Union	1
European Committee for the Defence of Refugees and Immigrants	2
European Solidarity with Chile	1
Fabian Society	1
Friedrich Ebert Stiftung	2
GDR ka foundation	1
Gulf Research Centre	1
Indian Council for Cultural Relations	1
International Institute for Strategic Studies	1

Table 9—continued

Political organizations and charities (continued)	Visits
Islington Muslim Association	1
Konigswinter Conference	2
North Atlantic Council	1
North Atlantic Treaty Organization	1
Parlt Association for European–Arab Co-operation	3
Parliamentarians for Global Action	2
Polisario Front	1
Royal Institute of International Affairs	2
Save the Siberian Seven Campaign	1
South African Sports Foundation	1
South African farmers	1
South African Council of Churches	1
South African Press Club	1
South Atlantic Council	2
Trades Unions (unnamed)	1
Turkey Solidarity Campaign	1
Turkey Foreign Policy Institute	1
UN Council on Namibia	1
United Nations	1
United Nations Relief Organization	1
United States National Defence University	1
War on Want	2
Wehrkunde Conference	3
West Berlin	1
West India Committee	2
Western Sahara Solidarity Campaign	1
World Peace Council	2
World Population Council	1
Total	77

Governments	
Bophuthatswana	2
Chinese People's Republic	3
Federal Republic of Germany	3
Hong Kong	9
Hungary	3
India	1
Iraq	1
Israel	3
Namibia	2
North Korea	2
Northern Cyprus	4
Norway	1

Table 9—continued

Governments (continued)	Visits
Oman	1
Panama	1
Saudi Arabia	2
South Africa	7
Sri Lanka	3
Taiwan	4
Thailand	2
Turkey	2
Union of Soviet Socialist Republics	3
United Arab Emirates	2
United States (USIS)	1
Total	63
Airlines	
British Airways	1
Singapore Airlines	1
South African Airways	1
Total	3
Grand total	147

Note: * Funding from IPU, CPA, BAG and the parliamentary assemblies (NAA, CUE, WEU) has been excluded. Figures relate to the forty-nine MPs who were most active on the floor of the House in foreign affairs in the 1983–87 Parliament.

Context of opinion

The second feature worth investigating is the direct interest now taken by governments and pressure groups in the volatility of public opinion, and in the means available for coming to terms with this sense of flux, particularly the targeting of parliaments. MPs mediate the flow of information; their reactions and interpretations belong more strongly to the interplay of international competition. They are vulnerable on two fronts. What they do abroad or with foreign links may signal British attitudes; what they do at home may stimulate demands from immigrant communities and from other constituents who are exposed to reports from overseas.

The impact of external events on the House of Commons can be seen in the orchestration of the occasions which MPs can create and in the forms of promotional campaign with which MPs engage. It is not easy to ascertain the full range of activities which arise either from projecting

British attitudes abroad or from reacting to external assaults on British opinion. Campaigns 'below the line' may be deliberately designed to be subliminal, and may involve questionable uses of traditional parliamentary procedures. For example to ask a Parliamentary Question may be a form of getting the Government to pay for the analysis of information on behalf of a sectional interest. The Labour party in 1990 blamed the increased costs of Parliamentary Questions on those Conservative Members who had set themselves up as consultants.[18]

There is a fairly extensive history of the parts played by parliamentarians in projecting favourable images of Britain to audiences overseas. The Commonwealth Parliamentary Association and the British group of the Inter-Parliamentary Union have for a long time been involved with influencing parliamentarians elsewhere. They not only send MPs abroad, but also receive inward delegations. Many MPs go to universities of international repute; several contribute to bodies such as the English-Speaking Union and the Royal Commonwealth Society. The quality of British stands in international trade exhibitions has been a subject of parliamentary concern since the end of the First World War when the Export Credit Guarantee Department and the Empire Marketing Board were created.

There was much less concern before the introduction of television about the need to educate domestic opinion on events abroad. There has never been a British equivalent of President Carter's call for a 'dual mandate' – official information services which educate Americans about abroad as well as foreigners about the USA. Apart from the Wembley Exhibition the colonial authorities were not very successful in recruiting parliamentarians to teach their constituents about the Empire. The art and literature in the metropole expressed the unity of the Crown's dominions overseas with the minimum of official interference. The attraction to most people of films from Hollywood during the 1930s led to demands for the protection of a British film industry.

Perhaps the major step in developing a parliamentary consciousness about the importance of professional publicity was the campaign begun in the late 1960s to promote the entry of Britain into the EEC. The Britain in Europe Group was a by-product of the Economist Intelligence Unit study (1957). The British Council of the European Movement formed in 1969 brought together such organizations, and proceeded to develop a consensus among them on the information policy required to put across their message to the general public. A series of 'media breakfasts' were inaugurated.[19]

In recent years MPs have had to come to terms with the ramifications of international news on television. Satellite hook-ups allow the transmission of pictures as events unfold, without the delay that ensues from flying in spools of film. These technical improvements of the media have transformed the signalling between governments that forms an essential part of foreign policy-making. Pictures convey messages. Issues can arise from these messages that have not been fully anticipated. Domestic public opinion may be caught up in a sudden wave of revulsion or disgust. Governments have to be ready for sudden contingencies; they have to be seen to be taking action. Television has been particularly important in arousing public interest in such issues as famine relief. Campaigns such as Live Aid and Band Aid led to a much publicized intervention in Ethiopia by established charities. For example the history of War on Want shows both a desire to act outside the framework of official government aid policy, and the way in which such campaigning can serve as a gateway to parliamentary politics for those who undertake the work.[20]

The impact of the decline in British power on the House of Commons was found in the continued doubts about what were the appropriate 'areas of concentration' – the phrase used by the Duncan Committee in 1969[21] – to indicate where resources devoted to the conduct of foreign policy should primarily be directed. Joining the European Community in 1973 defined the principal commitment of the country's future, but that very commitment complicated parliamentary approaches to foreign policy. On the one hand, Europe in some sense ceased to be foreign, and the provisions of EC legislation had to be incorporated into domestic life. On the other, joining Europe meant joining other Community members in foreign policy initiatives. Disputes about EC policies cut across Westminster party loyalties. The major parties were not initially very concerned to pay particular attention to the Members and proceedings of the European Parliament. Members of the European Parliament (MEPs) did not enjoy the privileges enjoyed by their European colleagues when they all returned to their respective capitals. Information about EC matters has been channelled informally to the back-benchers through the delegates to the COE/WEU assemblies. Some of these Members have contended that there should be a formal annual report to Parliament on the COE and WEU. The Government in 1987 conceded the preparation of reports on WEU, but not on COE. The only formal recognition of the opportunity to discuss these assemblies during the whole of the 1983–87 Parliament was in a single half-hour adjournment debate. The House continues to rely on the informal contacts which delegates establish.

There have been occasional rallies of parliamentary interest in the connections between the UK and the countries of the Commonwealth. In some cases, such as the repatriation of the Canadian Constitution in 1982, the House of Commons held a special position as the result of its own earlier legislation. In others, such as the international condemnation of South African apartheid, MPs have played a more ambiguous role. A significant proportion of parliamentary business on foreign affairs is concerned with the intractable problems of the former Empire. The most obvious post-imperial issues have been those which deal with the future of the remaining colonies, such as Hong Kong and Gibraltar, or of former colonies in which there is a division between opposing groups, such as Cyprus, Fiji and Sri Lanka. Some commentators would place Israel in this last category.

One reason why MPs are regularly caught up in Commonwealth affairs is that they respond to the questions raised by immigrant communities in their constituencies. MPs sitting in their 'surgeries' find that many of the cases on which they are asked to help come from recent immigrants. All Members of the House recognize the foreign affairs activities of their colleagues which stem directly from the patterns of immigrant settlement. Edmonton and Tooting, for example, are known to have Greek Cypriot constituents, while Bradford and Coventry have Asian constituents.

The forms of promotion

Parliament provides a wide range of points of access, from a full-dress debate on a Private Member's motion to the 'photo opportunities' of receptions on the terrace overlooking the Thames. Causes can be promoted by MPs both publicly and openly, particularly by using the procedures of the House, and covertly and secretly. A failure to speak on the floor of the House, which is sometimes judged a dereliction of duty towards constituents, is no handicap in the assistance of overseas interests or international civil rights campaigns.[22] Without speaking, MPs can put down Parliamentary Questions for a written reply, support Early Day Motions, or just simply act as the host to a delegation. Some campaigns can be conducted largely by taking MPs away from the precincts of Westminster. For example the campaign conducted by the Heritage Foundation in favour of persuading the British Government to cease its membership of Unesco was conducted through the press and through special meetings to which sympathetic MPs were invited. The Government announced Britain's withdrawal from Unesco in November 1984 without giving any opportunity for parliamentary debate.[23]

However, in all the forms of promotion that can be used, the product deemed most valuable seems to be parliamentary time. Debates and Oral Questions, or Supplementary Questions to ministerial statements, seem to ensure some kind of media coverage, however slight. Those who wish to place an issue of foreign policy or an issue of civil rights in another country on the agenda of British politics look for opportunities to take up parliamentary time. An adjournment debate, even if it involves few MPs and is held in the early hours of the morning, may well be a sufficient event for its promoters. Balloting for a place in the Consolidated Fund debate may also provide an opportunity for back-bench all-party country groups to be heard.[24]

The evidence 'on the record' seems to suggest that the promoters of special causes can in some sense 'buy' parliamentary time if a sufficient number of Members support them, and that major issues which do not generate their own lobby are likely to be neglected. For example the Parliament of 1983–87 devoted far more time to Questions about Chile, Central America, South Africa and Hong Kong, than to Questions of environmental pollution or of Anglo-American relations. When Members in these debates refer to the custom of 'leaving foreign affairs to the experts' they are usually acknowledging that both the Government and special interests have worked 'behind the scenes' to manage such parliamentary occasions.

Written Parliamentary Questions are a means whereby ministers can be asked to release information of value to overseas interests or particular campaigns for overseas groups. An analysis of such Questions brings to the fore the importance to overseas interests of back-bench sponsorship. An MP can act as the channel for an organized group which wishes to draw British attention to an overseas question.

In studying the staging of special events it is often difficult to decide who is using whom. The Inter-Parliamentary Union lays claim to the achievement of bringing together parliamentarians who might otherwise be kept apart by the policies of their respective governments. The history of the British group speaks of the 1980s as the 'bridge-building decade'. The group lists among its principal achievements the invitation of a Soviet delegation to London led by Gorbachev in 1984, the continuing dialogue with Guatemala and Argentina during breaks in diplomatic relations, and the establishment of the British–Irish Inter-Parliamentary Body.[25] But in all these cases other international forces are probably equally important.

The Commonwealth Parliamentary Association seems to make less impact on the discussion of foreign affairs than the IPU. The presence of the Commonwealth Secretariat in London means that the British branch and the Commonwealth Secretary-General stay at arm's length. The latter does not want the Commonwealth confused with the 'voice of Britain' and the former wants to have the freedom to speak in support of British interests. A symbol of the changing relationship between Britain and the Commonwealth was the redesignation in 1969–70 of the British branch's standard annual event for Commonwealth invitees. The eighteenth parliamentary course of 1969 became the nineteenth parliamentary seminar of 1970. This meant a shift from teaching British parliamentary procedure and practice to comparing experiences of parliamentary life. Another indication of changes in style was the funding of the international conference of 1986 in part with money from commercial sponsors rather than with British Government hospitality. The ten or twelve delegations which visit Commonwealth countries each year from Britain are funded partly by the Treasury grant-in-aid, which meets the cost of travel, and partly by the host country, which meets the expenses of the stay.

The 'domestic life' of Westminster provides a myriad of contacts between people who are seeking to influence each other. Apart from IPU and CPA delegations and receptions, there are a large number of *ad-hoc* visitors, special meals and receptions, and conferences or 'long week-ends' in which MPs learn of overseas affairs. *The House Magazine* provides a guide to the variety, including the opportunities to learn a foreign language. Those members who have mastered a foreign language or who were brought up with bilingual skills can play a major role in the general round of receptions and entertainments for foreign visitors.

MPs who devote a high proportion of their time to overseas affairs fall into a fairly distinct set of categories. An analysis of the 1983–87 Parliament provides some indication in round figures of the number in each category. If that Parliament is deemed to be representative of current practice, then the following general propositions seems to be reasonable assumptions to make.

The great majority of Members receive funds for overseas travel – at least 400 out of 650. There may be others who travel at the expense of their firms or who are paid by educational institutions for lectures or seminars. Of the 400 whose travel is publicly reported, about 200 receive foreign funding, but only about 70 of these will depend exclusively on foreign sources. About 140 Members will use the money from several different sponsors (in 1983–87 ten MPs in the Register of Interests declared more than five different sources). About 150 Members will travel solely under the auspices of IPU, CPA or BAG. About 50 Members will rely on NAA or COE/WEU activities.

Whatever the categories of funding, about 130 Members will devote a considerable proportion of their time to overseas affairs. There are at least four types.

1 About forty-five Members are principally committed to the promotion of overseas causes or overseas interests, including human rights. Some will work openly and use parliamentary procedures, such as Parliamentary Questions or Early Day Motions; others will prefer to work entirely by private contacts. This group will normally include a number of ex-ministers, former officers in the armed forces and former diplomats.
2 About thirty-five Members are 'organizational professionals'. They devote a high proportion of their parliamentary life to the committees

and other activities of the IPU, CPA and BAG, or to the NAA/COE/ WEU assemblies.
3 About twenty-five Members are 'loners'. They develop networks of contacts without the aid of a specific organization or company.
4 About twenty-five Members have a strong interest in particular regions of the world (often South Africa or the Middle East) which leads them to intervene from time to time in debates or to provide a channel for a visitor or a pressure group.

Set against these categories of 'promoter' are the professionals in Government who specialize in parliamentary liaison. The FCO's parliamentary liaison unit is supplemented by the day-to-day contacts of junior ministers. Perhaps it is truer to say that the ministers are supplemented by the unit. The unit is not always at the centre of FCO discussions, while ministers and senior diplomats see MPs on all kinds of occasions. The FCO maintains an arm's-length relationship with the IPU and CPA executives when they are deciding where to send delegations and whom to invite but is willing to give advice and make suggestions. The most deliberate cultivation of parliamentary opinion can be seen when an FCO agency wishes to improve its position in the allocation of public expenditure, particularly during the round of PESC (Public Expenditure Survey Committee) negotiations. The British Council for example may have improved its financial position by the skill of its presentations to Members.

Specialists in parliamentary liaison in the Embassies and High Commissions of other countries in London can sometimes be highly visible to members. For example James Kolker of the US Embassy cultivated the Labour party and followed its internal debates, particularly those on unilateral nuclear disarmament. The Indian Embassy has curry lunches. Some Embassies are keen to make presentations to private meetings of MPs or to back-bench committees. Ambassadors from time to time address back-bench groups.

Members themselves have in some cases become their own experts in parliamentary liaison because of the consultancy firms which they have established or by which they are employed. A service which their firms supply to clients is the monitoring of parliamentary proceedings in different policy areas. The Public Relations Consultants Association (PRCA) in its yearbook provides an indication of the increased importance of this kind of service. It is impossible to guess how many firms decline to join the PRCA because they hesitate to follow its rule that the names of clients should be made public. Peter Fry's evidence to the Select Committee on Members' Interests (25 April 1989) gave some indication of the degree to which the clients of Countrywide Political Communication Ltd are becoming more interested in the need to lobby not only in Westminster but also in Brussels.[26]

Options and opportunities

The front benches are nowadays sensitive to the influences that can shape the character of back-bench opinion. Ministers and Opposition spokesmen cannot afford to ignore the professionalization of opinion formation and interest presentation. They run the risk of finding some options closed if they are not properly briefed about the approaches being made by overseas interests and the activities staged by overseas groups, and if they themselves take no countervailing action. They may be tempted to 'play an overseas card' when such a tactic seems likely to open up latent divisions within their opponents. Debates may be a charade which conceals a 'party game'. But there are risks in staging a debate which attracts the attention of a well-organized 'foreign constituency'. The case studies in this book show how frequently options can be closed and opportunities lost. Party managers and senior officials need a detailed knowledge of 'behind the scenes', particularly when it looks as if parliamentary time is being purchased by a group with external funding.

It is commonplace to deplore the quality of Commons debates on foreign affairs. It is often said by one Member of another: 'When he stands up just to earn his corn I cease to listen'. Others comment that some MPs have reduced their vision of the scope of British foreign policy to 'fighting one's corner' in Europe and NATO and to limiting the influence of the USA and Japan on the domestic economy. Debates may sometimes look like the recital of briefings derived from conflicting outside sources. Members may seem too dependent on knowledge gained through 'corporate hospitality'. A great deal of energy goes into 'foreign junketing' with little visible result.

But the House of Commons cannot insulate itself from changes in the dominant system of international relations. Events overseas affect the behaviour of British parliamentarians much more strongly than they can ever hope to influence what happens in other countries. World affairs tend to shape the scope of parliamentary action, not vice versa. Interpretations of the treatment of foreign affairs have to be placed in the wider setting of political communications in general.

FIVE

The House of Lords and foreign affairs

■■■■■■

Introduction

The modern House of Lords has no pretensions to be a Chamber wielding power. It will contemplate contesting the will of the Government only in strictly limited circumstances, such as when some issue readily perceived as constitutional is at stake, or when it has good reason to believe that Government back-benchers in the Commons will support its action. The Lords is very much the junior Chamber to the Commons, and its role is minor compared to that of the lower House. But having said that it would be wrong completely to ignore the House of Lords: it is still a part of Parliament. Legislation must be debated and approved by the Lords as well as the Commons, and this means that the Lords has opportunities to suggest amendments to Bills. Apart from legislation the Government must make a response on any subject that is debated in the House, thus declaring what its opinion is on the issue concerned, even if this is simply to say that it has no view on the matter at all. Even when Government spokesmen are evasive or ill-informed the fact that the Government is officially answerable in the House marks the Chamber off from being simply another debating society. Leaders of interest groups, representatives of foreign governments, friends and opponents of the governing party alike, any or all of these can look to the House of Lords as one source within which the attitude of the Government of the day receives authoritative definition in the context provided by question and debate.[1]

Contributing to this context are peers with considerable experience and widely recognized expertise. This is a feature of the House well exemplified in relation to debates on foreign affairs. There is a considerable depth of knowledge about most parts of the world. Many peers have lived and worked overseas; many others have travelled extensively and become regular visitors to other parts of the globe. As well as former Government ministers, diplomats and defence chiefs, peers from the world of business, banking and the professions often have become knowledgeable of overseas affairs through personal experience. Composed as it is of a mixture of professional and part-time politicians and those who are not politicians at all, there is both a breadth and a depth of experience which is understandably lacking in a lower House ever more completely dominated by professional politicians.

These characteristics of the House do not of course in themselves ensure that it has any influence or significance in relation to the making of foreign policy. But it could well be argued that potentially they do give to the House certain advantages as a forum particularly in relation to foreign affairs. The intensification of competitive party politics has reinforced the adversarial character of the Commons to the point at which almost nothing escapes that mould. Traditionally foreign policy has been thought of as an area characterized by bipartisanship. The House of Lords with its much more consensual style of debate undoubtedly finds such a tradition easier to sustain than the House of Commons, though it may be argued that such a tradition has lost much of its former relevance given the changed character of foreign policy, in particular its assimilation with domestic policy.

It may further be argued that the very fact that the House of Lords can aspire to be only a Chamber of influence rather than one of power again potentially gives it a particular suitability as a forum for the consideration of foreign policy. Britain no longer exercises power on the world stage; British foreign policy is very much a matter of seeking to exert influence in situations where both resources available and room for manoeuvre are almost always extremely limited. The House of Lords deals naturally and unselfconsciously in the currency of influence rather than the currency of power.

It instinctively seeks consensus rather than confrontation. Its membership brings about a mingling of technical expertise and experience of all kinds with the professional politicians who nowadays tend to dominate all governments. It is probably these factors which have underlain the relative success with which the House of Lords has handled European Community policy proposals as compared to the House of Commons.

How much time does the House spend considering foreign policy?

Any answer to this question must presuppose some definition of the term 'foreign policy', a subject discussed in Chapter 2. From an organizational

Table 10 Time spent by the House of Lords on foreign affairs 1988–89

	Total and as proportion of total time of House	Number of foreign affairs items	Proportion of total on foreign affairs
Questions and Statements			
Starred	572 (6.0%)	70	12.0%
Unstarred	35 (4.5%)	2	5.4%
For Written Answer	1 202	123	10.2%
Statements	31 (1.7%)	5	16.0%
Motions			
For Papers	36 ⎫	5	17 hr 40 min ⎫
Take Note	6 ⎬ 15.9%	1	3 hr 50 min ⎬ 15.3%
Address	1 ⎭	part	5 hr 22 min ⎭
(Queen's Speech)			
EEC Reports	12	1	3 hr 21 min 11.0%
Other Select			
Committee Reports	2	0	
Legislation			
Government Bills	56.3%	2	1 hr 27 min 0.2%
Private Members' Bills	2.2%	0	
Private Bills	0.8%	0	
Statutory Instruments	3.2%	0	

point of view in analysing parliamentary business one might define foreign policy as anything for which the Foreign and Commonwealth Office provides ministerial spokesmen and parliamentary briefing. But that can be only a rough guide. In the Lords there is usually only one FCO minister, and hence ministers in other departments and Government Whips frequently have to deal with foreign policy questions. But apart from that point there is an external affairs dimension to numerous domestic policy issues, just as there are few foreign policy questions which do not have some direct relevance to domestic issues. At one stage it was probably appropriate to treat all European Community matters as questions of foreign policy, but this is certainly no longer the case. Most of the reports of the House of Lords European Communities Committee (ECC), and the debates which result from these reports, are concerned predominantly with issues which one or other domestic Government department regards very much as its own. This point may be more clearly appreciated if a full list of the reports debated in the 1988–89 session is given: these were Alternative Energy Sources, Package Travel, Financial Area, Visual Display Units and Occupational Health, Public Procurement Policy, Fraud, Disposal of Radioactive Waste, Merger Policy, Pensions, Nitrate in Water, Habitat and Species Protection, and Trade with Japan. All except the final one have been excluded from the statistical analysis that follows; our concern has been to try to identify those issues which would in a more traditional sense have been viewed as coming within the compass of foreign policy. Table 10 gives a breakdown of the time the House spent on foreign policy under various procedures in the 1988–89 session.

As can be seen from this table the House spends only about 5 per cent of its time on foreign affairs. But this is because the House spends the bulk of its time on legislation and very few items of legislation are primarily concerned with foreign affairs. If we exclude primary legislation the House spent approximately 12 per cent of its remaining time on foreign affairs.

This would appear to be fairly typical of other recent sessions. An analysis of time devoted to foreign affairs in the 1968–69, 1975–76 and 1984–85 sessions confirms this. The main variation between 1988–89 and the earlier sessions was that more Unstarred Questions (a procedure leading to a short debate) on foreign policy matters were then asked, ten in 1975–76 and twelve in 1969–70, though the total of all Unstarred Questions in the session was only slightly higher. Part of the explanation was the presence of Lord (Fenner) Brockway, much of whose life was given to unmasking the hypocrisies – supposed or otherwise – of the Foreign Office, and who asked three Unstarred Questions in each of the earlier two sessions. Otherwise, however, time spent on questions and motions has been very similar. The proportion of time spent on legislation devoted to foreign affairs has varied, but has always been lower, at least since 1968, than the proportion of time spent on other proceedings (mainly motions and questions) devoted to foreign affairs.

Analysis of 1988–89 activities

In the 1988–89 session only two Bills dealt with foreign affairs and both of these were of relatively minor importance and therefore took little time. One concerned the remnants of Empire, a gradually dwindling source of legislation, the other, environmental concerns, a growing area of legislative activity. The first, the Brunei Appeals Bill, took just twelve minutes to complete all stages; it adjusted arrangements for appeals to the Judicial Committee of the Privy Council from the Kingdom of Brunei. The other was the Antarctic Minerals Bill, which took seventy-five minutes; this ratified a convention signed by the British Government the previous year which regulated prospecting activities for minerals in Antarctica. The second reading debate drew front-bench speeches expressing satisfaction that nothing but prospecting would for the time being be allowed in Antarctica, but back-bench speeches expressed anxieties that even prospecting should be allowed in what could remain the last great natural wilderness on earth.

In some sessions more substantial legislation on foreign affairs subjects is debated. In the 1981–82 session the Canada Bill, patriating the Canadian Constitution, was debated for over seven hours. In earlier decades up to the 1960s considerably more time was spent dealing with legislation conferring independence on former colonies. The Lords have had a propensity for discussing the finer points of constitutional detail in such legislation.

Apart from legislation the House debates motions of various kinds and also deals with Questions. At the commencement of every day's business in the Lords up to four Oral (Starred) Questions may be asked. These are addressed simply to Her Majesty's Government, not to any particular minister; they are submitted in advance, and normally the four slots are taken almost as soon as they become available. There is no formal time limit on Questions, though by convention only about twenty minutes is reckoned to be available for dealing with the four Questions and supplementaries, though sometimes ten or even fifteen minutes will be spent on a single Question. This does mean that Questions can be a good deal more probing than in the Commons. On average about two Questions a week concerned foreign affairs. Slightly over half of these were answered by the Foreign Office Minister of State (Lord Glenarthur for most of the session, with Lord Brabazon of Tara taking over in July). Most of the remainder were answered by Lord Trefgarne, Minister of State at Defence, but a few were dealt with by Baroness Hooper, Parliamentary Secretary at the Department of Energy, who was listed as the third Foreign Office spokesman in the House. A total of thirty-two different peers asked foreign affairs Questions; those who know the House would not be surprised to learn that Lord Hatch of Lusby asked ten (eight of them on Southern Africa) and Lord Molloy asked seven. These two left-wing (in House of Lords terms at least) Labour peers were followed by Lord Eden of Winton, who asked five, and Lords Boyd-Carpenter, Kennet, Wyatt of Weeford and Orr-Ewing, all of whom asked three. The asking of Oral Questions in the Lords, as in the Commons, is an activity dominated by a comparatively small number of peers, most of whom are former MPs, who tend to specialize in particular areas of interest.

Since speeches may be made and in effect full-length debate take place on Unstarred Questions, it is more appropriate to consider them along with motions (despite the confusion of the nomenclature). Questions for Written Answer do not take up any time on the floor of the House, being merely printed along with the Answer given in *Hansard*, as in the Commons. But unlike the Commons only Questions put down for Written Answer actually get Written Answers in the Lords. Some 10 per cent of all such Questions concerned foreign affairs, with 34 different peers asking the 123 Questions so categorized in the 1988–89 session. One peer dominated here and that was Lord Kennet, a hereditary peer who held office in the Labour Government of 1966–70, served as chairman of the International Parliamentary Conferences on the Environment 1971–78, and joined the Social Democratic Party (SDP) in 1981, for which he was a foreign affairs spokesman until he rejoined Labour in 1990. His Questions mainly concerned defence strategy. Lord Hylton, an active hereditary cross-bench peer, asked thirteen Questions, mainly about human rights and overseas aid; Lord Avebury, the former Liberal MP Eric Lubbock, asked ten Questions, especially focusing on human rights issues. Lord Montgomery asked two Questions about Anglo-Argentinian relations, an area of particular concern to him because for some twenty-five years he has worked to develop trade with South America.

Most Questions for Written Answer are probably asked straight-forwardly to gain information, which may then well be used in debate in the House; certainly the examples given above were all of peers who spoke regularly on these subjects. But not infrequently there is also an underlying political attitude which motivates the asking of Questions and the form that these take. Lord Mayhew, another former Labour minister who had joined the SDP, and who for many years had taken an interest in the Middle East, asked two Questions (not included as foreign affairs questions in this analysis) about access to the wreckage of the Lockerbie plane crash afforded to Israeli security agents. Lord Callaghan, the former Prime Minister, asked if any previous Queen's Speech had included no reference to the attitude of Her Majesty's Government to the Common-wealth.

Ministerial statements, if repeated in the House of Lords, are made in the same form as in the Commons, which means that in the Lords a statement is usually repeated by a junior minister or Government Whip. As in the Commons, Questions may then be asked for clarification, which in practice allows Opposition spokesmen the opportunity to comment on the Statement. Exchanges may last for three-quarters of an hour or even longer. Of the thirty-one statements made in this session five concerned foreign affairs, a proportion typical for recent sessions. Statements tend to be made either in response to some crisis or in order to report on some diplomatic venture, such as an EC summit. Attention obviously focuses very much on the Commons, where the minister making the Statement has direct responsibility for the matter concerned. But the fact that in the Lords the Government spokesmen are normally no more than mouth-pieces for policy in the formulation of which they have had no part, a

Table 11 Foreign affairs debates in the House of Lords 1988–89

Date	Peer initiating	Number of peers participating	Total time
Motions for Papers			
14 December	Hatch of Lusby	13	2 hr 30 min
To call attention to the situation in Southern Africa			
14 December	Buckmaster	9	2 hr 30 min
To call attention to the continuing violation of human rights worldwide, particularly in Uganda, Iran and Chile			
25 January	Jenkins of Hillhead	19	4 hr 45 min
To call attention to Her Majesty's Government's method of conducting relations with foreign countries			
19 April	Home of the Hirsel	21	4 hr 30 min
To call attention to the importance, while acknowledging all proposals for the reduction of international tensions, of preserving the unity of the Western Alliance and its power to resist aggression			
7 June	Chandos	13	2 hr 30 min
To call attention to the case for Britain's full participation in a more integrated European community while maintaining Britain's national interest and cultural identity			
21 June	Ewart-Biggs	19	2 hr 30 min
To call attention to the problems facing the Government and people of Hong Kong and to the responsibilities of HMG in this matter			
Motions to take note			
13 July	Trefgarne	16	3 hr 30 min
To take note of the Defence Estimates			
15 November	Kearton	13	3 hr 21 min
To take note of the ECC Report on relations between the EC and Japan			
Motion for Address			
23 November	Glenarthur	21	6 hr
Address in reply to speech from the throne (day devoted to Foreign Affairs and Defence)			
Unstarred Questions			
15 December	Mayhew	4	1 hr
What action HMG proposes to take to prevent breaches of the 4th Geneva Convention in Gaza and the West Bank			
23 March	Wyatt of Weeford	8	1 hr 38 min
To ask HMG to reconsider its policy on the issue of British passports to Hong Kong citizens			

point widely appreciated in the House, is to some extent balanced by the fact that one or two peers present will almost certainly be able to ask Questions probing the Government from a perspective quite different from that found in the Commons.

This same point is more evident when we consider debates on motions. The subjects for debate are chosen partly by the party groups in the House and partly as a result of balloting. Table 11 lists the debates held in the 1988–89 session.

Debates such as those listed in Table 11 vary considerably both in terms of their quality and their effectiveness. Neither criterion is susceptible to easy or precise measurement. Some draw an impressive list of speakers, the best the House contains. Others seem overweighted with familiar, boring and platitudinous speeches. Seldom does real debate take place, because few speeches in the Lords are interrupted, and frequently successive speeches deal with quite different aspects of a subject. Thus in the Queen's Speech debate one peer dealt exclusively with the problem of AIDS in Africa, while another examined relations with South America, and so on. The debate initiated by Lord Home on 19 April elicited speeches from many of the peers foremost in the foreign affairs field, for example two other former Foreign Secretaries (Stewart of Fulham, Pym), four other former Foreign or Commonwealth Office ministers (Mayhew, Chalfont, Thomas of Gwydir, Cledwyn of Penrhos), as well as two former professional diplomats (Gladwyn, Greenhill of Harrow). Some contributions were, however, made by peers with no obvious qualifications or relevant experience, such as Lord Kagan and Baroness Strange, while other peers who might have made significant speeches chose not to do so, such as Lord Callaghan. Lord Trefgarne, a Minister of State at Defence spoke from the Government front bench early in the debate, with Baroness Hooper giving the Government reply to the debate; as a minister at the Department of Energy all she could be expected to do was to say the things she had been told to say by the civil servants on hand to provide briefing as the debate proceeded.

An unusual debate was that initiated by Lord Jenkins of Hillhead on 25 January, directed as it was to an examination of the conduct rather than the substance of foreign policy. His speech was critical of Mrs Thatcher for her 'megaphone diplomacy' or 'government by indignation'; if the object of policy was to achieve results rather than to strike attitudes then less stridency of tone and more regard for the authority of the Foreign Secretary and the expertise of the Foreign Office was desirable. Some other speakers echoed these sentiments; the former head of the Diplomatic Service, Lord Greenhill, referred to the disadvantages of 'Jericho diplomacy'! Other peers ranged widely in commenting on matters of both current concern and in drawing examples from the past, especially concerning relations between the Prime Minister and the Foreign

Secretary. The Minister of State at the Foreign Office, Lord Glenarthur, defined the aims of British foreign policy in an unexceptionable way, and then offered an equally unoriginal analysis of the constitutional relationship between ministers, civil servants and Parliament. The debate as a whole was disappointing because it was muddled and confused with peers simply talking past each other most of the time. One felt there was an important subject here, and a wealth of varied experience to offer in the discussion of it, but no possibility of imposing a clear enough framework on the contributions to give the debate a real sense of purpose.

Very few debates in the Lords receive any public attention. Press reporting of the House has declined steadily for many years. In the 1988–89 session there was only one occasion when a daily newspaper carried a report about the House which concerned foreign affairs (other than the brief summaries of proceedings in the House which the heavier press carries on most days); this was a *Financial Times* report on the House's European Communities Committee (ECC) Report on relations between the Community and Japan. Debates have of course been televised since 1985, and this results in a few extracts from some speeches being shown to several hundred thousand viewers weekly. If the vast majority of speeches go unreported in the media, do they also pass unnoticed within Government?

Ministerial representation in the House

Much depends on the performance of ministers. The total team of Government ministers and Whips in the House has not in recent years exceeded twenty-two. All ministers in the Lords have to get used to covering for other departments, and Whips too – who are silent in the Commons – speak for the Government in the Lords. The Foreign Office has always had one minister in the House, since 1975 at least at Minister of State level. Twice in the post-war period the Secretary of State for Foreign Affairs has been a peer, Lord Home from 1960 to 1963 and Lord Carrington from 1979 to 1982; on both these occasions a second Foreign Office Cabinet minister was appointed to speak for the department in the Commons. Occasionally there has been more than one Foreign Office minister in the Lords; in the late 1960s all three Ministers of State at the Foreign Office were peers, and during the latter part of Lord Carrington's time as Secretary of State – from September 1981 to April 1982 – Lord Trefgarne was Parliamentary Under-Secretary at the Foreign Office. But given that it has frequently been found difficult to appoint a single minister from each major department in the House of Lords, the luxury of having two ministers in the same department in the House can scarcely be allowed.

Peers welcomed the appointment of a Secretary of State from their House in 1960 but MPs understandably took a different view, with the Labour Opposition securing an immediate debate protesting at the appointment of a peer to so senior a post. The inability of a peer who is a Secretary of State to answer for his department in the Commons Chamber can be a real drawback, especially when the department is under heavy criticism for some reason. Furthermore any minister who is a peer is in danger of being isolated from the party mainstream in the Commons. Most Lords' ministers are well aware of this problem and do what they can to mitigate it, for example by taking very deliberate care to be available to back-bench MPs for discussions on matters within their area of particular ministerial responsibility. Close ministerial colleagues who are MPs can help avoid isolation by keeping ministers in the Lords in touch with back-bench opinion in the Commons. But Foreign Office ministers in the Commons can themselves easily lose touch with back-benchers simply because they need spend comparatively little time in the House, mainly because they seldom have responsibility for steering legislation through with the consequent numerous hours spent in Standing Committee.

The case of Lord Carrington is of particular interest in this respect. He had had experience of being a senior minister in the Lords from 1970 to 1974 (as Secretary of State for Defence, and then briefly as Secretary of State for Energy), and he knew the importance of keeping good communications with MPs. In his memoirs he paid tribute to the 'splendid team' of ministers he had in the Commons, which included a second Foreign Office Cabinet minister, first Sir Ian Gilmour then Mr Humphrey Atkins.[2] Lord Carrington himself had been very active in the House of Lords; while in Opposition he led the Conservative peers, and attended the House on over 75 per cent of the sitting days from 1977 to 1979. But after his appointment as Foreign Secretary he became much less regular, attending fewer than one-third of the sitting days in 1979–80 and then down to one-fifth in the year before the Falklands invasion. For him to attend the House of Lords more frequently as Foreign Secretary, listening to its debates on all and sundry topics, would no doubt have seemed a waste of time. Of course he was there to speak in foreign affairs debates, but in practice he became an infrequent attender in the minor Chamber of the British Parliament. Undoubtedly this added to his vulnerability when the Falklands crisis erupted. The Franks Report may show that he had been endeavouring to impress on his senior colleagues, especially the Prime Minister, the need to grasp the Falklands nettle, but he did not succeed in this.[3] When the Argentine forces invaded, his inability directly to answer his critics on the floor of the House of Commons was a serious handicap. Appearing before the 1922 Committee with MPs collectively in high dudgeon about an issue which few of them had bothered to make the effort to understand, Lord Carrington was not inclined to ameliorate their anger. His experience there settled his determination to resign.[4]

But if there are disadvantages to being in the House of Lords in terms of relative isolation from the heart of the party and the heat of party battle in the Commons, it can certainly also be argued that there are advantages to having ministers – particularly Foreign Office ministers – in the Lords. MPs who are ministers have many other things to do besides their ministerial duties. There is the regular pressure of constituency business. The summons of the Whips to divisions in the Commons must be heeded. Ministers in the Lords do not have to spend their weekends grinding through constituency chores. Nor do they have to hang around Westminster simply to keep up the Government majority, though because no 'pairs' are available in the House of Lords they can sometimes be under pressure to attend in order to vote, especially if there is a running Whip through the committee or report stages of a Bill. When Mr Wilson as Prime Minister decided in 1964 that he wanted a minister rather than a professional diplomat to be Britain's permanent representative at the United Nations, it was natural that such an appointment should be a peer (Lord Caradon) rather than an MP. At the same time Mr Wilson appointed someone who had hitherto not been a professional politician as Minister for Disarmament in the Foreign Office; this was Lord Chalfont, formerly Alun Gwynne-Jones, a journalist, who was given a peerage. By the end of the 1960s the Labour Government had all three Ministers of State at the Foreign Office in the House of Lords, the third being Lord Shepherd. When Mr Heath came to power initially the Foreign Office was reduced to a single Parliamentary Under-Secretary in the House, Lord Lothian, but he was promoted Minister of State two years later. In 1974 a Labour MP who had been a Foreign Office minister and then a front-bench spokesman when the party was in Opposition lost his seat in the election; a few days later as he sat at home brooding about his collapsed political career he received a telephone call inviting him to become a peer, and to resume once more his position as a Foreign Office minister. This was Lord Goronwy-Roberts, who remained at the Foreign Office throughout the 1974–79 Government.[5] Because of the precarious position of the Government in the Commons, Lord Goronwy-Roberts was for a time the only Foreign Office minister able to undertake overseas travel.

Ministers in the Lords, like their Commons counterparts, have their particular areas of ministerial responsibility. At the Foreign Office the allocation of responsibility is usually made on the basis of geography, with different junior ministers taking responsibility for policy in relation to various parts of the world. Clearly ministers speaking on matters for which they have direct ministerial responsibility can talk with greater authority than when speaking on matters for which they are simply spokesmen. Baroness Young was Minister of State at the Foreign Office during the 1983 Parliament; she had particular responsibility for Latin America, but as a former Cabinet minister and ex-Leader of the House she was also a more senior figure in Government than was customary for Ministers of State. As far as the Lords is concerned, having a minister who carries weight within the Government is important in gaining recognition for the views put forward in the chamber. Lord Glenarthur succeeded Baroness Young as Minister of State in 1987, and was in turn succeeded by Lord Brabazon of Tara in 1989. Both of these were less experienced ministers with no background in overseas affairs, though Lord Glenarthur had served overseas while in the armed forces from 1973 to 1975.

The Opposition parties in the House appoint front-bench spokesmen whose role has gradually become more formalized over the years. Since 1982 Lord Cledwyn of Penrhos not only has led the Labour peers but also has been Labour's chief foreign affairs spokesman in the Lords. As Mr Cledwyn Hughes MP he was from 1964 to 1966 Minister of State at the Commonwealth Relations Office. His contributions in the Lords on foreign affairs earned the respect of peers in all quarters of the House during the 1980s. When Labour had gone into Opposition in 1979 Lord Goronwy-Roberts continued with foreign affairs as Shadow spokesman in the Lords. The former Labour Foreign Secretary, Lord (Michael) Stewart of Fulham, took little active part in the House, making only the occasional speech, though he was a fairly regular attender. A number of other peers assisted on foreign affairs. Throughout most of the 1980s a Labour peer was specifically nominated to speak on overseas development matters; one of these was Baroness Ewart-Biggs, who then became the number two to Lord Cledwyn on foreign affairs. She had earlier been active in the Lords on behalf of Unicef and had also lobbied within the House at the prompting of Foreign Office friends whom she had got to know when her husband had been a professional diplomat.[6]

The other Opposition parties in the House tend to have fairly fluid and flexible arrangements, basically allowing any suitably experienced party member to speak from their front bench. Lord Kennet spoke regularly for the SDP in the 1980s and Lord Bonham-Carter for the Liberals. Lord Gladwyn spoke from the Liberal front bench on foreign affairs from the time of his arrival in the House in 1960 shortly after retiring as a professional diplomat. Generally the former professional diplomats like the former chiefs of defence staff who arrive in the House sit on the cross-benches, but Lord Gladwyn was not the only exception to this rule; Lord Brimelow, Permanent Secretary at the Foreign Office from 1973 to 1975, took the Labour Whip from the time of his arrival in the House in 1976, and though he very rarely made speeches in the

Chamber he was a regular attender and voter and he became one of the mainstays of the Lords' European Communities Committee.

While the contribution of front-bench spokesmen especially ministers is important for the satisfactory functioning of the House, its influence on both Government and the wider public is by no means simply dependent on the front benches. It is in the nature of the House of Lords that its influence is seldom direct, often uncertain, certainly hard to specify, and no doubt frequently marginal or non-existent. A look at some of the Questions which have come before the House in recent years may help to illustrate this.

Hong Kong

When introducing a debate on Hong Kong in June 1988 Lord Cledwyn referred to the fact that 'over the years this House has taken a close interest in the affairs of Hong Kong'.[7] If time spent in debate on the future of Hong Kong is a suitable yardstick for measuring interest then this would appear to be so. Throughout the 1980s the House usually debated Hong Kong at least once in each session. In 1981 Lord Brockway sought a Royal Commission to consider the colony's future, but his call received little support from other peers (24 February 1981). In 1984 (21 May) Lord Fanshawe of Richmond asked about the current approach of the Government to negotiations on the colony's future. The debate on this Unstarred Question lasted from 9.30 pm till midnight; among those who spoke were some of the peers who contributed regularly to debates on Hong Kong in subsequent years as the difficulties over the future of the colony mounted. Lord Fanshawe had in his previous incarnation been known as Sir Anthony Royle MP; in 1964 he had founded the Parliamentary All-Party Group on Hong Kong, and from 1970 to 1974 he had as Parliamentary under-Secretary at the Foreign Office ministerial responsibility for Hong Kong. Lord MacLehose of Beoch had spent his life in the diplomatic service, culminating in his appointment as Governor of Hong Kong in 1971, a post he held until 1982. Lord Tanlaw, a Liberal peer, was the second son of the Earl of Inchcape; he had worked as a businessman in the Far East for most of his life and in 1976 had married a Chinese lady. Lord Kadoorie, a prominent resident of the colony, who had been created a peer in 1981, flew to London especially to take part in this debate, but not having taken the oath of allegiance in the current Parliament was unable to speak; however, his friend Lord Rhodes – another peer with a good first-hand knowledge of the colony – in his own speech included the views and comments of Lord Kadoorie. Other peers such as Lord Shawcross and Lord Shepherd spoke in most debates on Hong Kong, drawing on their knowledge of the colony gained through regular business visits over many years.

On 10 December 1984 a Government motion expressing approval of the intention to sign the agreement negotiated with China over the future of Hong Kong was debated. Peers generally approved the agreement but without the enthusiasm shown by MPs in the Commons debate, a point made by Lord Fanshawe when he criticized the euphoria of the Commons debate as opposed to the more realistic tone heard in the Lords. When later in the session the Hong Kong Bill, providing for termination of links with the colony in 1997, was debated in the House of Lords, attention focused on the rights of British Nationality (Overseas) citizens in respect of UK entry; responding to an amendment moved from the Opposition benches Baroness Young announced that the Government would agree to an extension of citizenship to the grandchildren of current British Nationality (Overseas) citizens born after 1997. Lord Cledwyn welcomed this addition of a generation to British Nationality rights. Before the Government laid orders dealing with the nationality provisions of the Hong Kong Act it published a White Paper with 'green edges' (Cmnd 9637) embodying its proposals. This was debated in the House on 20 January 1986; Lord Glenarthur – at that time Under-Secretary at the Home Office – handled the debate for the Government. Baroness Young's Statement made during the passage of the primary legislation – that the Government would introduce a draft order in this way and then if necessary withdraw it for revision – was quoted in the debate; she was present during the debate but silent. There was clearly unease in the House, which was also reflected in Questions asked later in the year.

On 16 May 1986 when the draft order was laid, Lord Cledwyn moved that it be withdrawn. He argued that the view expressed in debate by the House in January had been hostile. Since then he had himself visited Hong Kong and was unhappy with the Government's proposals. However, during the debate Lord Glenarthur accepted that the Government had an obligation to look sympathetically at the cases of those ethnic minorities who were not Chinese and who lacked any other nationality than their British National Overseas status. This brought some satisfaction to Lord Cledwyn, who claimed that the minister had gone 'substantially further than any minister has done on any previous occasion' including his colleague in the Commons; as a result he withdrew his motion and the order was approved.[8]

On 10 June 1988 the House debated the Joint Anglo-Chinese Declaration on the future of the colony. Various aspects of the draft basic law were criticized, for example that concerning the freedom of the press, by Lord McGregor of Durris (who had chaired a Royal Commission on the Press in Britain in the 1970s). Several peers spoke of the debate being broadcast in Hong Kong; Lord Cledwyn believed this would enable the residents of the colony to 'appreciate the authoritative and impressive discussion' which had taken place and also mean that they were 'assured of our commitment to their interests'.[9]

That the House of Lords has a particular interest in Hong Kong is obvious. As a final remnant of the British Empire, it is hard to escape an element of nostalgia in discussing its affairs. But it is Hong Kong's astonishing business success which has probably been the predominant reason for engaging the interests of peers, so many of whom over the years have become very frequent visitors to the colony. By 1989, when anxieties over Hong Kong's future rapidly intensified, the Foreign Office minister with responsibility for the colony was Lord Glenarthur. Debates in the Lords might have done something to reassure the people of Hong Kong about the commitment and interests of the House, but given the weakness of the British position in relation to shaping the future of the colony, it is doubtful that the debates could do any more, simply because the policy options open to Britain were so limited.

The Falklands

The role of the House of Commons in relation to the Falklands crisis has frequently been the subject of discussion. Particular attention has focused on the reception given to Mr Ridley's statement in November 1980 about a possible agreement with Argentina involving the leaseback of the Islands, and also the highly charged atmosphere of the first Commons debate following the invasion of the Islands. On both these occasions MPs spoke with angry passion rather than sober realism. During the period of hostilities in 1982 the debates that took place in the Commons were important in sustaining public support for the actions taken by the Government. What role if any did debates in the House of Lords play?

The Statement made by Mr Ridley in November 1980 following his visit to the Islands was repeated in the House of Lords by Lord Trefgarne. But unlike the Commons, where the response was so hostile that it was thereafter assumed to be politically impossible to proceed with any leaseback proposal, peers gave a general welcome to the Statement. The Franks Report includes an extract from Commons *Hansard* which demonstrates not only how uninformed MPs were but also how unwilling they were to consider the arguments being advanced by the minister.[10]

Within the Lords there were two peers in particular who did know a great deal about the Islands. One of these was Lord Shackleton, a well-respected former Labour Leader of the House, the son of the famous explorer, and the man who in 1976 had completed a survey and report on the prospects for the Islands at the request of the then Labour Government; he had visited every part of the Islands and had given much thought to their possible future. The other peer who knew both the Islands and Argentina well was Lord Buxton of Alsa, a Conservative back-bencher who had received his peerage in 1978. His interest arose out of his extensive involvement in conservation and wild-life issues; he was a member of the Royal Commission on Pollution, a director of Anglia TV, and the father of Cindy Buxton, who had also achieved prominence through her films on Falklands wildlife.

On 30 June 1981 Lord Buxton initiated a debate on an Unstarred Question in the Lords on the future of the Islands. In a thirty-five-minute speech he stressed the urgency of the situation relating to the Islands following the breakdown of the Ridley initiative, and the need for negotiation between Britain and Argentina. Lord Shackleton spoke next and endorsed these views; he was followed by Lord Stewart of Fulham, the former Labour Foreign Secretary, who bemoaned the public ignorance and especially the ignorance of MPs about the Islands. Lord Trefgarne made a lengthy platitudinous reply for the Government, offering reassurance about the Islands, explaining why it was not possible on cost grounds to build an airport capable of taking long-haul jets, and generally exuding an air of complacency. In other words the concerns expressed very starkly by the two parliamentarians who knew most about the Islands had no apparent effect. It is interesting to note that according to the Franks Report on the very same day as this unnoticed debate was taking place in the Lords a 'major review of policy' towards the Islands was undertaken in the Foreign and Commonwealth Office at a meeting chaired by Mr Ridley and attended by the British Ambassador to Argentina, the Governor of the Falkland Islands, the Permanent Secretary of the Department, and several other high-ranking civil servants.[11] This meeting recommended that a major programme of public education should be undertaken. The speeches made during the debate in the Lords lent weight to the recommendation of this meeting. But no such programme was to be undertaken.

Later in the year when the House was dealing with the British Nationality Bill a Conservative back-bencher, Baroness Vickers, moved an amendment making special provision for the citizenship of all Falkland Islanders; the Government resisted this and on a division of the House voted 90–90, which meant under House of Lords rules that the amendment was lost.[12] After the military victory in the Falklands, the Government relented, but ironically a special Act of Parliament was then required to do what Baroness Vickers's amendment had sought.

Though the seriousness of the situation in the South Atlantic had been emphasized by Lord Buxton in the summer of 1981 he did not expect an Argentine invasion in 1982. At least that is what he said in the Saturday

(3 April 1982) debate immediately following the invasion. He had in fact visited Argentina and the Falkland Islands within the previous month and had had a 'long private talk' with Dr Costa Mendez, the Argentine Foreign Minister, which had not given him any expectation of an invasion, a fact he had reported to the Foreign Office upon his return. The contrast between the high excitement of the Commons debate and the much more subdued debate in the Lords is instructive. The Commons is open to criticism for its failure to grasp the issue concerning the future of the Islands, and for failing to make the effort to understand the complexities and the dangers that existed. But if the Lords' debates on the Islands both prior to and subsequent to invasion were better informed and much more realistic about the dangers that were faced, it has to be said that the House does not appear to have impressed its concern either on the public or on those within the Government, other than the minority who were already aware of the dangers. The supposed wisdom and experience of the House of Lords (evident in this instance in the persons of Lords Buxton and Shackleton) was to no avail. No one took any notice of the House.

Other foreign policy issues

Spain and Gibraltar (see Chapter 6) were frequently the subject of debate in the Lords, with no fewer than sixty-one Questions or Statements being made in the period 1977–78 to 1987–88. Again there were regular contributors to such debates, including Lord Selsdon, a banker with particular interests in European affairs, Lord Merrivale, who for thirty years took a close interest in Gibraltar, Lord Bethell the MEP, and others. During the passage of the British Nationality Act in 1981 the Government was defeated in the House of Lords on an amendment moved by Lord Bethell designed to alter the status of Gibraltarians. Some thirty Conservative peers defied the party Whip, including some prominent back-benchers such as Lord Boyd-Carpenter, the chairman of the Association of Conservative Peers (the Lords' equivalent of the 1922 Committee). Because the Government was also under a good deal of pressure from its back-benchers in the Commons on this issue it decided to give way, and the amendment was allowed to stand. As with most other Government defeats in the Lords the deciding factor in determining the Government's response appears to have been a calculation about the extent of a likely rebellion in the Commons if an attempt was made simply to reverse the amendment concerned.

In 1973 when the Grenada (Termination of Association) Order came before the House for approval Lord Shepherd moved a motion seeking the postponement of the order until a referendum had been held on the future form of Government. In doing so he argued that the Order was contrary to the spirit and understanding of the West Indies 1967 Act. He was supported by Lord Greenwood who had been the Secretary of State responsible for negotiating the Act. Lord Sainsbury spoke too, from a close personal knowledge of the island which he often visited, explaining that he would make a very undiplomatic speech because the Prime Minister of the island Mr Gairy had 'a very unhealthy lust for power and great skill but questionable methods in attaining his ends'.[13] Lord Shepherd pressed his motion to a division but it was lost by 55 votes to 80. The episode demonstrated the Lords' concern for constitutional matters especially in relation to the former colonies. It is also worth noting that subsequent events showed Lord Sainsbury to have been quite correct in his assessment of Gairy. This is another example of members of the House speaking on the basis of the particular knowledge and experience they have, but without avail as far as altering Government policy is concerned.

In what sense the House of Lords ever influences the course of events is difficult to assess. Individual peers who are thought to speak with authority on some matter may influence thinking elsewhere. In interview a former Conservative minister spoke of Lord Shackleton and Lord Buxton as a 'steadying influence' on the Falklands, and Lord Shackleton especially as having had an influence on both the Prime Minister and the Shadow Cabinet. But this was after the crisis had broken. The European Communities Committee reports are certainly read carefully not only in London but perhaps even more so in Brussels and Strasbourg. Sudden changes of policy do not result; rather it is a question of slow almost imperceptible changes in the climate of opinion which may have been influenced by the well-argued case put in a committee report, or possibly series of reports.

The greater freedom and flexibility the House has in arranging its business can enable it to hold debates which are more timely than the Commons. The device of the Unstarred Question in particular means that a debate lasting up to three hours or even longer can be held at short notice. The Commons may find it difficult to allocate time to debate matters of real significance, which the Lords is able to do with relative ease. In December 1989 both Houses held debates on the Report of the War Crimes Inquiry; the Commons debate was limited to three hours despite protests from several senior back-benchers. The Lords held a five-and-a-half-hour debate. The Commons debate was muddled, con-fused and generally unsatisfactory; most MPs who spoke were in favour of legislation to enable prosecutions to take place and the House voted 348 to 123 in support of this. No vote was taken in the Lords but peers' speeches ran overwhelmingly against the proposal to allow prosecutions. And the debate in the Lords included a string of extremely impressive speeches, giving it a quality – on this occasion – vastly superior to that achieved by the Commons.[14] However, later in the session the Government went ahead with legislation and introduced its War Crimes Bill. One wonders if anyone concerned (ministers in the Cabinet for example) bothered to look at the debate which had taken place in the Lords. The Bill was introduced into the Commons, passed all its stages in the lower House, but was then rejected overwhelmingly at second reading in the Lords by 207 votes to 74.[15] This was the first time a Government Bill had been so treated in the post-war period. However, it was not a manifesto Bill, and for the Lords to have done otherwise would have involved an abnegation of the view the House had clearly expressed in debate but a few months earlier. Though the Government announced its intention to re-introduce the Bill using Parliament Act procedures to ensure its passage, this had not been done by the end of 1990.

Occasionally the very timeliness of a debate in the Lords raises suspicions that events have been hastened on by the knowledge that a subject is to receive attention in the House. Lord Spens, a cross-bench peer, won a place for a balloted debate on Cyprus for 16 November 1983. He had put down a motion in June after visiting the island, and talking at length with Mr Denktash who was a personal friend. The day before his debate was held a coup took place and the Turkish Republic of North Cyprus was declared. Lord Spens believed the coup had been deliberately timed to pre-empt the Lords debate;[16] he himself was very sympathetic to the Turks, but of course others including the Government spokesman felt it necessary to make clear their feelings of strong disapproval for what had happened.

Very seldom do memoirs make any reference to debate in the Lords. Lord Callaghan for example refers only incidentally to the House of Lords in his memoirs and never to a debate that took place there, despite his quite lengthy and detailed discussions of problems over Cyprus, Rhodesia and other matters which were being debated in the House. References to Commons debates are not numerous but recur regularly in his book. Likewise with Healey's memoirs. A former Permanent Secretary at the Foreign Office was asked in interview if he could remember any occasion when as a diplomat he had really taken notice of debate in the House of Lords. The only occasion that came to mind was the 1977 debate in the House on the Central Policy Review Staff (CPRS) report on Overseas Representation; the House provided an excellent forum for the Establishment to fight back against a report which had recommended substantial cuts in overseas representation. According to the authors of a study of the CPRS

The debate opened with a speech in defence of the British Council by Lord Ballantrae, who until a year earlier had been its chairman. Many of the subsequent speakers also had been or still were in some way directly connected with one or more than one of the organisations being reviewed. Many of them clearly felt passionate about the need to defend these organisations . . . Out of 29 speakers, only 4 were in favour of the report.[17]

Conclusion

It is hard to summarize the role of the House of Lords in relation to foreign affairs. Part of the reason for that lies in the highly curious character of the House. It contains many people who have held positions of great importance in Government and society. To some extent their opinions and experience do have significance. Yet by the time they reach the Lords most of them are retired, elderly and – as they themselves are often the first to admit – out of touch. (See also the case study on Libya, Chapter 7.)

It was suggested earlier in this chapter that the European Communities Committee was not primarily concerned with foreign affairs. Yet it is worth noting what a high reputation the ECC has established. It may be thought rather typically British that active retired folk of great experience should be accorded places in the Lords, and should then spend much of their time working on a committee examining in a shrewd and fair-minded way detailed policy questions, and doing this without remuneration. Even if it were true that little good came of this activity it could hardly be thought harmful. But in fact much that is worthwhile does result from the work of this committee in the identification of British interests and contributions to the work of EC policy-making. The same sort of point can be made of other activity within the House.

Some very perceptive and extremely interesting speeches are made in the House (along with many others which lack not only these but perhaps any other desirable quality too). The facility for such speeches to be made, with Government required to listen and to make some sort of response, may be considered a worthwhile feature of the bicameral British Parliament. (If such a matter as the report of the War Crimes Tribunal could be debated only in the Commons, this would represent an impoverishment of parliamentary debate.) It is, however, easy to criticize the Lords as being simply a rather self-indulgent debating club. As a number of examples given above indicate the House appears to be so peripheral as far as Government is concerned that at least in its deliberative role it can easily be forgotten about altogether. And in its legislative role it has very little to do with foreign affairs.

SIX

Case study I: Gibraltar and the House of Commons 1977–88

The problems of Gibraltar constitute only one small part of the huge range of foreign policy business which even today preoccupies British decision-makers. In its turn, foreign policy is a minority interest in both Whitehall and Westminster, where domestic business proliferates and tends to have priority. It would be reasonable, therefore, to expect that a specialized and relatively low-profile issue like Gibraltar would not come to the attention of Parliament very often, or generate much expertise among MPs. A close look, however, at the practice of the last decade compels us at least to qualify this picture.

By studying *Hansard* over the period since Franco's death in November 1975, it is in fact possible to glean a great deal of information about Gibraltar. Certainly the essential components of what discussion has taken place on the subject in the public eye are to be found in the proceedings of the House of Commons. Many aspects of Gibraltarian life and of the relationship between the colony and Britain have been aired in the House, from the impact of Spanish entry into NATO to the conditions of Moroccan guest-workers. The principal focus, however, has been on the question of sovereignty and the possibility of a new relationship between Gibraltar and democratic Spain. Of a total of 876 separate Parliamentary Questions (PQs), replies and statements on Gibraltar between November 1977 and June 1988, 420 related to Spain.[1] It is clear that had the status of the colony not been in doubt during the period, there would have been very little parliamentary activity on Gibraltar. Yet the unpredictable turn of events can turn the spotlight even on a quiet and strategically redundant rock of 29,000 inhabitants from time to time. The

Table 12 Parliamentary Questions, replies and ministerial statements in the House of Commons on Gibraltar November 1977 to June 1988

Session	Number of statements and PQs
1977–78	29
1978–79	7
1979–80	107
1980–81	81
1981–82	150
1982–83	63
1983–84	119
1984–85	131
1985–86	71
1986–87	23
1987–88	95
Total	876

Source: Hansard, House of Commons Debates

reviews of Royal Naval dockyards announced in November 1983, leading to the closure of that in Gibraltar, are a major case in point, since the consequences for the Rock were severe and led to a good deal of lobbying. Even more unexpected was the furore produced by the events of March 1988, when three members of the IRA were shot dead by British under-cover soldiers while reconnoitring for a possible bombing. Out of the 876 Commons references already referred to, 127 dealt with the dockyard question, and 68 with the shootings (no doubt a proportion which would be greatly expanded by any data collected after June 1988).

Not surprisingly, some years were more active than others in terms of parliamentary interest in Gibraltar (see Table 12). The peaks were in 1979–80 when the joint British–Spanish Lisbon Statement was issued, 1981–82, when Spain postponed the expected reopening of the borders between Spain and Gibraltar, and 1984–85, when the opening was finally achieved, but essentially the whole six-year period from 1979 to 1985 was one of consistent interest in Gibraltar in the Commons.

This was the result, not simply of the claims of an historic imperial possession, but of the linkages between Gibraltar and much more wide-ranging political issues at home and abroad. If it can be said that no man is an island, then certainly no island (poetic licence, with respect to Gibraltar) can be entire of itself. Gibraltar touches on, and is affected by, the question of Spain's entry into NATO and the European Community, which has been one of the central dilemmas for the West European states in the 1980s. If Spain had not been willing to behave reasonably towards Gibraltar, then the unstated possibility was always that Britain would use its position in the two major Western groupings to obstruct Spanish diplomacy. Equally, once Spain was in NATO and the EC, it would be more constrained in the pressures it could bring to bear on Gibraltar. Finally, Gibraltar's anomalous position as a colony within the EC creates certain complications for the functioning of the Community, as was evident in recent difficulties over the restructuring of airfares, caused by a dispute over whether Gibraltar came within the scope of an agreement.[2]

On the domestic front, Gibraltar has been entangled not only with the question of naval dockyard facilities, close to the hearts of the senior service and trade unionists alike, but also with the debate about immigration and citizenship, which has stirred up even stronger emotions. The British Nationality Act 1981 was one of those pieces of legislation which by its nature straddled internal and external consider- ations, and therefore increased parliamentary interest in foreign policy. It also called into question the rights of Gibraltarians to reside in the UK. Parliamentary interest here (most effectively from the House of Lords) almost certainly concentrated the Government's mind and led to the clear acceptance of the Gibraltarians' right to apply for full British citizenship that followed.[3]

It took the Falklands war in 1982 to secure a similar privilege for the inhabitants of those Islands, and also to stimulate comparisons in the House of Commons by Members between the situations of the two dependencies. In particular, Denis Healey for the Labour party used the example of warmer relations with Spain over Gibraltar to press for renewed contacts between Britain and Argentina.[4]

If, then, Gibraltar was of rather more significance than might be at first assumed, how did MPs actually respond? In what ways, and to what effect, did they contribute to the debate that has intermittently been taking place within and between governments, on the future of the Rock?

A surprisingly large number of individual MPs – 133 in all, contributed to the discussion of Gibraltar during the period 1977–1988 although this cannot be expressed as a percentage of the total of 650 Members of the House (635 until 1983), as the formal total considerably understates the number of elected representatives actually in the House during three Parliaments, when MPs regularly drop out and are replaced. (On the other hand it should also not be forgotten that a large number of MPs are on either the Government or the Shadow 'payroll'.) The figure of 133 may, however, not be too far from the number of constituencies whose MPs have spoken on Gibraltar during the years in question.

The contributing MPs were from a cross-section of the House as a whole, with the Conservative party's majority during the majority of the

Table 13 Leading back-bench activists in the House of Commons on the subject of Gibraltar November 1977 to June 1988

Member	Number of PQs asked
McQuarrie, A. (C)	151
Latham, M. (C)	27
Dalyell, T. (L)	24
Wall, Sir Patrick (C)	20
Van Straubenzee, W. (C)	20
Taylor, J. David (UUP, also MEP)	13
Stanbrook, I. (C)	12
Craigen, James (L)	10
Hooley, F. (L)	10
Young, David (L)	10
Johnston, R. (Lib)	10
Biggs-Davidson, J. (C)	9
Brocklebank-Fowler, C. (SDP)	7
Colvin, M. (C)	6
Mills, Sir Peter (C)	6
Roberts, Allan (L)	6
Brown, Gordon (L)	5
Stern, M. (C)	5

Notes: C = Conservative; L = Labour; Lib = Liberal; MEP = Member of European Parliament; SDP = Social Democratic Party; UUP = Ulster Unionist Party

period naturally giving them the numerical edge. Of the total of 133, about 18 were really active, asking five or more Questions on Gibraltar during the period 1977–88, as well as taking part in debates and responses to ministerial statements (see Table 13). Most of the remaining 115 asked one or two Questions only, but some clearly held a watching brief and also participated in debate from time to time. It seems likely, again rather like the case of the Falklands (this time before 1982), that without this persistent back-bench interest (even if in this case not of one mind) the Government would have felt under very little domestic pressure at all in its policy on Gibraltar, and would have come to the House far less frequently to put its views and actions on the record. Perhaps the average back-bencher without hope of preferment identified with the small dependency, and refused to allow its cause to go undefended.

The ten activist MPs were headed decisively by Albert McQuarrie, the Member for Banff and Buchan, who had lived on the Rock for six and a half years. He asked 151 Questions before losing his seat in the 1987 General Election. No one else approached this level of activism, with the next most busy being Michael Latham (27), Sir Patrick Wall and William van Straubenzee (20 each), and Ivor Stanbrook (12). The highest Labour scorers were Tam Dalyell (24), James Craigen, Frank Hooley and David Young (10 each), while Russell Johnston submitted 10 for the Liberals. The Official Unionist John David Taylor submitted 13 Questions. These figures should be kept in proportion, of course. In the 1977–78 session of Parliament a total of 36,435 Questions was asked of ministers in the Commons, and the pressure of business has increased in the decade since then. On Gibraltar, about 50 Questions are asked each year, on average, which is about 0.14 per cent of the whole.

Yet even the individual Member can pack a hefty punch, if the timing is right. Albert McQuarrie, for example, seems to have commanded respect from ministers for his knowledge and persistence. When he was defeated by a Scottish Nationalist, the House lost an important source of practical expertise on Gibraltar, and the inhabitants lost an indefatigable supporter. The latter was perhaps the more important quality. Deep technical knowledge was not really necessary to monitor the international politics of Gibraltar. Instead, the traditional House of Commons back-bench skills came into their own – keen interest, doggedness, a sharp eye for detail, and the capacity to lobby while the Government was likely to be distracted with other, apparently more weighty, matters. And on such issues, back-benchers tend to make the running. Ministers make such statements as they have to, or are useful to them as part of 'megaphone diplomacy'. Front-bench Opposition spokesmen come in when events take a serious turn, as after the 1988 shootings, or Spanish indignation at the honeymoon of the Prince and Princess of Wales being started from Gibraltar in 1981. But Gibraltar is precisely the kind of issue where a back-bencher can carve out a reasonably discrete area of expertise for himself (no women MPs seem to have shown an interest), and where, accordingly, he can sometimes make a mark.

On the principle that numbers mean strength, MPs should be more effective in the various subject groups which they form than as isolated individuals. So far as Gibraltar is concerned, there exists an All-Party Gibraltar Parliamentary Group, under the auspices of the Commonwealth Parliamentary Association (CPA). McQuarrie was its chairman from 1983 to 1987; he was succeeded by fellow-Conservative Michael Colvin. The Labour Member David Young was a long-time vice-chairman, while Sir Russell Johnston (Liberal) and James Kilfedder (Ulster Popular Unionist Party) have also served as officers. The group obviously forms a focus for lobbying by Gibraltarians, and a source of instant expertise for the mass media whenever Gibraltar hits the headlines. It also makes possible visits by MPs to Gibraltar, whether funded by the CPA or the local administration itself. Such visits are ostensibly fact-finding affairs, and it would be overly cynical to suggest they are no more than boondoggles in sunny climes. There is no hard evidence either way on the effectiveness of such trips in promoting understanding. It is difficult to believe, however, that the delegations who visit Gibraltar come back with a *decreased* sense of loyalty to its inhabitants.

In the period 1977–88 there were two parliamentary visits to Gibraltar: the first delegation, in October 1980, consisted of Michael Latham, John Carlisle and Neville Sandelson, as well as the Labour peer Lord Hughes, who led the party. In the subsequent debate on 10 December only Latham was present, although he apologized for the absence of Carlisle and Sandelson 'for very good reasons which they have explained to me'. The second visit which included the Labour MP James Craigen, arrived on 27 November 1984, the very day that Sir Geoffrey Howe and Sr. Fernando Moran issued a joint communiqué in Brussels on Gibraltar, and it continued during one of the rare debates on the subject in the House, prompted by Sir Geoffrey's statement of the 28 November. With Denis Healey, David Owen, Michael Foot, Sir Anthony Kershaw, Sir John Biggs-Davison and Ian Paisley taking part in the debate, however, this was a high-profile affair, and with McQuarrie, Stanbrook, Johnston, Sir Kenneth Lewis and Sir Bernard Braine among the back-bench contributors, there was no serious depletion of the all-party group's representation.

In foreign policy debate at the national level, there is always something of a presumption that bipartisanism is to be expected, as both an inevitable consequence and a good in itself. On the question of Gibraltar, it is clearly true that there was no obvious divide between the Government of the day and the Opposition parties on how to handle Spanish pressure and the other problems which occurred. There was a natural tendency for Tory and Unionist traditionalists to rally to the flag, and for Labour's trade union wing to be concerned about the employment implications (in Britain and Gibraltar) of the dockyard closure, but in general both sympathy and advice tended to cut across party lines. In relation, for example, to the ministerial statement of February 1985 which followed on the opening of the border with Spain, Sir Geoffrey Howe received the support of Denis Healey and the congratulations of Russell Johnston; the tone of most remarks was that of support and concern not to exacerbate a still delicate situation.

In the very different circumstances of the immediate aftermath of the SAS shootings of March 1988, the Government was also relieved to be able to rely on the support of the House across party lines. This dramatic incident aroused concern primarily because of the alleged 'shoot-to-kill' policy towards the IRA, but the status of Gibraltar and Anglo-Spanish relations were also important issues at stake. At first the Government had a free hand. Although party political argument on the affair was to become steadily more inflamed, Sir Geoffrey Howe escaped remarkably lightly at the time the story broke. George Robertson, for Labour, condemned the IRA and congratulated the Army, and although his statement contained a sting in the tail, in its asking about whether those shot had received any warnings, the Foreign Secretary was able blithely to ignore the question, which was not followed up. Only Eric Heffer asked whether what had happened would actually help in the fight against terrorism, a stance which Sir Geoffrey neatly stigmatized: 'I am afraid that the hon. Gentleman must stand almost alone in the House in offering that point of view'.[5]

The advantages of the Government over the House in the midst of confusing, shocking events where accurate information is at a premium, were dramatically evident during these proceedings. Whether by design or not, what took place in the Commons on 7 March 1988 constituted a most effective piece of public relations from the Government's point of view, with potential critics disarmed by a strong ministerial input and an equally firm closing of national ranks on behalf of the Opposition front bench.

The forms of discussion of a foreign policy issue in the House can vary, although the lack of a legislative component usually restricts the opportunities for sustained investigation. On the subject of Gibraltar, most references occurred in the context of responses to ministerial statements (themselves possibly often made in anticipation of Parliamentary unrest), and Parliamentary Questions. Formal debates were inherently unlikely given the specialized nature of the problem, and indeed during the 1977–88 period only one took place, the adjournment debate of 10 December 1980, opened by Michael Latham.[6]

This debate, furthermore, took place between 1.09 am and 1.35 am, with very few Members in the House – a not untypical state of affairs (in 1988 the first general debate for thirty-eight years on Britain's relations with Latin America took place, between 2.51 and 4.21 in the morning: five MPs spoke).[7] In the Latham debate, the only other speakers were Albert McQuarrie and the Under-Secretary of State for Foreign and Commonwealth affairs, Richard Luce. In such instances Parliament is not a place for the real conflict of views; it is a vehicle for creating an historical record. Of course, the record can itself be a powerful political instrument and a means of sending storm signals. No doubt the Foreign Secretary's officials would later have drawn his attention to Latham's remark that were Gibraltarians to become subject to more restrictive immigration controls, 'I do not believe that there would be a majority in this House for such a deplorable proposition'. Such warnings of back-bench rebellions are pregnant with significance for governments, although they can get lost in the 'noise' of information overload. It is also true that the bluff is called more often than not. In the case of the Latham debate for example, the Government did introduce the British Nationality Bill within a few weeks without making any provision for Gibraltar. The inhabitants of the Rock were granted full British citizenship only by virtue of an amendment in the House of Lords on 22 July 1981, a defeat which conceivably did not distress the Government overmuch. Certainly when the Bill returned to the Commons the amendment was allowed to stand.

It is an open secret that Parliamentary Questions are often used as plants by ministers. On an issue like Gibraltar, however, there is rarely the need for such manoeuvring. George Robertson's request for a statement on the SAS shootings ('by private notice') probably suited the Government as much as the Opposition, but that was an exceptional event, loaded with potential political difficulties for both front benches. In any case, PQs are parried easily enough, and are not the best means of extracting new information. On Gibraltar, as on other subjects, they provided simply the means of keeping a persistent drip of pressure on the administration, a reminder that ministers and officials did not have *carte blanche* on Gibraltar.

Since 1979 the House of Commons has had at its disposal in the pursuit of foreign policy accountability a Select Committee on Foreign Affairs. This Committee has been over-worked and under-valued, but it did produce a Report on *The Situation of Gibraltar and UK Relations with Spain*, published on 22 July 1981 (the date of the Lords' amendment of the British Nationality Act.[8] The Report contained useful historical and analytical material. It was, however, a rather bland and understated document, careful to avoid controversy. The slight leaning that is evident is of interest given the Falklands analogy (not apparent until a year later) in that the committee accepted that the *wishes* of the Gibraltarians to remain British constituted a veto, but also warned the Government that

the United Kingdom might well come to find itself in grave difficulties if it does not make clear to the Gibraltarians that though the colony is in many aspects unique, the British Government's prime responsibility is to this Parliament.[9]

Essentially the committee favoured new diplomatic initiatives with Spain to explore 'possible constitutional solutions'. They can be said to have been on the right side of the argument, but not to have carried much political clout at the time. A single report is easily buried in a mass of later business. After the 1983 election, indeed, the composition of the committee changed, and none of its members was to figure among the ranks of the Gibraltar specialists. The successes of diplomacy between London and Madrid to some extent obviated further committee attention, but lack of continuity is also a major problem for the parliamentary scrutiny of foreign affairs. This was accentuated in the period 1977–88 because of the changes between Foreign Secretaries in the Commons (1977–9, 1982–8) and a Foreign Secretary in the Lords (Carrington, 1979–82).

Parliament itself has developed an international dimension in an attempt to cope with the foreign policy expertise of the Government. The Commonwealth Parliamentary Association is explicitly designed to promote co-operation between members of the various legislatures of the Commonwealth and, as we have seen, it promotes exchange visits. Similarly the larger Inter-Parliamentary Union (IPU), with 110 parliaments affiliated, holds conferences to 'debate any questions of an international character suitable for settlement by parliamentary action'. Unhappily, however, disputes between countries are as evident at the parliamentary as at the inter-governmental level, as can be seen in the case of Gibraltar.

The Foreign Affairs Committee Report of 1981, for example, pointed out that 'the democratic parties in Spain share the long-standing insistence on Spanish sovereignty over Gibraltar', as well as the fact that the two countries perceived the Lisbon agreement of 1980 to mean radically different things. The FAC concluded that

> whether or not the Spanish Foreign Minister of the time understood in Lisbon that Spain was to lift the restrictions [on Gibraltar's frontier] unconditionally and that only thereafter there would be 'reciprocity and equality of rights', the Lisbon Agreement would not have been acceptable to the Spanish Parliament on that interpretation.[10]

It is possible that the visit of Spanish parliamentarians to Britain in December 1979 under the auspices of the IPU may have at least prevented illusions at Westminster. It clearly did not lead to much softening of positions in either Commons or Cortes. No doubt this was partly because of the closer links between Westminster and the Gibraltarian House of Assembly. The internationalization of parliamentary life is by no means necessarily a process of widening co-operation. The European Parliament perhaps has the greatest long-term potential to build bridges between Spanish and British political parties (although contacts in the Council of Europe framework should not be overlooked), but so far it has been only a cause of suspicion in the Commons on the Gibraltar question. John David Taylor MP, in particular, has asked hostile Questions of the Foreign Secretary as to why Gibraltarians have no representatives at Strasbourg, and why they cannot vote in European elections. He has also objected to what he sees as the illegitimate interest of the European Parliament's Political Affairs Committee in the affairs of Gibraltar.

Parliament's ability to intervene directly, therefore, at the international level is not wholly without foundation. But the Commons is just as likely to be used by the Government as a factor in its own diplomacy, as to be a constraint. It is clearly very useful for the Foreign Secretary, assuming that he does not *want* to give up Gibraltar, to be able to say to the Spanish Government that his hands are tied by parliamentary opposition to any deal at home – just as Madrid plays the same card in its turn. This was particularly evident during Spain's negotiations to enter the EC, when MPs were willing to make the explicit linkages that the Government preferred to leave unstated. The Spanish Ambassador in London, however, no doubt faithfully relayed home these indications of 'British opinion' on Gibraltar.

In conclusion, we need to ask the question of whether the House of Commons has made any real difference to British policy over Gibraltar. The general rule seems to be that British governments have a fairly free hand in foreign policy-making, and that Parliament is weak. Does the Gibraltar case sustain such a generalization? On the face of it, the answer is yes. The amount of time devoted to the subject is small, often when the House is empty, and in the watches of the night. The specialists on Gibraltar are rarely individuals who carry much political weight in the House. The Foreign Affairs Committee Report made little impact. The leads given by ministers are difficult to resist, and the Government can set the tone of debate. There is little direct evidence for the expression of Members' opinions having influenced the course of official policy. Much secret diplomacy takes place which MPs do not hear about and may be disclosed (if then) only after the passage of thirty years. Where the Government was embarrassed, as with the impact of the British National-ity Bill on Gibraltar, it was as much the result of interest and expertise in the House of Lords as of debate in the Commons.

On the other hand, a case can be made for an important role for Parliament on the kind of issue which Gibraltar represents. The Rock is loaded with symbolism. It has been of great strategic importance to Britain. Its acquisition (1713) came at the end of a famous series of victories. Its people are fiercely British at a time when self-doubt has set in even amongst the metropolitan British themselves, and they have fought bravely in war on Britain's behalf. They are the underdogs in a dispute with a powerful neighbour. These are sufficient reasons for enough MPs to feel strongly about Gibraltar's fate, and to hold a watching brief for the colony. The practical instruments at their disposal are not many or very impressive, but there are still enough opportunities to act as a persistent lobby against any sell-out to Spain, and to monitor any developments which might endanger the economic and other well-being of the inhabitants of the Rock.

In this sense, the Falklands analogy is correct. Just as a vocal and determined minority of Members stepped into a political vacuum in the 1970s to torpedo all diplomatic efforts to reach a compromise with Argentina, and the Government let it happen because it had other priorities and did not want more embarrassment over what seemed a small matter, so the supporters of Gibraltar have managed to emphasize the narrowness of the options of the Foreign Office in its diplomacy towards Spain. The 1969 Order-in-Council on the Constitution of Gibraltar states that

> Gibraltar will remain part of Her Majesty's dominions unless and until an Act of Parliament otherwise provides, and furthermore that Her Majesty's Government will never enter into arrangements under which the people of Gibraltar would pass under the sovereignty of another State against their freely and democratically expressed wishes.[11]

This in itself gives the House of Commons a crucial potential role in any future 'solution'. The ten to fifteen Members who have taken it upon themselves to safeguard Gibraltar's interests have continually reminded the Government of this fact by the very fact of their Questions, however technical and apparently tedious. Whitehall cannot therefore afford to ignore them, and in practice takes notice by anticipating what it knows they can say and do. Whether this example of an issue imbued with the emotional significance of both imperial residue and embattled community is typical of the modern foreign policy process must, however, be very much open to question.

SEVEN

Case study II: the Libyan raid

During the night of 14/15 April 1986, US Air Force planes based in the UK and with the US Sixth Fleet in the Mediterranean bombed targets in and near to the Libyan cities of Tripoli and Benghazi in response to terrorist acts, and in particular to the bomb attack on the La Belle discotheque in West Berlin on 5 April, for which the US Government held the Libyan Government responsible. In the days immediately preceding the raid the US Government had sought the assistance of several Western European countries, but only the UK had responded affirmatively.[1] The decision to allow the use of US bases in the UK to attack Libya had been taken by Mrs Thatcher in accordance with the UK-US agreement of 9 January 1952, which states

> Under arrangements made for the common defence, the United States has the use of certain bases in the United Kingdom. We reaffirm the understanding that the use of these bases in an emergency would be a matter for joint decision by HM Government and the US Government in the light of the circumstances prevailing at the time.

Since this was not an issue on which Parliament could have been consulted (except in a very general hypothetical way) in advance, the question for Parliament to resolve in the immediate aftermath of the attack was whether or not the Prime Minister's judgement and method of handling the decision had been correct and whether any additional or different political guidelines should be established for any future occasion when a Prime Minister might have to take a similar decision.

This chapter examines the immediate reaction to the US raid on Libya in

Table 14 Parliamentary Questions and interventions on the Libyan raid 15–17 April 1986

Occasion	Members referring to Libya
Prime Minister's Questions (15th)	PM + 14
Statement (15th)	PM + 22
Business Statement (15th)	Leader + 7
Debate (16th) – speeches	33
– interventions only	15
Prime Minister's Questions (17th)	PM + 7
Business Questions (17th)	Leader + 3
Statement on Lebanon (17th)	Minister + 13

the House of Commons, the House of Lords and (though only briefly) in the European Parliament.

Proceedings in the House of Commons

The fact that the bombing raid had taken place was broadcast on radio and television on the morning of 15 April 1986. It being a Tuesday, the House of Commons sat at 2.30 pm and the first opportunity to refer to the raid came at 3.15 pm with Questions to the Prime Minister. At 3.31 pm the Prime Minister made a formal statement 'about Libya' which, with Questions, ran until 4.14 pm. The Leader of the House then made a Business Statement in which he announced that there would be a debate on Libya on a motion for the adjournment the next day (Wednesday 16 April), displacing the business already announced. This debate duly took place and ran from 3.40 pm to 10.00 pm, followed by a vote. The matter arose again at Prime Minister's Question Time on Thursday 17 April and during a statement on terrorism in the Lebanon which followed. A further statement on the European Community response to the events was made on 23 April 1986. After this, Written Questions and Answers on the consequences of the raid continued more sporadically. Questions about the incident which directly led to the raid, the bomb attack on the La Belle discotheque, were still being tabled from time to time in the parliamentary session of 1987–88.

In the course of the three days immediately following 15 April 1986, eighty-eight individual MPs (including the Prime Minister and three other ministers) were able to express an opinion on the matter on the floor of the House of Commons, whether by making a speech in the debate, by intervening, or by asking a pointed question. There were twenty-two back-benchers who spoke on more than one occasion. Table 14 gives the numbers who contributed at each stage. Only Questions and interventions concerned with the Libyan raid are counted.

The sequence of speakers over the three days partly reflected the usual conventions of the House of Commons, but there were also some surprising features. The balance of speakers as between the political parties was governed by the usual convention of alternation, so that the number of speakers from the Government side (though not all of them were supporting the Government on this matter) was exactly equal to the number of speakers from the Opposition side, including all the minor parties. As on any major occasion, Privy Councillors were much in evidence, with fourteen speaking in the debate on 16 April out of thirty-three speakers. Apart from the four principal speakers (Mrs Thatcher, Mr Kinnock, Mr Healey and Sir Geoffrey Howe), the Privy Councillors consisted of two former Prime Ministers (Heath and Callaghan), three minor party leaders (Steel of the Liberal Party, Owen of the SDP and Stewart of the Scottish National Party), four former Conservative ministers and one former Labour minister.

Two surprising features were the absence of women MPs and the absence of members of the Foreign Affairs Committee. Though in April 1986 there were twenty-five women MPs, only one (the Prime Minister) made any contribution to the proceedings on Libya. This may reflect the fact that in the 1983–87 Parliament women MPs still played a disproportionately small part in foreign affairs and defence as a whole. The FCO has rarely been without at least one woman minister since the 1960s, but few women back-benchers feature in any of the case studies in the present volume. One reason for this seems to be that women MPs with foreign affairs interests (e.g. Ann Clwyd, first elected in 1984, and Joan Ruddock, first elected in 1987) tend to be recruited rapidly to their front bench, but rarely with a foreign affairs portfolio. None of the eleven members of the Foreign Affairs Committee participated in the Libya debate. Eight members of the FAC were absent on a visit to South East Asia at the time; the other three members of the committee took part in the vote on Wednesday evening, but did not speak on Libya. The Defence Committee was much more in evidence. Four members of the committee made contributions, three of them in the debate, and all but two took part in the vote.

Of the twenty-nine back-benchers who spoke in the emergency debate, a very high proportion had an established interest in defence or foreign affairs. There were five former Foreign Office ministers (Callaghan, Owen, Gilmour, Amery and Onslow), the chairman of the Conservative back-bench defence committee (Buck), vice-chairman of the Conservative back-bench foreign affairs committee (Temple-Morris), chairman and

vice-chairman of the Labour back-bench foreign affairs committee (Clarke
and Winnick). As has already been mentioned, there were three current
members of the Commons Defence Committee (Churchill, Douglas and
Gilbert) and two former members of the Foreign Affairs Committee
(Griffiths and St-John Stevas). Several others were active in the North
Atlantic Assembly or WEU (Wall, Hardy, Goodhart) and towards the end
of the debate came a succession of speakers well-known for their interest
in the Arab world (Walters, Marlow, Faulds, Ron Brown). It would not be
unreasonable to conclude that the great majority of speakers in the debate
had some specialized knowledge relevant to it. The same would be true,
but perhaps to a slightly lesser extent, of the longer list of MPs who asked
Questions or otherwise intervened at various stages during 15–17 April,
many of whom also come into the categories mentioned above.

The debate ranged far and wide over the way in which the Prime
Minister had reached her decision, the degree of consultation, the
position in international law, the nature of the US–UK bases agreement
and precedents for its application, the underlying causes of tension and
terrorism emanating from the Middle East, the evidence for Libyan
complicity in terrorism and the likely consequences of the raid. The
detailed background knowledge which some speakers brought to the
debate was generally of two kinds: familiarity with the region and its
politics, or else knowledge of relevant precedents, usually obtained from
previous occupation of high office. As often on similar occasions the
ghosts of Suez were again disturbed.

Speakers arrived at widely divergent judgements on what had occurred. All of the Labour and Liberal/SDP Alliance speakers were
strongly critical of the Prime Minister's handling of the matter. For
example the former Prime Minister James Callaghan commented,

> The obligation on the Prime Minister was to consider whether this was in
> the best interests of Britain and the United States, as well as in the interests
> of promoting the object that she had in mind. On all these matters I answer
> no.
>
> (16 April 1986, col 894)

Equally critical was the sole Ulster Unionist to speak, Enoch Powell, in his
intervention on 15 April: 'Has it not become clear from these events to the
people of this country how flimsy would be our protection against the use
of bases on British soil for the launching of nuclear operations?' (15 April
1986, col 733). The great majority of Conservatives rallied to the Prime
Minister's support, but there were notable dissenters. Among the
loyalists on this issue, for example, Sir Antony Buck declared

> In my view, we are right now to take a firm line in the face of the precipitate
> action and the statements which have been made by a very dangerous

dictator. I think it was right for Her Majesty's Government to support what the Americans planned to do and did.

(16 April 1986, col 908)

On 15 April four Conservatives put critical or highly sceptical Questions to the Prime Minister and three made dissenting speeches in the debate on 16 April. For example Sir Ian Gilmour said

> I believe that, difficult though the decision was, my right hon. Friend made the wrong decision. I believe that when an ally does something wrong, it is the right and the duty of a good ally to try to persuade them not to pursue that course of action. If they continue to pursue it, we should disassociate ourselves from it.

(16 April 1986, col 918)

Several others were less than whole-hearted in their support and hinted that they would not be able to support any repetition of the raid. One Conservative back-bencher (Marlow) argued that the US action had been a terrible mistake, but that the Prime Minister had none the less been right not to refuse the US request to use the bases.

In a frequently interrupted reply to the debate, the Foreign Secretary, Sir Geoffrey Howe, gave a further detailed account of all of the circumstances which the Prime Minister had taken into account and repeated her assurance to the House that 'our position on any question of further action which might be more general or less directly targeted against terrorism was explicitly reserved' (16 April 1986, col 956). When it came to the vote (on the proposition that this House do now adjourn) the Government had a comfortable majority. One Conservative voted with the Opposition and several abstained.

From the procedural point of view the whole episode passed smoothly. No one was in any doubt as to the seriousness of what had occurred and the Government had readily accepted the need for an immediate statement followed by an emergency debate in Government time.

Proceedings in the House of Lords

Shortly after the Prime Minister had begun her statement to the House of Commons on 15 April, Lord Whitelaw rose to read out precisely the same statement to the House of Lords. He then responded to questions for almost an hour. The following day the House spent four minutes on Libya, during which the Minister of State at the FCO (Baroness Young) replied to questions from Lord Kennet and others. However, a debate had been fixed for Friday 18 April and duly took place, two days after the emergency debate in the House of Commons.

The debate in the House of Lords differed in a number of respects from that in the Commons. There were far fewer interventions in the middle of speeches and the speeches were on average shorter than in the Commons (9 minutes as against 11.5). The tone of the debate was calmer and less adversarial. This was partly due to the fact that in the House of Commons the Prime Minister had been speaking in defence of her own judgement, whereas in the House of Lords Lord Whitelaw was able to take a slightly detached view and to speak of 'those who took that decision'. There was no vote at the end of the debate.

Thirty-three peers took part in the debate. Of these, eleven were former MPs; the others had never sat in the Commons. Exactly two-thirds (twenty-two) were life peers; one sat as Archbishop of York and the remainder were hereditary peers, but these included two of the first generation (Whitelaw and Gladwyn). Of the other hereditary peers, most were of the second or third generation; one was a viscount of the fifteenth generation.

Since the House of Lords is renowned for the expertise which it can bring to bear on complex subjects, it is worth considering the background and experience of those who spoke in the Libya debate. These included a former Prime Minister (Home), who had also served as Foreign Secretary, and another former Foreign Secretary (Stewart). There were also four former junior ministers in the Foreign Office or Commonwealth Relations Office (Mayhew, Chalfont, Caradon, Cledwyn), one of whom (Caradon) also had long experience as a diplomat and colonial administrator. Among the senior retired officials who contributed to the debate were Lord Gladwyn (senior posts in the FO, including UK permanent representative to the United Nations 1950–54), Lord St Brides (Colonial Office and CRO) and Viscount Buckmaster (FO Arabist with service in Libya). Lord Carver spoke as a former Chief of the Defence Staff and there were a host of contributions from former ministers in other departments. Legal expertise was provided by Lords Elwyn-Jones and Broxbourne, ethical expertise by the Archbishop of York and Lord Soper.

In some respects the expertise available was very impressive. Whereas the Commons could argue over the interpretation of Article 51 of the UN Charter, the Lords could boast the man who drafted it (Gladwyn); whereas the Commons could field a man who knew Colonel Gadafi (Ron Brown), the Lords were able to compare him with his predecessor, King Idris ('What a charming fellow he was!': col 913). These may be trivial examples but they illustrate one of the shortcomings of the House of Lords, namely its bias towards the fairly distant past, for of the undoubted experts on Middle East affairs in the House, the great majority had acquired their knowledge many years earlier; those who focused their attention on the present in general spoke with no especial authority and some acknowledged this (e.g. Lord Graham, col 927).

It is true, nevertheless, that the debate in the Lords gave expression to a wider range of views than that in the Commons and that a number of original notes were struck. On the other hand not all of the reminiscences and historical allusions which were heard were strictly relevant to the matter in hand. In replying to the debate, Baroness Young did not, on the whole, respond specifically to those speeches which had displayed historical or personal knowledge of the Middle East; instead she concentrated her attention on the fairly small number of contributions which had raised questions about future policy.

The debate in the Commons was undoubtedly the more dramatic and politically charged of the two, because it was closer to the event, because of the presence of the Prime Minister, Foreign Secretary and Leader of the Opposition, and because of the voting at the end. The debate in the Lords was bound to echo and partially duplicate the proceedings two days earlier in the Commons and although it produced some distinctive points of view and thoughtful speeches, it could not, in the circumstances, make much of a political impact. The case of the Libyan raid appears therefore to reinforce Donald Shell's general conclusions about the House of Lords and foreign affairs in Chapter 5.

The European Parliament

While the proceedings which are described above were unfolding in the two Chambers at Westminster, a third parliamentary Chamber with British members participating was also considering the implications of the US raid on Libya. The monthly session of the European Parliament at Strasbourg was scheduled for 14–18 April 1986 and so coincided with the raid and its immediate aftermath.

On Tuesday 15 April the proceedings commenced at 9.00 am and the Presidency was immediately asked about a possible change to the agenda. The Bureau of the Parliament met during the morning and before lunch-time the full assembly was informed that at 3.00 pm there would be an opportunity for all the chairmen of political groups to make short statements on Libya. This duly took place against a background of cheers and jeers from various sections of the hemicycle.

On the following day (16 April) questions to the President-in-Office of the EC Foreign Affairs Ministers were scheduled to follow questions to the Council of Ministers. The normal order was reversed to take account of the concern about Libya and the Dutch Foreign Minister (it being the Dutch Presidency of the EEC in the first half of 1986), Mr Van den Broek, responded to questions for an hour. He explained that European Community Foreign Ministers had met on Monday and had called for moderation on both sides in the dispute between the USA and Libya. He acknowledged that the US action a few hours later had heightened tension and announced that the ministers were about to meet again, but he also stated 'In my present capacity I cannot become involved in any assessment of the justification for the American military intervention.'[2]

On 17 April the European Parliament held a brief debate on the 'Libya-USA conflict and terrorism' under its procedure for 'topical and urgent debate'. The debate was noisy and emotional and concluded with the adoption of three resolutions, two of which condemned the US action and contained implicit or explicit criticism of the British Government for its supporting role in what had occurred.

Few MEPs commented on the British role in the course of the debate. Perhaps this was not surprising since neither in the Treaty of Rome nor in practical politics was there any basis for harmonization of policy between the members of the EEC on so sensitive a matter as the rules governing the use of US bases in Europe. In a matter such as this it was clear to all that the national parliaments retained full sovereignty and were unlikely to relinquish it.[3]

On 23 April Sir Geoffrey Howe reported to the House of Commons on the meeting of the Foreign Ministers of the Twelve which he had attended and which had been dominated by Libya. He did not find it necessary to refer at all to the proceedings which had taken place in the European Parliament.

Conclusions

For British parliamentarians the main political interest in the Libyan episode described in this chapter concerned the judgement of the British Prime Minister in agreeing to the US Government's request for permission to use bases in the UK. The wisdom or otherwise of the US action itself was an important but secondary issue. This being so it is not surprising that the focus for the British political reaction to the event was the House of Commons where the Prime Minister had to meet her critics face to face and satisfy her supporters that the decision had been correct. By contrast the proceedings in the House of Lords and in the European Parliament seemed almost academic in their detachment.

In the Commons both Government and Opposition recognized that the Libyan raid was a significant political event which required an immediate debate, pushing aside normal business. The normal Questions to the Prime Minister on 15 April together with her statement gave an opportunity for initial reactions and these were followed by more considered responses in the emergency debate the following day. A surprisingly large number of MPs were able to express a view. The result was an endorsement of the Prime Minister's decision, but one delivered with some reservations which appeared to have set limits to any similar decision in the future.

EIGHT

Case study III: the INF Treaty

■■■■■■

This book is primarily concerned with the business of the FCO, but the FCO does not hold a monopoly on 'dealing with foreigners'. When such dealings take place against a background of actual or potential military threats, it is the responsibility of the Ministry of Defence (MoD) to organize a suitable military response; when international negotiations take place in order to reduce or place limits on the development and deployment of arms the FCO has to work very closely with the Ministry of Defence, using a network of ministerial and official committees. The FCO provides the negotiating and presentational skills and generally takes the lead at international meetings; the MoD not only provides the technical input, but also bears the ultimate responsibility for military security and hence plays the major part in deciding what can be offered, what, if necessary, can be abandoned and how forces may be adjusted to meet a new situation. When Parliament takes an interest in arms control it questions both departments and expects both to field ministers for debates. The purpose of the present case study is to examine the parliamentary handling of a single arms control episode which stretched over three parliaments.

It is doubtful whether any arms control episode involving the UK can be regarded as typical. The long negotiations leading to the INF Treaty of December 1987 were mainly concerned with European security (rather than the global balance of power) and were therefore of particular significance to the European members of NATO, including the UK. The UK had been directly involved in the discussion of theatre nuclear weapons within NATO in the later 1970s. The UK was also involved as one of the states on whose territory the weapons dealt with in the negotiations of the 1980s were to be based. However, no weapons actually belonging to the UK were involved and in that sense the UK was not a principal party to the talks. These were to be conducted exclusively between the USA and the USSR with only such consultation of their allies as the principals found expedient.

The contrast between the formal situation, which was that the UK was not a participant in the negotiations, and the reality, which was that British security was vitally affected by them, was striking and made it difficult for the Government to present its position to Parliament. It also made it difficult for Parliament to grasp the subject effectively. In respect of other arms control talks, such as the tortuous multilateral effort on chemical weapons at Geneva, the British Government could make policy statements, table papers and provide full details to the House of Commons, but where intermediate-range nuclear forces (INF) were concerned, despite the missiles and demonstrations at Greenham Common, it could only repeat the formulae adopted in public by NATO ministers, or point to statements made by the US President and officials. Though in theory the negotiations were conducted in confidence, there was a good deal of leaking to the press. Often this was deliberately intended to influence the debate in Western European parliaments. As Lawrence Freedman comments, 'It has become a truism that the United States and the Soviet Union have been gearing their statements as much to Western public opinion as to the other side'.[1]

The origins of the deployment of new generations of US and Soviet intermediate-range nuclear forces in Europe go back to the mid-1970s. There was a strong element of competition involved. The Soviet decision to deploy large numbers of SS20s in Eastern Europe and the western USSR from 1977 was seen in NATO as a crude attempt to alter the balance of nuclear firepower in Europe under the umbrella of global nuclear parity between the USSR and the USA. The NATO response was presented as restoring the balance ('tit for tat'), but also had an ulterior motive: to make manifest the official NATO strategy of 'flexible response' whereby the West could make a nuclear response to Soviet aggression at a series of graduated levels, a 'seamless web' of deterrence which would enable NATO to avoid using the incredible threat of an all-out US-Soviet nuclear exchange to deal with aggression against Western Europe alone.

The NATO decision on how to 'modernize' nuclear forces in Europe crystallized during 1978–79 and was finalized in December 1979. It was announced to the House of Commons on 13 December 1979 in an oral statement by the Defence Secretary, Francis Pym (HC Deb, vol 975, cols 1,540–56). This was the 'dual-track' decision: NATO would introduce Pershing II missiles to replace Pershing IAs and a completely new force of ground-launched cruise missiles (GLCMs or, more commonly, 'Cruise'), but was also prepared to negotiate about their numbers; if the USSR were prepared to agree to equal numbers of missiles in the upper part of the intermediate range (i.e. 1,000 km or more) then a balance might be struck at a lower level of deployment; if not, NATO deployment would proceed in full. The NATO meeting on which Mr Pym was reporting involved both Foreign Ministers and Defence Ministers. Over the coming years there would be a roughly equal division of labour on this topic between FCO and MoD ministers in the House of Commons; the choice of the Defence Secretary to make the first statement may possibly have been determined by the fact that the then Foreign Secretary, Lord Carrington, sat in the 'other place'. Mr Pym's statement was read out to the House of Lords by a junior defence minister, Lord Strathcona.

In the course of Questions following the Commons statement a succession of Opposition MPs, including the Shadow Defence Secretary, William Rodgers, and the Leader of the Opposition, James Callaghan, criticized the Government for not holding a Commons debate before making the announcement; several drew adverse comparisons with other Western European parliaments. One back-bencher, Tam Dalyell, asked whether 'this complex subject is adequately dealt with by necessarily haphazard questions and answers' and demanded a serious debate (col 1,550). Mr Pym denied that there had been a deliberate decision to avoid a debate and hinted that one might be arranged before long. The Conservative chairman of the Foreign Affairs Committee, Sir Anthony Kershaw, opined that it is 'traditional in matters of foreign policy and treaties for the Government of the day to come to a decision, to convey it to the House and to ask for its approbation' (col 1,554). In reply to the Conservative back-bencher, Julian Critchley, Mr Pym confirmed that any arms control negotiations would be bilateral between the USA and the USSR, that is excluding the UK, but in replies to others he offered reassurance that there would be special provision for consultation within NATO (col 1,556). Immediately after the statement William Rodgers applied unsuccessfully to the Speaker for an emergency debate under Standing Order no 9 (now no 20).

Soon after the Christmas recess the Government announced a full-day debate on 'Nuclear Weapons' to be held on 24 January 1980, the first specifically on this subject since 1965. The long gap reflected a distinct reticence on the part of successive British Governments where nuclear weapons and strategy were concerned, a reticence which cannot be explained by attachment to ancient prerogative powers and consider-ations of national security alone. During this period NATO had formally adopted the strategy of 'flexible response' (1967) and the UK had modernized both its strategic deterrent (the Chevaline programme) and its sub-strategic nuclear weapons. There had also been an intensive debate elsewhere in NATO Europe about the need for the alliance to modernize its theatre nuclear capability – a problem with political dimensions which exercised foreign ministries as much as defence ministries. Lawrence Freedman comments, 'In Britain there was none of the intensive discussion on the merits of theatre nuclear modernization found in the rest of Europe – not even a Parliamentary debate'.[2]

For the Secretary of State, Mr Pym, the debate of 24 January 1980 was to serve a number of different purposes: it would give the Commons the opportunity to debate the dual-track decision recently announced, but it would also enable the Government to unveil the Chevaline programme (which had been authorized by the previous Labour Government and kept secret) and to pave the way for the coming decision to buy Trident as a replacement for Polaris. Clearly these were matters primarily within the competence of MoD rather than FCO and Mr Pym set the tone with the comment, 'Obviously defence considerations must predominate in the ultimate decision' (HC Deb, vol 977, col 681). In the course of the debate only a few MPs dwelled for long on the arms control aspect of the dual-track decision. Partly this was because the Soviet intervention in Afghanistan during the recess had made the prospect of successful negotiations seem even more remote than before. The Government treated the debate as essentially one about defence and had a junior defence minister wind up. The official Opposition took a different view and used their Shadow Foreign Secretary, Peter Shore, to wind up the debate. He asked for reassurance that the Government would still pursue arms control seriously, despite the events in Afghanistan (col 722).

The talks were to be held up by Afghanistan and the US elections and did not commence in earnest until November 1981. Then President Reagan seized the initiative and advanced a more radical proposal not envisaged by NATO at the time of the dual-track announcement. This was the 'zero option', that both sides would agree not to possess missiles in the longer-range INF bracket: the SS20s would be removed and the NATO missiles never deployed. According to an official source quoted by Jonathan Haslam, this offer was 'crafted mainly to appease the anti-missile movement and not as a real negotiating goal'.[3] The offer was rejected by the Brezhnev Politburo. In the summer of 1982 the two principal INF negotiators, Nitze and Kvitsinsky, took their celebrated private walk in the Jura mountains and arrived at a possible compromise level of deployment, only to find that their governments were not prepared to accept the deal.[4]

These events found only a distant echo at Westminster in occasional Parliamentary Questions and Answers. However, the death of Brezhnev in November 1982 and the approach of the deployment of Cruise missiles in Britain, together with the prospect of a General Election, gave the subject new parliamentary interest. On 14 December 1982 the Shadow Foreign Secretary, now Denis Healey, applied under Standing Order no 9 for an emergency debate on the NATO ministerial meeting, citing in support of his application reports that the new Soviet President, Yury Andropov, had offered to cut the SS20s by 50 per cent and that there was now little time left for negotiation before deployment of Cruise and Pershing II was due to begin. The application was granted and the debate took place on 15 December.

This time it was, from the ministerial point of view, entirely an FCO day. The Government fielded the Foreign Secretary (now Pym) and Minister of State Douglas Hurd. The Labour Opposition fielded Denis Healey to open and close the debate. Healey made a point of stressing that the House of Commons was in the dark about the talks and was aware of the new Soviet proposal only because of a leak in the *New York Times* (HC Deb, vol 34, col 312). He hoped that it would be possible to strike a bargain somewhere between the new Soviet position and President Reagan's 'zero option', which few now considered viable. The Foreign Secretary responded by giving a general outline of the negotiations to date, but then continued

> I hope the House will understand that if negotiations of this difficult and delicate kind between the Americans and the Russians are to get anywhere, and be successful, as the House will want, confidentiality must be respected. This has always been an essential part of successful arms control negotiations in the past. . . . I do not therefore intend to go into details.
>
> (col 320)

The former Foreign Secretary, Dr David Owen, now speaking for the Social Democratic party, said that his new party, unlike the Labour party, had been consistent in its support for the dual-track approach, but also distanced himself from the Government by arguing for a 'dual-key' arrangement or even British ownership of the missiles should deployment become necessary. He also commented on the role of the House of Commons in these matters. He felt that the Foreign Secretary's contribution 'justifies the need for the House of Commons to debate these issues at fairly regular intervals as we go into the complex and difficult period of negotiations' and the debate already demonstrated 'that the House of Commons can grapple with this issue'. Finally he criticized the Prime Minister for hinting that the decision on deployment was not a matter for Parliament: 'The people of this country must have more confidence in the House of Commons to assert its own judgement' (col 317).

Since this was a three-hour debate under Standing Order no 9 only nine back-benchers were able to make speeches. By and large they represented the opposite poles in the debate more starkly than the front-bench speakers. The four Labour speakers all belonged to the CND-unilateralist wing of the party. The Conservatives included Michael McNair-Wilson, the MP whose constituency contained Greenham Common with its now famous women's peace camp.

Outside of Parliament the missile issue was now attracting considerable public and media attention, much of it focused on Greenham Common. The whole question of British nuclear defence policy was to be debated in the General Election campaign of May–June 1983. In January 1983 an opinion poll found 54 per cent of respondents opposed to the deployment of Cruise missiles in Britain.[5] According to two British MPs reporting to the North Atlantic Assembly, 'Opposition to the possession of nuclear arms and the location of American nuclear bases on British soil was running higher than in the heyday of the CND in the 1950s'.[6] Despite the public agitation against deployment, enough voters were prepared to support the Prime Minister's judgement on security as well as other issues to return her Government with a greatly increased majority in June 1983. On the eve of the election a MORI opinion poll found that a majority of poll respondents (52 per cent) now favoured the deployment of Cruise, should negotiations fail.[7]

The negotiations did not succeed and when the House of Commons next debated the whole matter it was on a Government motion paving the way for almost immediate deployment of Cruise in the UK. The Government motion was put on 31 October 1983 by the Defence Secretary, Michael Heseltine, with a junior FCO minister, Richard Luce, winding up, while the official Opposition led once again with Denis Healey, with the Shadow Defence Secretary, John Silkin, winding up.

Michael Heseltine vigorously defended the dual-track approach and attacked the Labour party, and especially Denis Healey, for allegedly retreating from it. On the negotiations themselves and any future negotiations involving British nuclear weapons he roundly declared, 'It would be quite impossible for a Government to conduct negotiations with the Soviet Union, the United States or the French over the Dispatch Boxes of the House of Commons' (col 625). In reply Denis Healey stated, 'We are debating the most important decision that Parliament will be asked to approve in the lifetime of this Government' (col 630). He cast doubt on the military rationale behind NATO deployment of INF and urged acceptance of the Andropov offer to have the force of SS20s as a basis for negotiation. The third contributor to the debate was David Steel for the Liberal/SDP Alliance, whose amendment had been selected by the Speaker. Steel spoke for a settlement based on the 'walk in the woods' formula, with limited deployment allowed on both sides, NATO using a 'dual key' to share control of the missiles between the USA and the basing countries. However, he regarded this as a 'second best' to the zero option.

The back-bench contributions which followed were understandably pessimistic about the prospects for arms control. NATO deployment was now regarded as inevitable and, following the 1983 General Election, the

Conservative Government had a very large majority. Even those on the Conservative side like Sir Ian Gilmour, who were very critical of US policy on the invasion of Grenada (which had taken place a week earlier), rejected Healey's assertion of US unreliability over nuclear missiles in the UK. Few MPs in any party held out much hope of a rapid change in Soviet policy given Andropov's illness and the continued domination of the Politburo by Brezhnev's aged friends. The Liberal/SDP amendment was rejected by 360 to 22 and the main motion passed by 362 votes to 218.

Two weeks later the Defence Secretary informed the House that the first Cruise missiles had arrived in the UK. In his statement of 14 November 1983 Michael Heseltine recalled that the dual-track policy had recently been reaffirmed by the Commons with a majority of 144. Deployment was the logical outcome because negotiation had so far failed: 'The twin-track decision was essentially about trying to persuade the Soviet Union that it could not introduce a class of weapon system without expecting us to deploy an equivalent modernised system' (HC Deb, vol 148, col 627). Mr Heseltine also insisted, in contradiction of Opposition comments, that this was a NATO decision, not an American one. He also confirmed that the zero option was still available should the USSR change its mind (col 619).

On the morning of 23 November 1983 the Soviet delegate at the INF negotiations announced that the USSR would withdraw in response to NATO deployment of Cruise missiles and would set no date for the resumption of the negotiations. The fact was announced to the House of Commons by the Minister of State at the FCO, Mr Richard Luce (HC Deb, vol 49, col 326), who answered Questions on the matter for almost an hour. All of the questioners, including Denis Healey for the Labour party and David Steel for the Liberals, deplored the Soviet withdrawal, but, as on 31 October, they differed widely in their interpretation of the event.

Though the Government clearly believed that it had received the Commons' endorsement for its policy and could proceed with deployment over the next few years with the necessary political support, the official Opposition was not yet ready to let the matter drop. On 24 May 1984 it used a half-day of Opposition time for a further debate on Cruise missiles, which was opened by the Shadow Defence Secretary, now Denzil Davies. Davies cited various authorities to support his case that the NATO deployment of INF was not really a military response to the Soviet deployment of SS20s and that as a tactic to make the USSR negotiate it had manifestly failed. Michael Heseltine counter-attacked with quotations suggesting that both before and after the 1979 General Election Labour defence spokesmen had been in favour of modernizing INF. The party-political argument was continued by Francis Pym and Michael Foot, both now on the back benches. In the second half of the debate the partisan spirit was less evident. One Conservative back-bencher (Nicholas

Soames), after a trenchant condemnation of the paranoid mood in Moscow, where he had recently been, also criticized the stance and rhetoric of the Reagan administration.

Another (Richard Shepherd) expressed doubts about basing US nuclear weapons in the UK: 'I am worried that another nation, albeit with which we have had the greatest alliance and one with which we have lived in friendship for many years, and which I count most highly, may hold the final decision as to whether this country goes to war' (col 1,331). Enoch Powell (Ulster Unionist) delivered a comprehensive critique of British nuclear defence policy concluding, with reference to Cruise, 'that this is not a weapon which it is in the interest or need of this country to possess, or to allow to be stationed or operated upon its soil' (col 1,335). Taken as a whole the debate confirmed that the House was capable of reflecting the nuances of the INF debate as well as the stark political choices.

The commencement of NATO deployment of INF in November 1983 had been marked by a Soviet walk-out at the negotiations in Geneva. Throughout 1984 there were no negotiations. Yury Andropov died and was replaced by the geriatric Konstantin Chernenko. Mikhail Gorbachev moved up in the Kremlin hierarchy and began to look and act like Chernenko's eventual successor. In December 1984 he visited the UK and was found to be a man with whom Mrs Thatcher could do business, but no breakthrough in arms control was yet in sight. The first sign of a thaw came in January 1985 when the US and Soviet Foreign Ministers met and agreed on a new agenda for arms control talks at Geneva. The agenda was to consist of space weapons, strategic weapons and INF, all to be treated in their interrelationship. The public agenda was to be dominated by the first of these issues; during his visit to Westminster (where he met the Foreign Affairs Committee and Opposition leaders), as later during his first two years in office as General-Secretary of the Communist Party of the Soviet Union (CPSU), Gorbachev was to insist that his first priority was to halt the Strategic Defense Initiative (SDI) and reaffirm the ABM (Anti-ballistic missile) Treaty of 1972, which blocked the development and deployment of anti-missile weapons in space.

Mikhail Gorbachev's succession to the Soviet leadership in March 1985 was to transform East–West relations. During the next few years he would meet President Reagan on five occasions, visit all the major Western countries and take a series of new initiatives designed to improve relations. According to Haslam he was 'redefining security as a political problem requiring a political rather than a military solution'.[8] At first he took the Geneva agenda as a single package and tried to obtain a grand settlement of all three parts in a framework which would lead ultimately to complete nuclear disarmament. This effort culminated in the Reykjavik summit of October 1986 where President Reagan appeared ready to agree on everything except the abandonment of SDI. With this avenue blocked Gorbachev began to untie the grand package in the spring of 1987 and seized upon INF as the most likely topic for a separate agreement.

On 28 February 1987 Gorbachev announced that the USSR would accept an INF agreement based on the zero option in Europe: both sides would eliminate their longer-range INF (LRINF) in Europe and retain only a hundred missiles each away from Europe. NATO governments were quick to point out that they had been insisting for several years on some collateral restraints on missiles in the 500–1,000 km range, that is the shorter-range INF (SRINF) in which the USSR had a clear numerical advantage. When British ministers, including Mrs Thatcher, mentioned this in reply to Parliamentary Questions they were greeted with some scepticism from the Opposition, members of which clearly believed that they were trying to find obstacles to the zero agreement, which many NATO planners had never really wanted (HC Deb, vol 112, col 461). The Soviet leadership, however, had an answer ready. On 14 April 1987 Tass (Telegraphic Agency of the Soviet Union) announced that the USSR was prepared for a second 'zero' in Europe for shorter-range INF – the 'double zero'.

This presented NATO with a challenge. Double-zero removed the anxiety that the SRINF could be built up to circumvent the LRINF prohibition, but did the double-zero deal also remove vital rungs from the 'ladder' of NATO's flexible response strategy? Would it 'de-couple' the USA from Western Europe? These questions caused much concern in Western Europe, especially in political parties belonging to the centre and right where suspicion of Soviet motives was very strong. The divisions were particularly apparent in the Federal Republic of Germany. Intense debates took place in each NATO country and in most cases the arguments were fully aired in Parliament.[9] This did not happen in the UK because of the coincidental circumstance that a General Election was imminent and Parliament was prorogued on 15 May 1987. Because of this the House of Commons missed its opportunity to deliver a verdict on the emerging INF agreement. However, the Government issued a qualified endorsement of 'double-zero' early in the election campaign. On 14 May an FCO spokesman stated that 'the British Government could accept the zero-zero SRINF, provided that the conditions adequately safeguard Western security' (*Guardian*, 15 May 1987). On the day of the election, in which the Conservatives were returned with a majority of 101, Sir Geoffrey Howe (Foreign Secretary since 1983) went to Reykjavik to join in a general NATO endorsement of the principle of the double-zero proposal.

The first opportunity for the Commons to debate the agreement properly came after the summer recess, not on a substantive motion or motion to adjourn, but on the second reading of the Arms Control and Disarmament (Privileges and Immunities) Bill, which was held on 22 October 1987. This Bill arose directly from the appointment of arms control inspectors and observers under the Stockholm Document of 1986 on confidence-building measures, but it was drafted as a general measure enabling the Government to take powers to confer diplomatic status on arms control inspectors under other agreements too. The draft INF Treaty was not to be completed and signed until December, but it was already clear that the new legislation would be relevant to the comprehensive verification measures planned for INF, which would involve visits by Soviet inspectors to Greenham Common and Molesworth. Thus a Bill which might otherwise have received perfunctory treatment late at night in the House of Commons was given a full day's second reading which turned into a debate on the INF Treaty and nuclear weapons in general. It was too late now to oppose the principle of the INF Treaty so the argument turned instead to the question of what had brought it about and who could claim the credit. A newspaper report about the arrangements for the servicing of UK Trident missiles in the USA, though irrelevant to the contents of the Bill, provided a second theme for argument between the front benches.

It was clearly the will of the House that the rules of order should be interpreted broadly for the purposes of the debate. Many speakers agreed that the technical contents of the Bill were symbolic of a greater shift in international relations. The new Shadow Foreign Secretary, Gerald Kaufman, declared, 'This is a tiny, two-clause Bill, but in its implications it is almost certainly more far-reaching than any piece of legislation that this House has debated during the last forty years and more' (col 952). In the closing speech the Minister of State at the FCO, David Mellor, stated more circumspectly, 'This debate – which has properly ranged very wide, as it was intended to do – is based on a little Bill that deals with the building of confidence between East and West' (col 1,006). Most of the back-bench contributions in between concentrated on the party-political arguments referred to above. A few returned to the derogation of sovereignty which they saw in the whole INF episode. A Labour member of the Defence Committee, Dick Douglas, questioned the wisdom of granting rights to Soviet inspectors in the UK without reciprocal British rights in the USSR (col 977). A convinced Labour unilateralist, Bob Cryer, felt that the Government had been foolish all along 'to allow the stationing of weapons of a foreign state on our soil' (col 987). In response to arguments like this David Mellor insisted in his winding-up speech that 'the Labour Party, with its policies, could not possibly have obtained this deal' (col 1,007).

After four committee sittings, during which the chairman allowed the debate to go wide enough for the Government to provide more information on the INF negotiations, the Bill returned to the floor of the House for its third reading on 10 December 1987, two days after the signing of the INF Treaty by President Reagan and Mr Gorbachev in Washington. This time the goodwill which had allowed considerable latitude in the debates on the earlier stages of the Bill's passage was markedly absent. The Minister of State, David Mellor, insisted that the INF Treaty was not directly relevant to the Bill, while the Shadow Foreign Secretary, Gerald Kaufman, backed up by the Shadow Defence Secretary, Denzil Davies, argued that the Foreign Secretary should have come to the House himself to share his assessment of the INF Treaty and that all the texts including the as yet unsigned UK–USSR agreement should have been made available (col 609). The debate was marked by numerous points of order and interventions, many of them acrimonious, and almost every contributor was at some point warned by the Deputy Speaker to stick to the Bill before the House.

At this point we may review the involvement of Parliament in the INF episode from the initial statement in 1979 to the signature of the Treaty in 1987. During this period the House of Commons was given three formal statements (one in 1979 and two in 1983) and debated the matter more or less specifically on six occasions. This total excludes general foreign affairs debates and debates on the defence estimates and also a small number of short adjournment and Consolidated Fund debates on limited aspects of the matter. For example there was a half-hour adjournment debate on Greenham Common on 25 July 1983 and two short debates on the 'dual-key' idea on 7 February and 1 March 1983. The sequence of events leading to the eventual treaty included three important decision-making phases: the adoption of the dual-track strategy; the decision to proceed with deployment; and the decision to accept Gorbachev's version of the zero option. On the first of these the House of Commons was presented with a decision and debated it a month later; on the second, the House of Commons was invited to debate and endorse deployment two weeks before it actually happened; on the third, the House of Commons played no part because of the General Election. The final debates of October and December 1987 came too late to have any influence on the negotiations.

The House of Lords has rarely been mentioned in these pages. Each of the three statements on INF was repeated in the House of Lords and some of the Commons debates were echoed there. For example the House of Lords, like the House of Commons, held two short debates specifically on the dual-key issue in 1983 (on 3 May and 15 November). On 9 December 1987 (the day following the signature of the INF Treaty) the House of Lords debated 'the progress made in disarmament negotiations and the improvement in East–West relations'; on 14 January 1988 the House of Lords was to give a second reading to the Arms Control and Disarmament

Table 15 Parliamentary Questions on INF and related issues 1980–88

Session	Number of sitting days	Number of PQs	PQs per sitting days
1980/81	163	48	0.3
1981–82	174	26	0.1
1982–83	115	105	0.9
1983–84	213	256	1.2
1984–85	172	123	0.7
1985–86	172	76	0.4
1986–87	109	76	0.7
1987–88	218	180	0.8

Bill, which had already passed its Commons stages. During this period the House of Lords also held a number of short debates on Unstarred Questions on more general aspects of nuclear defence and disarmament.

At no point between 1979 and 1987 was the INF issue examined by either the Foreign Affairs Committee or the Defence Committee. It was possibly not an issue which lent itself to Select Committee treatment given the entrenched party positions and the difficulty of extracting detailed information. Similar problems did not prevent the Defence Committee in 1980–81 from undertaking a detailed inquiry into the issues arising from the replacement of Polaris, but INF offered fewer peripheral topics of political interest.[10] On the central questions it would have been very difficult to arrive at a cross-party consensus. The Foreign Affairs Committee did carry out an inquiry into the political impact of arms control agreements, but this was after the signing of the INF Treaty.[11] The fact that the INF issue fell squarely between the remits of the two committees may also have discouraged both from taking it on.

A great many Parliamentary Questions on INF and related matters were tabled over these years. Table 15 summarizes a rough count of the numbers of Parliamentary Questions (PQs) in each parliamentary session.

It will be apparent from these figures that both in terms of debates and Parliamentary Questions the high point of parliamentary activity on INF was in the 1983–84 session, when the first Cruise missiles arrived in the UK. It is scarcely a coincidence that this was the period when public interest in INF was also at its peak. The preparations at Greenham Common and Molesworth were highly visible and there was an emotional reaction in the media and in the public at large. The fact that these nuclear weapons had to be carried out of their two bases periodically in order to rehearse their firing from dispersed sites in the event of war made them somehow more shocking and worrying than nuclear weapons on submarines. It was, no doubt, partly because of this reaction that the Government felt it necessary to obtain specific parliamentary approval of the decision to deploy in 1983, but was content to announce decisions first and gain specific approval later in 1979 and 1987.

Throughout the entire episode the House of Commons lacked detailed information on the negotiations and ministers had repeatedly to justify their inability to provide more. They cited the need for confidentiality in negotiations and the sensitivity of information on nuclear matters in particular. The fact that the UK was not participating in the negotiations may have made little real difference, since ministers assured Parliament that they themselves were kept fully informed by the Americans, and could not have been more forthcoming had they been negotiating themselves. If, in the end, the Government had a fairly easy ride in Parliament over INF, this was largely due to the very poor public image of the Soviet leadership in the early 1980s and the existence of big Government majorities at Westminster. The absence of either of these two factors could have turned a merely uncomfortable episode for Parliament into one of considerable stress and strain.

NINE

Case study IV: Chile

The long, thin country on the far side of the Andes is physically almost as far removed as is possible from post-war British foreign policy preoccupations: East–West relations, the development of Europe and the withdrawal from Empire. Nevertheless, historic links of investment in, and cultural exchange with, Latin America's Southern Cone are surprisingly strong. As Jacobo Timerman has written, 'Chileans regarded their cultured and well-ordered society . . . as a European nation. To them, Chile was "the England of the South".'[1] In the mid-nineteenth century the UK had been Chile's principal trading partner, and British diplomacy had resulted in substantial privileges for the Empire. By the early 1970s there were still about 4,000 British subjects living in Chile, and British investment and trade remained important, particularly in the copper industry.

Through the 1940s, 1950s and 1960s the British Parliament concerned itself very little with this mirror of England in the southern hemisphere. Most years saw one or two references to Chile in *Hansard* – the refusal of wine import licences was raised in 1946–47, whisky exports in 1948–49 and earthquake aid in 1959–60 and 1964–65. Bilateral squabbles about the Falkland Islands and the British Antarctic Territory were also the subject of Parliamentary Questions in 1947–48, 1948–49, 1950–51, 1953–54 and 1955–56, but Chile was basically absent from the parliamentary agenda.

In September 1970 the ill-fated leader of the left-wing coalition *Unidad Popular*, Dr Salvador Allende Gossens, was elected President. Chile embarked upon a radical change of direction – though Allende was not the first socialist to lead the country. Socialism was not a majority creed.

The system of presidential election was 'first past the post' and Allende had won with only 36.3 per cent of the vote. The middle class became increasingly distraught at the radical policies which he tried to put into effect. Allende, however, retained and increased his working-class support and *Unidad Popular* won 43.4 per cent of the vote in the March 1973 congressional elections. The opposition remained in control of Congress, and helped to whip up an atmosphere of chaos in Chile. A military coup on 11 September 1973 was the culmination of this chaos. Allende was killed and a military junta took office. *Unidad Popular* was banned, the trade unions and Congress were dissolved, and a secret police formed. One member of the junta, General Augusto Pinochet Ugarte, emerged as President of Chile in 1974.

Unlike many of its Latin American neighbours, Chile had a history of democratic government going back to the early post-independence years. It also had a tradition of military neutrality. Pinochet, however, secured the 'recession' of the Christian Democrat, National and Democratic Radical parties, while the Communists, Socialists and Radicals, which had made up *Unidad Popular*, were banned. In 1975 his junta formed a National Unity Movement (*Movimiento de Unidad Nacional*) to replace the parties of the past. Pinochet's role was endorsed by a plebiscite in 1978; a further plebiscite in 1980 allowed the introduction of a constitution permitting him to remain in office at least until 1989. However, the 1970s and 1980s saw considerable unrest in Chile, which was met by a harsh government response, including censorship, torture, arrests without trial and the proclamation of a state of emergency. Pinochet, however, honoured the terms of the 1980 constitution which required a referendum in 1988, effectively on the question of whether or not he should remain in power. The opposition was able to secure a 53.3 per cent majority against Pinochet, and in December 1989 presidential elections took place, won by Patricio Aylwin.

The House of Commons appears to have paid scant attention to Chile while Allende was in government. A handful of Labour MPs made encouraging noises, especially Stanley Clinton Davis, who asked Oral Questions of the Foreign Secretary in 1971–72 and 1972–73. Other Labour MPs who displayed a public interest included Nigel Spearing, Frank Judd and Tam Dalyell. There was also interest from the Conservative benches. Ronald Bell, the Conservative Member for Beaconsfield, asked a Written Question on the takeover of British banks in 1970–71, while Ian Lloyd, called to ask a supplementary to Davis's Oral Question in 1972–73, referred to the 'devastating consequence of the application of the extreme measures of socialism' which the Foreign Secretary would be able to see if he were to visit Chile.

But it was the overthrow of Allende and the subsequent behaviour of Pinochet which struck chords among the Left in Britain as it did in many other countries. This brought Chile to the centre of the Parliamentary stage. The idea of democracy subverted by military oppression is a potent one, particularly when the example is drawn from an exotic but not too different country like Chile. For the Left, Chile presented two further bogeymen. The first was the foreign policy of the USA. It had been clear that the US administration regarded Allende as inimical to US interests in Latin America, and it seems likely that the CIA had worked to destabilize Allende. The second bogeyman was monetarism, an economic theory enthusiastically adopted by Pinochet at the behest of advisers who had studied under Milton Friedman.

Although the left was very prominent in Parliament during the years of the Pinochet regime, concerns about human rights abuse were also taken up by the churches and by other non-political organizations, like Amnesty International. These, too, brought influence to bear by lobbying parliamentarians of all political parties.

This chapter will look at parliamentary coverage of Chile during the Pinochet years. It will look especially at the post-Allende months, and then at the period 1983–89.

Stanley Clinton Davis secured the first Oral Question to the Foreign Secretary on 7 November 1973. He criticized the Government for supplying weapons to the Chilean military regime and for denying asylum to those trying to escape 'the barbarities practised by that wicked regime'. He cited Sweden as an example of a country which had stood up to the military government, and James Callaghan, the Shadow Foreign Secretary, added Belgium, the Netherlands, Denmark and Ireland. A Conservative MP, John Temple, deplored the 'temporary suspension of parliamentary government in Chile', told the House that the military regime would restore democracy 'just as soon as the present situation has been stabilized' and reminded members of his view that Allende had himself been guilty of abrogating the constitutional guarantees he had given. It is clear that passions among Labour MPs ran high. Interjections in Temple's Question and in the minister's Answers are recorded by *Hansard* from Eric Heffer, Judith Hart and Gerald Kaufman.

Labour passions were able to find more lengthy expression when on 28 November 1973, eleven weeks after the coup, the Labour Opposition in the House of Commons devoted half of a Supply Day to Chile.[2] Their motion read

> That this House deeply deplores the armed overthrow of democracy in Chile, and condemns the continuing murder, torture and imprisonments carried out by the military junta; regrets the hasty recognition of the new regime by Her Majesty's Government; and, bearing in mind the strength of feeling in Great Britain, now condemns the refusal of the Government to offer refuge in its Embassy in Santiago to those in danger of their lives, in sharp and deplorable contrast to other Western European embassies, and

calls on the Foreign Secretary to issue fresh instructions to our Ambassador, to press for the immediate release of all political prisoners and an end to executions, to prevent any sale of arms from Great Britain to the junta, to ensure that refuge in Great Britain is provided for Chileans who seek it, and to withhold future aid and credits from the present Chilean regime; and to use his influence to ensure that World Bank and IMF [International Monetary Fund] assistance is also withheld.

In moving it, Judith Hart felt obliged to justify such a debate: 'it is not our normal practice to comment unduly on the internal affairs of another country'. Mrs Hart outlined the ties between Britain and Chile and between the Labour party and the Chilean Radical party, one element of the Allende coalition, and set the coup in terms of socialist ideology: 'the real crime of Popular Unity was that the poor were becoming less poor and the rich were becoming less rich'. This was particularly repugnant to the USA's interests. Mrs Hart was forthright in describing her view of the military junta's repression. Her forty-minute speech ended with the justifications for each of the actions proposed in her party's motion. These ideas – pressing for human rights, preventing arms sales, helping refugees and withholding economic assistance from Chile – were to be the watchwords of Labour pressure in Parliament over the next fifteen years.

The FCO case was put by its Minister of State, Julian Amery. He justified recognition of the Chilean junta as a recognition of reality (the FCO some years later in 1980 sought to resolve this problem of criticism for recognizing governments by announcing a new policy of recognizing states, not governments), and a means of protecting British citizens and interests. On human rights, the British Ambassador had made representations but 'it would be invidious to intervene in Chile and not in other countries where there are more political prisoners and where there have been even more political executions'. Amery also refused to sanction special measures to help Chilean refugees or to suspend arms sales or aid. The minister did say that the British Government 'regret that a country which has enjoyed many generations of constitutional government should see that government overthrown' but did not 'regard it their duty to pass judgement on what is an internal Chilean conflict'. He concluded his speech by telling the House 'this is a quarrel of limited concern to the people of this country'.

The debate which followed was passionate if predictable. Labour Members denounced the minister's 'disgraceful' and 'odious' speech, compared the Chilean junta with Hitler and criticized the activities of US Government and business. Eric Heffer made a spirited defence of socialist internationalism: 'democracy is indivisible'; he was echoed by Neil Kinnock: 'Are we on the side of brutality and the suppression of civil rights, or are we on the side of maintaining our own parliamentary traditions and freedom of speech?'

Conservative Members, beginning with the veteran Sir Robin Turton, criticized Allende's record. One described the ex-President as 'a man who brought his country to absolute ruin, chaos and abject poverty'. Several alleged that the Labour party indulged in double standards: Sir Frederic Bennett pointed out that there had been no criticism from the Labour benches of the recognition of the post-Dubcek Czechoslovak Government. They repudiated the idea of severing links with Chile. A return of democracy was more likely to be achieved if links were maintained, and all Conservative speakers made it plain that they hoped for an eventual return to democratic government in the country.

Mrs Hart, summing up for Labour, detected a 'Chilean Embassy Lobby' among Conservative MPs. Mr Amery concluded by expressing his scepticism about the commitment to democracy of any avowedly Marxist government, and by accusing the Labour party of adopting the Chilean crisis as a diversionary tactic for its own problems.

In all, five MPs from the Conservative party and five from the Labour party spoke, including Mrs Hart and Mr Amery. *Hansard* records interventions from two other Conservatives, one of whom, Christopher Woodhouse, was mildly critical of the Government. (He did not vote for the Government motion, though that may have been because he was paired.) Eight Labour MPs intervened. According to Mrs Hart, no Liberal MPs were present during the whole debate. However, the Liberals voted solidly for the Labour motion. On a division, this was lost by 280 votes to 262. By this stage in the Parliament, the Conservatives had an overall majority of 20.

The debate took place after a British State of Emergency had been declared and as petrol rationing coupons were being issued. The Labour party would three months later win a General Election. When it had done so, Government policy on Chile changed. Aid was stopped and future arms sales banned. In parliamentary terms, the period 1974–79 saw two elements in the House keeping Chile on the agenda. The Right, represented by MPs like Ernle Money, Evelyn King, Frederic Bennett, Ronald Bell and Robert McCrindle, argued that sanctions against Chile were inconsistent with policies towards left-wing dictatorships in Eastern Europe and harmful to British trading interests. On the Left, MPs like Dennis Skinner, Martin Flannery, Neil Kinnock, Phillip Whitehead and Stan Newens ensured that there was no backsliding by the Labour Government. Typical of the last was the exchange at Oral Question Time on 28 January 1976 between the left-wing MP Stan Thorne and James Callaghan, the Foreign Secretary. Two submarines had been constructed and, under an old contract, were destined for Chile. Callaghan was prepared only to say that the future of the submarines was under review. This exchange then followed

> **Mr Thorne:** Will my right hon. Friend take into account whilst reviewing this subject that torture and crimes by the Chilean junta continue and that to allow the submarines to leave for Chilean shores is almost tantamount to supporting its activities?
>
> **Mr Callaghan:** I do not think that the last part of my hon. Friend's question follows from the first. There is strong feeling about the actions of the Chilean Government, which I wholly share. However, when considering these matters we must realise that a different category is involved when we are talking about long-standing and binding contracts negotiated many years ago. We shall keep all these matters under review.

During this period of Labour Government one particular event in Chile captured British public attention. Dr Sheila Cassidy, a British Christian missionary doctor who later went on to run one of Britain's leading hospices, was expelled from Chile on 29 December 1975. Arrested in an armed police raid while visiting a sick nun on 1 November, she was subsequently subjected to electric shock torture and held in solitary confinement. Her case produced public outrage, and James Callaghan, the Foreign Secretary, recalled the British Ambassador from Chile on 30 January 1976. The Chilean authorities denounced Dr Cassidy's story of torture as 'unfounded and malicious', but their accusation against her of 'moral cowardice' in not complaining officially about her torture before she was released cut little ice with enraged British public opinion.

Dr Cassidy's case was naturally raised in Parliament. Neil Kinnock had a Written Parliamentary Question answered on 11 November, and he and Judith Hart tabled Oral Questions for 17 December.[3] Their concern was also shared by Conservative Members who had shown an interest in human rights like John Biggs-Davison and Bernard Braine. Dr Cassidy's suffering was particularly repugnant to church groups, and her case was taken up much more widely than by just the political left.

The new Conservative Government elected in 1979 announced in January 1980 its decision to re-establish normal diplomatic relations with Chile.[4] Speaker Thomas, who rarely granted Private Notice Questions, allowed one to David Winnick on this new policy. Not everyone who wished was able to intervene, but, extraordinarily, the Leader of the Opposition, James Callaghan, did so, raising the issue of Sheila Cassidy. He was echoed by the Liberal Foreign Affairs spokesman, Russell Johnston. Conservative MPs appear to have welcomed the announcement. From the liberal wing of the party, Cyril Townsend said that the new ambassador will 'not only give Britain's approval, but disapproval from time to time', while others endorsed the view of the junior minister, Nicholas Ridley, that ambassadors would need to be withdrawn in many other countries if human rights infringements were the cause. Anthony Kershaw, the newly elected chairman of the Foreign Affairs Committee, asked simply 'Are we proposing to keep our Ambassador in Moscow in this regard?' Other Conservatives referred to trade possibilities and Winston Churchill proposed the restoration of trade in arms.

Although the themes raised by the Labour party throughout the Pinochet years remained those of the 1973 debate, it is interesting to analyse in more detail how these themes were raised in one specific period, 1983–84 to 1988–89. These years are interesting for a number of reasons. First, Pinochet was well established in power in 1983, but beginning to have to cope with better articulated dissatisfaction at home. By the end of the 1988–89 session, he was a lame duck President. Second, the Conservative Government in Britain was well established, and Labour MPs could attack any dealings by the Government with Chile without any concern about scoring an own goal – a problem with which they had to cope from 1974 to 1979. Finally, the period does not include the temporary distortion of UK perception of Latin America during the Falklands campaign when Chile may have played a covert role in aiding Britain against its old rival Argentina.

One measure of parliamentary interest is the use of Parliamentary Questions. Over these six sessions, a total of 335 Questions relating to Chile were asked. These include a small number of Questions asked in the House of Lords. Table 16 gives a more detailed breakdown.

Among the Labour MPs who asked questions, we find few with a sustained interest (see Table 17).

It is particularly noteworthy that a large number of Scottish Labour MPs asked questions about Chile – about half of those sitting in the 1988–89 session had done so, and this probably bears some relation to the fact that the most persistent questioner on Chile, the junior Opposition spokesman on Foreign Affairs, George Foulkes, is a Scottish MP (the third,

Table 16 Parliamentary Questions in both Houses on Chile 1983–89

Session	No. of PQs relating to Chile						Average per day	No. of questioners (MPs + peers)		
	PM	FCO	MoD	DTI	Other	Total		Con	Lab	Other
1983–84	3	28	7	3	1	42	0.19	2 + 0	13 + 0	0 + 1
1984–85	15	50	16	7	4	92	0.53	1 + 0	16 + 1	2 + 0
1985–86	0	39	6	2	1	48	0.28	2 + 0	14 + 0	2 + 1
1986–87	0	11	2	0	1	14	0.13	1 + 0	5 + 1	1 + 0
1987–88	1	66	6	13	3	89	0.41	3 + 2	30 + 2	1 + 1
1988–89	0	27	1	0	2	30	0.17	1 + 0	21 + 0	1 + 0

Table 17 Numbers of Labour MPs asking Questions on Chile 1983–89

	1 PQ	2–4 PQs	5–7 PQs	8–15 PQs	16+ PQs
No. of MPs	43	18	3	4	3

fourth and fifth questioners were also Scots – Tam Dalyell, Judith Hart and Jimmy Wray).

The second most assiduous questioner was Jeremy Corbyn. He is secretary of the Parliamentary Labour Party Latin America Group, and is married to a Chilean.

The Parliamentary Questions of the Opposition parties had a number of purposes. All dealings between British ministers and officials and their Chilean counterparts were the subject of questions. For example in July 1985 Corbyn asked for details of meetings between the Chilean military and British officials, and Foulkes asked for a list of official Chilean delegations which had visited the UK. Questions also attempted to ensure that the British Government accounted for its actions in international forums – such as the UN or IMF – when votes relevant to Chile were expected. A number of Questions dealt with individuals whose human rights were under attack in Chile. These served to alert the British Embassy in Santiago, and might do something to alleviate the position of the person concerned. Finally, there was a consistent series of Questions asking ministers to account for their trade, military and human rights policies in Chile. Most Questions were given written answers, but on virtually every occasion when FCO ministers answered Oral Questions (approximately nine times each calendar year), Questions about Chile were tabled. In recent years, Oral Questions have been subject to attempts at co-ordination by front-benchers, and Chile was regularly a subject on which the Labour front bench wished to test the FCO. Other ministers also occasionally faced Oral Questions on Chile.

In effect, Oral Question Time is an opportunity for a mini-debate. But there were several other methods by which MPs used House of Commons procedures to give prominence to Chilean issues. The principal of these was the Early Day Motion (EDM). From June 1983 to June 1988, thirty EDMs relating to Chile were tabled by Labour and Liberal MPs. Some of them were gestures of defiance. For example Jimmy Wray's EDM of December 1987 expressed solidarity with dissident Chilean actors, but EDMs were also frequently used – in a technique Amnesty International has employed in other contexts – to bring the names of threatened individuals to public attention. Seven Chilean dockers held in Valparaiso Gaol are, for example, mentioned in an EDM tabled by Terry Fields in 1986.

Occasionally other public parliamentary opportunities were used. The House of Commons allows a limited number of debating opportunities to back-benchers, and demand is heavy. However, Pat Wall spoke on Chile in the summer adjournment debate in 1987 while Jeremy Corbyn spoke in a Consolidated Fund debate of 1986 and used a half-hour adjournment debate in 1985 to discuss Chile.

As well as these public opportunities, the private means of writing to ministers, taking delegations to meet them, and buttonholing them in the Lobby will also have taken place, as well as meetings with Chilean visitors – official and unofficial – and meetings with Embassy staff. The only involvement of the Foreign Affairs Committee with Chile during these years consisted of meetings with Chilean visitors, and Labour front-benchers were in the late 1980s prepared to visit the Chilean Embassy.[5]

One difficulty in analysing the involvement of Parliament in Chilean affairs is the impossibility of measuring the extent to which these sorts of private activities took place. This is especially so when they were at the initiative of those Conservative MPs who were in favour of a thawing in relationships between the UK and Chile. Ivan Lawrence in December 1983 in a Christmas adjournment debate called for a 'little goodwill towards Chile'. He told the House that he was not an apologist for Pinochet, but he had been there with a Bow Group delegation. Although he acknowledged that there had been 'considerable bloodshed, torture, police repression and censorship', he believed that Chile was changing. John Biffen, the Leader of the House, in replying to the debate said merely that Lawrence's speech had been 'contentious'. However, as well as these rare and almost maverick appearances of Chile on the parliamentary stage at the behest of Government supporters, it is likely that a number of Conservative MPs will have taken a rather different view of Chile from that of the Left, and will have used their own private means to ensure that ministers were aware that there were two sides to the perception of Chile in Parliament. Sympathetic Conservative MPs certainly retained contact with the Embassy throughout the Pinochet years.

The changes in Chile in 1989 allowed an opening up on all sides. An all-party *ad-hoc* committee in support of human rights in Chile was set up that year led by George Foulkes (Labour), Russell Johnston (SLD), Cyril Townsend (Conservative) and John Cartwright (SDP). In May 1989 the Conservative peer Lord Torrington and two MPs, Calum Macdonald (Labour) and Jacques Arnold (the Conservative secretary of the All-Party Latin America Committee), visited the country at the invitation of the Chilean Embassy. Mr Macdonald later raised the topic of Latin America in the Consolidated Fund adjournment debate on 27 July. He told the House that he had 'returned full of a greater confidence and hope' for Chile's future than he could have imagined before he went. His faith was based upon the ability of the Chilean people to return to traditional values, and he was critical both of the Pinochet regime and of the British Government. Other speakers, ranging from Ray Whitney (a former Conservative FCO Minister and one-time official, with a particular interest in Latin America and chairman of the All-Party Latin America Committee) to Jeremy Corbyn, welcomed the changes in Chile, and Jacques Arnold, while criticizing the regime's human rights record, asked the House to recognize 'the determined way' in which Pinochet had led Chile back to democracy.

From the front benches, Donald Anderson for Labour referred to his party's rejoicing that Chile was returning to democracy, 'although that is no thanks to the British Government who seemed happy and at home with dictators'. Tim Sainsbury – who had been transferred to the FCO only two days before – replied to the debate. Interestingly he set relations with Chile in the context of the European Community: the Twelve would collectively encourage democracy, while the unified EC market in 1992 would offer Chile trading opportunities. He applauded Chile's economic success in recent years, and stressed that the UK and other EC states had frequently protested about human rights abuses in Chile, just as they had about abuses elsewhere in the world. Perhaps with a hint of impatience, he told the House that the issue of human rights in Chile had 'been referred to rather too often, one might think'. His speech may in retrospect have signified the drawing of a line which separated the way Parliament dealt with the Chile of Pinochet with the way in which the Chile where democracy was restored was treated.

Certainly Conservatives were able to speak more freely about Chile after the 1989 Chilean election. Neil Hamilton, who introduced a Private Members' motion on the future of socialism on 15 December 1989, perhaps expressed a typical Conservative view:

> I am delighted that today we have heard the results of a free election. President Pinochet, whom I have not come here to defend, took over the Government of Chile in the midst of much turmoil and confusion. I am delighted that his undemocratic regime has now been translated into a democratic one, and in the process, over the past 15 years through the application of Thatcherite nostrums, the economy of Chile has transformed from one of the most shambolic countries in South America into one of the most advanced.[6]

It is also interesting that four out of the five MPs who tabled Oral Questions on Chile for the first FCO Oral Question Time of the 1990s were Conservatives.

However, taking the Pinochet years as a whole, the principal parliamentary activity in respect of Chile was initiated by the Left. Their natural sympathy with the anti-Pinochet forces in Chile was supplemented by information coming from two lobby groups organized in Britain, the

Chile Solidarity Campaign and the Chile Campaign for Human Rights (CCHR). There is also a Spanish-language group of Chilean exiles, *Chile Democratico*. The English-language bodies were heavily influenced by the large number of well-informed and articulate Chilean exiles (perhaps 350,000 Chileans lived outside their country in the Pinochet years, many in Western Europe and Britain), and it was they who principally targeted MPs. As one CCHR publication said, 'CCHR is lobbying hard, informing MPs and future parliamentary candidates about Chile's grave human rights situation and seeking commitments from them for greater action on Chile. But lobbying by concerned individuals like you will achieve much more.' The CCHR leaflet went on to show how to contact an MP or a parliamentary candidate, and what points should be made to him or her.

Since it shows how pivotal a role an MP has in the lobbying process, it is worth reproducing what the CCHR leaflet says in full:

Lobbying actions should raise awareness of the human rights situation in Chile with the British government and individual politicians. They should also seek to obtain, from the politicians and government alike, commitments to future action on Chilean human rights. The following are just some suggestions for action:

1. Write to your current MP and to the parliamentary candidates of all parties, telling them of your concern for human rights in Chile, and of your belief that the British government should be more actively involved in the defence of human rights and promotion of democracy in Chile.

Ask your MP and candidates the following questions:

a) Do you believe Britain should sell arms to the Chilean regime?

b) Do you think Britain should sell to the Chilean regime communications equipment that could be used in operations involving internal repression?

c) Should Britain offer training to members of the Chilean armed forces and police?

d) Should the British Ambassador to Chile make human rights a major and public concern?

e) Should Britain make its support for international financial packages for Chile dependent on improvements in human rights?

f) Are you prepared to take action to encourage the British government to play a more active role in the defence of human rights in Chile?

If you feel that six questions are too many for one letter, why not make a selection from these above: *but don't omit (f)*.

2. When you receive replies: (a) write again on points that you do not feel are adequately answered (b) send copies of replies to CCHR.

3. Ask your MP/candidates for a meeting to discuss the issue of British action on human rights in Chile. You may prefer to do this in conjunction with a small group of likeminded friends. CCHR will supply you with back-up information on request.

At the meeting ask your MP/candidate his/her view of the points raised under 'What CCHR Wants', above. Ask him/her the policy of his/her party on British relations with human rights violators, and with Chile in particular.

Ask your MP/candidate what action he/she will take on human rights violations in Chile as a result of the meeting. You could suggest:

a) A letter to the British Foreign Minister asking for Britain to step up pressure on Chile on human rights issues.

b) A letter to Foreign Affairs spokesperson of the MP's/candidate's own party (if not the present Foreign Minister) asking the spokesperson what action the party is prepared to take on human rights violations in Chile.

c) A letter to the Chilean Ambassador to Britain, protesting at continuing human rights violations in Chile, and calling for a swift return to full and free democracy.

Send reports of your meetings to CCHR.

4. Organize a public meeting locally, to which local party candidates are invited, to speak on their parties' policies on British links with human rights violators, and Chile in particular. You might find it easier to do this in conjunction with other local human rights/solidarity/development groups.

CCHR can provide written information, slide-tape shows, videos and speakers to assist at such meetings.

5. Scan your local newspapers and notice-boards to discover forthcoming meetings at which your MP/candidates will be present. Go along yourself and raise publicly the question of the British response to human rights violations in Chile.

6. If you are a member of a political party, trade union, or other group, try to get a resolution passed supporting the demands in 'What CCHR Wants'.

7. Try to get the support of local candidates for any campaigning events you organize locally.

8. Once you have established contact with local candidates, remain in touch with them, passing on relevant news and information on Chile and calling upon them to take action on specific issues concerning the UK–Chile link and human rights in Chile.

For many MPs, lobbies like this are a wearisome fact of parliamentary life, to be dealt with by diplomacy and a promise to write to the Foreign Secretary. In most cases, the effect is minimal. A photocopied letter passed on by an MP to the FCO with a covering note has very little result. However, effective lobbying will result in an awareness of which MPs are really interested in a subject, and the lobbyists will feed them with appropriate briefing material. In the case of Chile, the two lobbying organizations were responsible for making the core of MPs who showed sympathy aware of what was happening in Chile, who was visiting the UK and who, most importantly, was being threatened with human rights abuse there. Skilful deployment of their parliamentary resources meant that the Government was boxed in so that no cordial relation could develop with the Pinochet regime without public scrutiny, and a small group of informed and well-briefed MPs could be mobilized to defend the interests of the Chilean Left, calling, where necessary, on the support of other MPs who were sympathetic but not Chile specialists.

The specifically Chilean lobbying organizations were supplemented by the activities of charities such as CAFOD (Catholic Fund for Overseas Development), Oxfam and Amnesty International. The lobbying of non-political groups, especially the churches, will certainly have resulted in a considerable body of cross party knowledge of human rights abuses in Chile, though there appears to have been little pressure on Labour MPs from individual constituents.[7]

What purposes did this parliamentary activity serve? First of all, it was not confined to the UK nor were the British Left in the lead. In the run-up to the 1989 Chilean plebiscite, 100 parliamentarians from 28 countries visited Chile. US politicians played a major part, but in Europe, Spain, the Federal Republic of Germany, France, Italy, the Netherlands and the Nordic countries (as well as the European Parliament) showed at least as much parliamentary interest in Chile as did the UK.

In domestic terms, so far as British Government policy to Chile was concerned, the FCO and British Embassy in Chile could privately discount the bulk of parliamentary pressure upon them as tedious, poorly thought out and unchallenging.[8] However, they acknowledged that the constant spotlight of world parliamentary and media attention, each of which sustained the other, meant that forging close links with the Pinochet regime was difficult, and that certain options – for example the sale of arms which could be used for internal repression – were impossible. There was also a more subtle use to which parliamentary pressure could be put. British Government policy was to limit public criticism of Chile in order not to devalue the currency. A low-key approach was thought more fruitful. But the Chilean Government was also made aware that this low-key policy was always under parliamentary scrutiny at home, and that parliamentarians did not believe enough was being done to attack the Pinochet regime. The line played in Chile, as elsewhere in the world, was 'We'd like to help, but we can't because Parliament wouldn't stand for it. But if you move back towards democracy, then we'll reassess the position'.

As far as the Chilean Government itself was concerned, the views of the UK were of importance. Although the vast bulk of their effort was directed towards the British Government, Parliament was not disregarded. Early attempts to market Pinochet-ruled Chile through glossy propaganda such as *Chile Today* (copies liberally distributed inside Parliament) and to rely on the British Right for support, were replaced in the later Pinochet years by attempts to make politicians across the spectrum aware of developments in Chile. The Embassy acknowledged that contact with Labour became easier as memories of the Sheila Cassidy affair waned.[9] Parliament was certainly monitored at the Chilean Embassy. All Parliamentary Questions and Early Day Motions concerned with Chile were carefully read, and their contents sent by telegram to Santiago. Officials of the Embassy believed that this sort of parliamentary pressure from the Left had exerted an influence on British Conservative Government policy towards Chile and therefore monitored Parliament conscientiously. No doubt British parliamentary activity cut less ice in the Interior Ministry in Santiago – or a police station in Valparaiso – than it did among Chilean Embassy staff in London, but European parliamentary activity was an important measure of how the regime was regarded by European opinion-formers.

This case study leads to no very startling conclusions. However, it does illustrate one small aspect of Parliament in general and of one part of Parliament's interest in foreign affairs in particular. Until the overthrow of Allende in 1973 Chile occupied a very minor place in the world as seen from Westminster. The events of 1973 evoked an emotional response from some British politicians because of their dramatic nature and their impact on certain sensitive nerves (the overthrow of parliamentary democracy; socialism frustrated; CIA plots). The change of government in Britain in 1974 brought a modification of policy towards Chile and changed the role of the Labour parliamentary lobby against the Chilean junta from one of opposition to one of critical support. Only in 1979 with the return of a Conservative Government interested in resuming normal relations with Chile did the lobbying effort at Westminster settle into a regular pattern. Lobbying organizations outside the House who have a cause to which a group of Members of Parliament are sympathetic can use the House as a megaphone for their views, particularly when elements of the media are prepared to co-operate. In this sense, Chile is no different from campaigns to open shops on Sundays or ban Rottweiler dogs. The genesis of the interest in Chile was largely outside the House, through exile groups and international socialist organizations. Other equally worthy potential foreign affairs parliamentary campaigns were not mounted: there was no sustained parliamentary campaign against Ceauşescu in Romania or Stroessner in Paraguay or Ne Win in Burma. But the haphazard coverage of overseas abuses does not mean that the Chilean campaign should not have been mounted. It is clear that the British parliamentary support for a democratic Chile was one part of the patchwork of extraterritorial support which the victors of the 1989 elections acknowledged as sustaining the Chilean campaign to eliminate the military dictatorship.

The return to democratic ways in Chile was welcomed by Government and Opposition in Britain and will in all probability mark the end of the Chilean question as a party-political issue at Westminster. It is perhaps appropriate that one of the most senior officials of the House of Commons should have been invited to Chile in 1990 to advise on the re-establishment of a democratic Parliament.[10]

■ TEN

European Political Co-operation

■

European Political Co-operation (EPC) is the process of information, consultation and common action among the twelve Member States of the European Community ('the Twelve') in the field of foreign policy. Its aim is to maximise the Twelve's influence in international affairs through a single coherent European approach. It is the essential counterpart to progress towards European unity in the Community framework.[1]

The evolution of EPC

The Single European Act of 1986 for the first time sets out the phrase 'European foreign policy', stating that the Twelve 'shall endeavour jointly to formulate and implement a European foreign policy'.[2] But it has taken almost thirty years for the member states to reach agreement even to aspire to a joint foreign policy. This chapter seeks to trace the evolution of EPC, with all its significance for the work of the British Parliament on international relations; and to describe the efforts of the European Parliament in bringing pressure on the member states to adopt as an objective the establishment of a European foreign policy and to monitor its operation.

The three Reports by the Foreign Ministers

EPC was launched in 1970 with the First Report by the Foreign Ministers to the Heads of State and Government of the Six Member States (the 'Luxembourg Report'). The Foreign Ministers stated that

The present development of the European Communities requires Member States to intensify their political co-operation and provide in an initial phase the mechanism for harmonising their views on international affairs.

The objectives of political co-operation were

● to ensure, through regular exchanges of information and consultations, a better mutual understanding of major international problems;
● to strengthen their solidarity by promoting the harmonization of their views, the co-ordination of their positions and, when it appears possible and desirable, common actions.

The ministers also reached agreement on a structure involving at least two ministerial meetings per year; a committee composed of the directors of political affairs from the foreign ministries, meeting at least quarterly; provision for emergency meetings; and the involvement of the Commission. Significantly two colloquies per year (one in each presidency) were to be held with the Political Affairs Committee of the European Parliament; and the chairman of the Council of Ministers was to inform the Parliament on the progress towards the drawing up of a Second Report on political unification and co-operation in foreign policy matters.

The Second Report (the 'Copenhagen Report') was approved by the Heads of State and Government (this time of the Nine) in 1973. Having reiterated the objectives of political co-operation already set out, the Report recorded that the member states had been able

to consider and decide matters jointly so as to make common political action possible. This habit has also led to the 'reflex' of co-ordination among the Member States which has profoundly affected the relations of the Member States between each other and with third countries. This collegiate sense in Europe is becoming a real force in international relations.[3]

The ministers took several steps to strengthen and intensify their co-ordination on foreign policy matters. They agreed to meet four times per year, and more often as necessary; the Committee of Political Directors would meet as frequently as was required; each Foreign Minister would establish a 'correspondent' with EPC who would meet with his or her colleagues in a Group in order to prepare meetings of the Political Committee. In addition, *ad-hoc* working parties would be established to ensure more thorough consultation on individual questions; medium and long-term positions in EPC should be prepared by groups of experts or research officials.

The faster rhythm of ministerial and directors' meetings was matched by an increase from two to four in the number of colloquies held each year with the Political Affairs Committee of the European Parliament. An annual statement on EPC would also continue to be made to Parliament.

With hindsight it is possible to detect the initial appearance in the Second Report of two major problem areas, which were to cause concern both to the Foreign Ministers and to the European Parliament. These were the realization of the importance of the Presidency of EPC and of the burden beginning to fall upon it, and the relationship between the work of EPC and that of the European Community proper. It is also highly significant – and this point was not lost on the European Parliament – that the ministers considered that 'co-operation in foreign policy must be placed in the perspective of European Union'.[4]

Within a few months of the agreement on the Second Report, the Foreign Ministers found it necessary at an informal meeting under the German Presidency at Gymnich Castle, near Bonn, further to intensify foreign policy co-operation. They reached agreement that, if any member state

> raises within the framework of EPC the question of informing and consulting an ally or a friendly state, the Nine will discuss the matter and, upon reaching agreement, authorise the Presidency to proceed on that basis.[5]

This new 'Gymnich arrangement' had become essential under the impact of the oil crisis, the 1973 war between Egypt and Israel, and the launching both of the Euro-Arab Dialogue and of the Conference on Security and Co-operation in Europe, in order to assure full consultations with the US Government. It was to stand the Nine in good stead in the turbulent years ahead.

The 1970s produced one crisis after another for the Nine, and the machinery of EPC was put under strain in different directions. The oil crisis, the Arab-Israeli dispute, events in Rhodesia and Southern Africa, and latterly the Soviet invasion of Afghanistan all tested to the limit the will and ability of the member states to co-ordinate their foreign policies, and also the efficacy of the structures of EPC.

In response in part to these challenges, the Heads of State and Government created the European Council, which first met in Dublin in March 1975. This new body was to meet both 'in the Council of the Communities and in the context of political co-operation' in order to meet 'the need for an overall approach to the internal problems involved in achieving European unity and the external problems facing Europe'.[6] The importance of the Presidency was emphasized, and it was given the new task of replying to questions on EPC put by Members of the European Parliament (who heretofore had been able to put questions only to the Council and the Commission). Furthermore, the election of the Parliament by direct, universal suffrage was foreseen.

The first direct elections to the European Parliament in June 1979, by legitimizing Parliament and strengthening its capacity to participate actively in political co-operation, led it to play a considerably enhanced role therein. In July 1981 Parliament, in a resolution on EPC and the role of the European Parliament,[7] called for a Third Report by the Foreign Ministers on EPC, to include specific measures for improving foreign policy co-operation: in December 1981 the Foreign Ministers adopted such a Report.

The Third Report on EPC (the 'London Report') stated that 'The Community and its Member States are increasingly seen by third countries as a coherent force in international relations.'[8] EPC had steadily intensified and its scope had continually broadened. This development had contributed to the ultimate objective of European Union. But despite these favourable developments,

> in spite of what has been achieved the Ten are still far from playing a role in the world appropriate to their combined influence. . . . the Ten should seek increasingly to shape events and not merely to react to them.

The most important advance marked by the Report, however, was that the ministers agreed

> to maintain the flexible and pragmatic approach which has made it possible to discuss in EPC certain important foreign policy questions bearing on the political aspects of security.

The delicacy of the drafting of this sentence reflected on the one hand the restrictions forced by the policy of neutrality in Ireland, hesitations on the part of some Danish parties, and of the new Greek Socialist Government. On the other hand it reflected the paramount need of the Ten to achieve common positions on overall matters of European security, as defined in the Final Act of Helsinki of 1975, in the context of follow-up meetings to the Conference on Security and Co-operation in Europe.

The inclusion in EPC of the 'political aspects of security' finally met the demand of the European Parliament in this sense, which had been put forward in a resolution of January 1976 for which the rapporteur was Lord Gladwyn. The scope of EPC was widened, as was that of proceedings in the European Parliament on European security matters within EPC. Henceforward, both Parliament's Political Affairs Committee and Parliament itself felt justified in devoting more attention to the political aspects of security.

The Third Report emphasized once more the need to associate the European Parliament with EPC, and extended the ambit of this association by providing for informal meetings between ministers and the leaders of the different political groups represented in Parliament. This was a useful new area of contact between Parliament and EPC, achieved just over two years after direct elections and unheard-of in the British Parliament. And the burden on the Presidency was relieved by the invention of the 'Troika', a small team of officials from the preceding, present and succeeding Presidencies.

Thus the European Parliament could take credit for its persuasiveness in that, three months after adopting a resolution in July 1981 based on the Elles Report,[9] some 60 per cent of its requests to the Foreign Ministers contained therein had been accepted and implemented.

The Solemn Declaration on European Union 1983

Only one month after the Third Report had been agreed, however, in a dramatic declaration to the European Parliament, Mr Hans-Dietrich Genscher, Foreign Minister of the Federal Republic of Germany, and Mr Emilio Colombo, Italian Foreign Minister, put forward a draft European Act on European Union. This contained proposals for the further deepening of EPC and for further powers to be attributed to the European Parliament within the framework of progress towards European Union.

After many months of discussion, the Genscher-Colombo Act, which had been welcomed by Parliament, was adopted – in a considerably weakened and limited form – by the European Council at Stuttgart in June 1983.

The Solemn Declaration of Stuttgart formalized current practice as regards the functions of the European Council and relations between the other institutions and Parliament in regard to EPC. In particular, it set out a list of measures to be taken to reinforce EPC. Although many of these measures constituted no more than an intensification and codification of current practice, two served to indicate the continuing development of EPC:

> co-ordination of positions of Member States on the political and economic aspects of security, and increasing recognition of the contribution which the European Parliament makes to the development of a co-ordinated foreign policy of the Ten.[10]

The Single European Act of 1986

Although the burden of the Presidency of EPC had been relieved by the introduction of the Troika teams by the Third Report in 1981, the Presidency's work-load – not least because of its increasing accountability to the European Parliament – continued to increase. The dichotomy between EPC and Community functions proper continued to impede the hoped-for improvements in co-ordination and the realization of common action in EPC. And the adoption by the European Parliament in 1984 of its Draft Treaty on European Union, calling for the progressive introduction of a new framework for Community policies as a major step towards European Union, widened the horizons of those member states which were impatient to arm the Community to beat off the economic challenges of the USA and Japan and to reduce unemployment in the EC.

The Single European Act finally brought EPC within the Treaty framework of the EC (as Parliament had demanded) in order to end the pointless dichotomy encapsulated in the Second Report of 1973. The quotations at the head of this chapter recall the present stage of development of EPC (or should it be 'FPC': Foreign Policy Co-operation?) But a Declaration annexed to the Single European Act has acquired new significance with the dramatic moves towards democracy in Eastern Europe. The Declaration states that the member states

> reaffirm their openness to other European nations which share the same ideals and objectives. They agree in particular to strengthen their links with the member countries of the Council of Europe and with other democratic European countries with which they have friendly relations and close co-operation.

As regards security, the member states agreed to work to maintain 'the technological and industrial conditions necessary for their security', while reaffirming their readiness to 'co-ordinate their positions more closely on the political and economic aspects of security'.[11]

The European Parliament was not overlooked, and the member states undertook to associate it closely with EPC, and to ensure that its views were duly taken into consideration.[12] Articles 237 and 238 of the Treaty of Rome were also amended to require the assent of Parliament by an absolute majority of its Members to applications by European states for membership of the Community and to commercial agreements with other states (see pp. 149–50). The Presidency's authority was extended and it was finally granted the support of a small Secretariat of five officials, based in Brussels, drawn from five Presidencies – the two past, the present one and the two future Presidencies.

On the signing of the Single European Act, the Foreign Ministers adopted 'Provisions of Practical Application', which set out in detail the manner in which the Parliament would be associated with EPC (see pp. 156–9).[13]

But if accountability to the Parliament has increased, has foreign policy co-operation intensified and improved since the Single European Act came into force in July 1987?

The Single European Act has set for the first time the objective of formulating and implementing 'a European foreign policy'. If member states cannot be expected to have attained this objective in the period since the Act came into effect, they can nevertheless be expected to have made progress towards it.

In this period the Foreign Ministers have been concerned primarily with Southern Africa (Namibia and the Code of Conduct), Afghanistan, Central America, human rights and East–West relations, including the Conference on Security and Co-operation in Europe (CSCE) and relations with East European countries. It is significant to note in how many of these subject areas the functions of the EC as such (common commercial policy, trade and economic agreements, and development and co-operation) have been intimately linked to foreign policy issues. These links testify to the necessity – so long argued by the European Parliament – of mounting a unified policy covering all EC external relations: political, economic and commercial.

The role played by the Commission has become central in EC external relations, but the Commission appears to exert comparatively little influence in EPC.

The European Council does not neglect its role in EPC. At its Madrid meeting in June 1989, for example, it adopted statements on East–West relations, the Middle East, the Maghreb, Latin America, Asia, and Southern Africa, as well as formal Declarations on the Middle East and China.

It must be said that the content of statements and Declarations, both by the European Council and the Foreign Ministers, is largely hortatory and declaratory, often recalling in detail a series of previous statements before urging those concerned to certain courses of action. On the other hand the greater the number of member states in the Community and in EPC, the more difficult it is to achieve the necessary consensus on any basis other than one of a *reductio ad minimum*.

The European Parliament and EPC

Methods of proceeding

From the Second Report of the Foreign Ministers of 1973, the European Parliament set itself to adapt its proceedings, the better to monitor and to influence the evolving process of political co-operation. From the outset, responsibility for these functions was vested in the Political Affairs Committee, with which it has remained.

It is open to members of the Committees of Parliament to decide whether or not to act upon motions for resolutions which, having been tabled, translated and circulated, are referred to them under Rule 63 (Motions for resolutions). By Rule 121 (Own-initiative reports) a committee requires the authorization of the enlarged Bureau (the political steering committee of Parliament) to draw up a report on a matter within its competence. These provisions together endow any committee with a large area of freedom to pursue inquiries into a wide range of subjects within its competence.

Thus the Political Affairs Committee drew up reports specifically on EPC in 1973, 1978, 1981 and 1988. Of the sixty-three reports adopted by the committee between July 1984 and May 1989, twenty-four related to subjects dealt with by the Foreign Ministers in EPC, including several on human rights.

The 'Provisions of Practical Application' of Title III of the Single European Act (see pp. 156–9) record the procedures for the holding of four colloquies per year between the President-in-Office of EPC and the Political Affairs Committee of Parliament. Ministers are briefed in advance of EP resolutions on EPC matters; the Political Affairs Committee and Presidency agree in advance on the three or four topics on which the latter will make a short statement at each colloquy, on each of which committee members pose several rounds of brief questions.[14]

In addition the Provisions foresee 'special information sessions at ministerial level' on specific EPC topics, at which by joint agreement the Presidency briefs the Political Affairs Committee informally in addition to the normal colloquies. This new provision, which was first formalized only in 1986, adds an element of flexibility to the Presidency's task of informing Parliament regularly of the issues discussed in EPC.

The Political Affairs Committee has also since 1979 held four public hearings, two on security and disarmament, and two on human rights matters, at which experts were invited to inform the committee and to answer questions on specific topics. Internal hearings with experts (for example with the Secretary-General of NATO, with the Israeli and Jordanian Ambassadors to the EC, and with Commissioners) also serve to provide committee members with the information essential to them in the drawing up of reports and in participation in debates.

The 'Provisions of Practical Application' also set out the obligations of the Presidency of EPC to Parliament as a whole (see pp. 156–9). They provide for

1 an oral report by each Presidency at the beginning and end of its six months' term
2 an annual written report on EPC
3 replies by the Presidency to oral and written questions
4 responses to be made to resolutions on EPC 'of major importance and general concern' adopted by Parliament
5 the transmission to Parliament of declarations by the Foreign Ministers on EPC.

Unfortunately Parliament has not yet secured the agreement of the Presidency to reply to topical and urgent debates (under Rule 64), which occupy three hours of each session and which often cover subjects within the scope of EPC. However, each of these obligations by the Presidency has been requested – often several times – by Parliament since 1973. Taken together, they represent the acceptance by the Foreign Ministers of substantive accountability to the European Parliament and represent a remarkable achievement by Parliament in a period of only seventeen years.

Members of the Political Affairs Committee, in addition to enjoying these opportunities of calling the Foreign Ministers to account, are regularly appointed to the EP's inter-parliamentary delegations to parliaments of other countries. Of these, the most important is that to the US Congress from the European Parliament, which meets delegates from the Congress twice per year. Other major delegations meet with those from Eastern European countries, Canada, Australia and New Zealand, Japan and China, Central and Latin American countries, Israel, and so on. The inter-parliamentary delegations act as the eyes and ears of the European Parliament, and discuss political, economical and commercial relations between the EC and the country in question, as well as, where appropriate, respect for human rights.

It is difficult to escape the conclusion that the European Parliament, by developing its procedures and by securing from the Foreign Ministers clear obligations of accountability, has since 1973 achieved a status and a role in regard to EPC which the House of Commons might well envy in regard to its attempts to monitor British foreign policy.

Scope of EP proceedings on European foreign policy

Little indication has so far been given of the principal areas within EPC which are addressed by the European Parliament. These are broadly

1 political and institutional aspects of relations with third countries (e.g. the political relations between the EC and the USA; relations between the EC and the countries of East and Central Europe)
2 questions pertaining to co-operation in the sphere of foreign policy and the policy on security and disarmament (e.g. the situation in Afghanistan; the security of Western Europe)
3 problems concerning human rights in third countries (e.g. biennial report on human rights in the world; human rights in Turkey)
4 political aspects of international problems (e.g. the political situation in Southern Africa; the situation in Chile).

Parliament's impact on EPC

Any assessment of the impact on EPC made by the European Parliament since 1970 gives rise to certain difficulties. Unfortunately neither the

Presidency, the Foreign Ministers themselves, nor the European Council are normally prepared to admit openly that any of their actions or Declarations have been influenced by the EP – despite repeated questions by Members of the Parliament. Assessments of Parliament's impact are bound to include elements of subjectivity.

As has already been noticed, each one of the 'Provisions of Practical Application' of the Single European Act had been requested by the EP, and each exemplifies its direct impact on the formal procedures of EPC. But, as a European Parliament Research Paper of 1988 notes: 'In the vast majority of cases, [the EP's] impact is necessarily indirect and complementary to other factors which will determine decision-making in a highly complex area of policy.'[15]

Nevertheless, Article 238 of the EC Treaty has given Parliament significant powers, which it has used to influence the Foreign Ministers. Article 238 reads

> The Community may conclude with a third State, a union of States, or an international organisation agreements establishing an association involving reciprocal rights and obligations, common action and special procedures. These agreements shall be concluded by the Council, acting unanimously and after receiving the assent of the European Parliament, which shall act by an absolute majority of its component members.

Without any doubt the EP made a direct impact on EPC (and on EC commercial relations with Israel) when in March 1988 it refused on a vote to give its assent under Article 238 to the financial protocols amending the 1963 association agreement between the EC and Israel. The votes of 260 MEPs were necessary to give Parliament's assent, but they were not attained. Many Members expressed in the debate anxiety about the methods used by the Israeli authorities to control the *intifada* or uprising in the Occupied Territories of the West Bank and Gaza. Other Members drew attention to the discrimination by Israel, in exporting agricultural produce to the EC under the Association agreement, against the products of Palestinians from the West Bank and Gaza. Such discrimination was directly contrary to the terms of the agreement.

Only after the Government of Israel had given assurances to the Commission about the methods used to control the *intifada*, and that commercial discrimination against Palestinian producers had ceased, did Parliament in October 1988 give its assent to the financial protocols with Israel. The EP also delayed its assent to protocols to the EC agreement with Syria concurrently with the delay in agreeing to the Israeli protocols.

On another occasion, in December 1987 Parliament used its power under Article 238 to delay for one month the vote on its assent to a financial protocol to the EC Association agreement with Turkey. The delay enabled the political groups in Parliament to consult their political friends in Turkey as to whether the latter favoured the giving of assent to the protocol. This being so, assent was given in January 1988.

The Parliament has on several occasions since 1979 expressed in strong terms its anxiety about continued violations of human rights and lack of democracy in Turkey under both the military and civilian governments. One resolution of 1981 led the Commission within forty-eight hours to 'freeze' the operation of the Association agreement with Turkey for several years. Thus Parliament's resolution was the signal for which the Commission was waiting before acting to suspend the operation of the agreement – a suspension which displeased the Turkish Government but which demonstrated (even before the Single European Act) the powerful influence of the European Parliament.

Furthermore, Parliament's oft-expressed and continuing anxiety about imperfect democratic practices and human rights violations in Turkey encouraged the Commission to treat with reserve Turkey's application for membership made in 1987 and, in late 1989, to reject it.

Parliament's impact on EPC in the field of security has been particularly marked. It is largely due to the insistence of the European Parliament since 1976 that security matters should form an integral part of foreign policy that, seven years later, the Solemn Declaration of Stuttgart included 'the political and economic aspects of security' as an integral part of EPC. Parliament has set as its objective a European security policy within NATO and is using its not-inconsiderable powers of persuasion to secure its achievement within EPC and the EC.

It is perhaps in the field of ensuring respect for human rights in the world that the impact of Parliament is most difficult to assess. The most fruitful approaches to governments responsible for violations of human rights are often made by 'quiet diplomacy', conducted by the Presidency and by the Ambassadors of the Twelve in third countries.

In this field two statements may be made with certainty, however. First, successive Presidents of Parliament, heading an inter-Parliamentary delegation to a third country, have made *démarches* to ministers and MPs of that country, which have resulted in greater respect for human rights.

Second, Parliament is contributing to setting the agenda for the work of the Foreign Ministers on human rights. For example in March 1984 the President-in-Office M Claude Cheysson, then French Minister for External Affairs, told the Political Affairs Committee of Parliament that the Foreign Ministers had adopted as a declaration of their policy a resolution on human rights in Chile which Parliament had just agreed to. Parliament's resolution thus became within days official EPC policy, to which the Chilean Government was invited to respond.

The direct impact of Parliament's resolutions on violations of human rights in Turkey have been noted above. By using its assent power under Article 238 of the EC Treaty, Parliament can now ensure that, in any new trade and co-operation agreement made by the EC, respect for human rights is included as a *sine qua non* of the continued validity of such an agreement. It was Parliament, after all, which insisted, successfully, that the Fourth Lomé Convention should contain in its preamble a reference to the necessity of respect for human rights in all African, Caribbean and Pacific Territories.

The impact of EPC on Westminster

The impact of EPC on Parliament at Westminster may be examined in a variety of ways. This section postulates an ideal model and moves on to consider how well reality stands up to the ideal.

In an ideal model Westminster (taken here as referring to both Houses of Parliament) would monitor continuously the flow of events in the outside world and provide a continuous commentary which would feed into the deliberations of ministers and their consultations with their European counterparts. Ministers and officials engaged in formulating EPC declarations and *démarches* would therefore know the views of the British Parliament and take them into account. Steps taken in EPC would promptly be reported back to Westminster, where there would be an opportunity to check that any changes of policy or new initiatives were broadly acceptable to Parliament and compatible with the British Government's other policy commitments, for example its obligations to NATO, the Commonwealth and the United Nations, its responsibilities towards dependent territories, and its bilateral relations with individual countries.

In the real world some parts of the ideal model sketched above are impractical. Parliament does not sit continuously and cannot therefore provide ministers with a continuous commentary on world events. In order to have their maximum diplomatic impact EPC *démarches* cannot wait for the end of a long summer recess, or sometimes even for the end of a weekend. EPC activities may be divided into long-term positions, for example on Afghanistan or the Middle East, and instant reactions, such as to the Iranian threat to murder the author Salman Rushdie or the massacre in Tiananmen Square. While Parliament would have many opportunities to contribute to the first set of EPC activities, it rarely has the time to contribute much to the second.

Taking the EPC positions adopted during the first half of 1989 during the Spanish Presidency as a sample, we find a number of subjects which the House of Commons had debated in the fairly recent past (e.g. Poland, Afghanistan and Central America). During this period there were also four EPC Declarations relating to the Lebanon (20 March, 31 March, 17

April and 12 June). The first three could not have been influenced by any recent debate or Oral Question in the Commons, because there had been none, but the last might have been influenced by an adjournment debate on the Lebanon held on 16 May.

Most of the other topics covered had been the subject of fairly frequent exchanges at Foreign Affairs Questions (e.g. South Africa, Sudan, Egypt, Romania and Namibia). A few, such as the EPC Declaration on the Maghreb Summit, had not been considered at Westminster at all and were of much greater interest to the Mediterranean members of the EC.

Two 'emergency' positions were adopted in EPC, on Salman Rushdie and China. In the first case the EPC statement preceded the statement in the House of Commons; in the second the Foreign Secretary was able to tell the Commons on 6 June that the matter was being discussed urgently in EPC, and the EPC statement came a few hours later.

The record of the first six months of 1989 suggests that (apart from occasional exceptions, such as the statement on the Maghreb Summit), the agenda of EPC is similar to the foreign affairs agenda in the House of Commons. However, since the attention paid to particular foreign countries and situations at Westminster is sporadic and depends to some extent on individual whims and the randomness associated with ballots and 'shuffles', there is never any guarantee that a topic discussed in EPC will have been ventilated in the recent past at Westminster.

The next stage in the ideal model is the report back. All texts adopted in EPC, regardless of the form and manner of their adoption, are placed in the Library of the House of Commons by the Foreign and Commonwealth Office, usually within a day or two of their adoption. They are not formally brought to the attention of the House, but are available to any MP alerted by press reports or ministerial references. MPs interested in a particular topic will frequently ask Library research staff about EC activity in that area and will be given copies of any relevant EPC statement.

Some EPC statements are reported to the House, but only when they are adopted in the course of a meeting of the EC Foreign Affairs Council. Recent practice has been to issue brief statements on all Foreign Affairs Councils in the form of Written Answers to Parliamentary Questions. Statements adopted in EPC are referred to briefly at the end of such answers. Occasionally a Foreign Affairs Council acquires a higher political profile and earns a full oral statement, in which case EPC activity is also reported on the floor of the House and can be questioned by Members. This was the case with the Foreign Affairs Council of 14 June 1989, which was overshadowed by the violent suppression of dissent in China. On this occasion the Foreign Secretary was able to make an oral report on the response which had been worked out in EPC and also to refer to other topics (Lebanon and South Africa) which had been the subject of EPC declarations on 12 June. It also occasionally happens that an EPC topic is debated in the Commons in the weeks following an EPC initiative, in which case it is likely to be mentioned by ministers in the course of their speeches.

Finally, a short report on all EPC activity under a given EC Presidency is issued as part of the regular six-monthly White Paper on *Development in the European Community*. These have sometimes emerged long after the six-month period in question, but recently an effort has been made to catch up. The White Paper on January–June 1989 was published in September 1989 (Cm 801) and debated on 15 November. The House of Commons Select Committee on Procedure has recently recommended that such retrospective debates be discontinued and replaced by twice-yearly debates on the *forthcoming* European summit. The Procedure Committee saw this suggestion primarily as a means of improving the scrutiny of European legislative proposals and made no recommendation that EPC should also fall within the terms of reference (HC 622 of 1988–89, para 47). In May 1990 (Cm 1081) the Government indicated its acceptance of the general principle of forward-looking debates. At the time of writing it is not clear whether in future the Government intends to report more fully on EPC matters for these debates; if it does then the House of Commons may acquire a valuable new opportunity to debate current developments in EPC.

We have seen that the topics which arise in EPC are, by and large, ones which are also discussed fairly frequently in the House of Commons and that the House is informed of developments in EPC (if only, in many cases, through the mechanism of texts being placed in the Library). We have also seen that where a topic arouses considerable interest at Westminster the EPC dimension is usually referred to in statements or debates.

However, it is also apparent from a study of the first six months of 1989 that EPC impinges only slightly on foreign affairs consideration at Westminster and one is bound to conclude that awareness of EPC among MPs is not high. The fact that EPC declarations are necessarily consensual also means that they are generally brief and blandly phrased and this too seems to detract from their significance as political statements.

Some MPs have discovered that EPC can form a useful peg on which to hang a Question (and, if called, a Supplementary Question) designed to support a particular policy or point of view. The initial question usually runs: 'When is it next proposed to have discussions with EC partners concerning development of common European foreign policies?' Some have also found that EPC can serve as a special route by which to promote a particular point of view. For example the Venice Declaration of 1980 committed the then members of the EC to the view that the PLO must be 'associated' with any negotiations for a solution of the Palestinian problem. This proposition was not, at the time or subsequently, accepted by Israel or the USA and was controversial in the House of Commons, but it has continued to be one of the main planks of collective EC policy on the Middle East and allows supporters of the Palestinian cause to press the British Government to observe its 1980 commitment.

The Venice Declaration was unusual in attracting controversy. Most EPC statements are based on a firmer consensus and are most unlikely to offend majority opinion at Westminster. As Lynda Chalker MP (then Minister of State, FCO) told the Foreign Affairs Committee on 21 June 1989:

> Member states are no more likely to take up positions in European Political Co-operation that would be unacceptable to national parliaments than they would on a national basis. In other words, we do not change our stance in co-operation of a political nature from that which we hold here in Westminster. We discuss things together and seek to find a way forward but there is no change of basis.[16]

The reason for this confidence is, of course, that there is no majority voting in EPC. Whereas the Single European Act extended majority voting for certain types of European legislation and therefore increased the number of areas on which the UK could be out-voted and obliged to swallow unwelcome legislation, it did nothing to modify absolute national sovereignty in the area of foreign policy as covered in EPC. At the same time there can be no confidence that EPC is acceptable to national parliaments unless they are kept fully informed of what is happening in EPC and how it relates to other dimensions of national foreign policy. If national parliaments neglect EPC while the European Parliament devotes more time to it, then there is bound to be a shift in influence from the former to the latter, *de facto* if not *de jure*.

Conclusions

EPC has made great strides forward since its tentative launching in 1970, as this brief study has shown. The European Parliament has, however, often pointed out its weaknesses, which the new approach embodied in the Single European Act may or may not help to overcome.

EPC has been slow to encompass security and disarmament policy. The reasons are not far to seek: the Irish Government's policy of neutrality; Danish and Greek unwillingness to concur in progress towards a European security policy, even within NATO; difficulties in constructing an EPC/EC security policy within NATO; the unwillingness of some governments to pool sovereignty in this field.

Against this shadowy background, the European Parliament's success in contributing to the inclusion within EPC of the political and economic aspects of security becomes clearer.

In the second place, the Foreign Ministers have never succeeded in developing a closer relationship with the USA through EPC. The Gymnich approach of 1974 never elicited a reciprocal 'consult-first' approach by the US Administration. As a result, EPC appears to have had, especially since 1985, little influence on US policy on the Arab-Israeli dispute. The Nine's Declaration at Venice in 1980 on the Middle East has, with hindsight, given rise to hopes which, without US collaboration, could not be realized.

Again, the Ten or Twelve have never been able to achieve unanimity in sufficient areas to pursue a coherent policy towards the Republic of South Africa. Apartheid has been continuously condemned, but deep divisions on further policy initiatives have resulted in – as in so many other fields – anodyne declarations based on a *reductio ad minimum*.

The European Parliament has been criticized for casting its net too wide in seeking to influence, and even to guide, the external relations of the European Community. It has not hesitated to deploy to the full the power, granted to it by Article 142 of the EC Treaty, to draw up its own rules of procedure. Parliament has thus created a structure of three committees and twenty-four inter-parliamentary delegations which enable it to conduct its own external relations and to make an impact, not just upon EPC, but also on the external economic relations and development and co-operation policies of the EC. Although the net may have at times been cast too wide, the breadth and depth of Parliament's approach have brought it considerable success.

In short, the European Parliament has influenced, is influencing, and will increasingly influence decisions and actions taken by the Foreign Ministers.

This being so, the opportunities open to national parliaments to bring influence to bear upon EPC, already narrow, could further diminish unless their members are active in keeping abreast of developments in EPC. National parliaments will always be able to use their tried procedures to bring home to their Ministers of Foreign Affairs or European Affairs the views either of the House or of its appropriate committee or committees. Intelligent anticipation of the agenda of the next quarterly meeting of the Foreign Ministers (or of their next Gymnich-type meeting) would enable a committee to press its views on the relevant aspects of EPC sufficiently in advance to make an impact on the national minister. National ministers in turn require sufficient time to seek support among their colleagues for the point of view of their parliaments or of their committees.

Equally the dates of European Council meetings are known months in advance, and the subjects to be discussed there within EPC can be established – or guessed at – some weeks beforehand. Thus national parliaments can make their impact by making their views clear in good time on these subjects and – just as important – by studying the Declarations made by the European Council and in questioning national ministers on any discrepancies with the position of the national parliament in question.

But the final conclusion must be that in fact only the European Parliament has the freedom, the instruments, the procedures, the experience and the status within the Community structure to maintain a coherent, constructive and fruitful collaboration with the Foreign Ministers in their quest for a joint European foreign policy.

European political co-operation[17]

Decision adopted by the Foreign Ministers on the occasion of the signing of the Single European Act

3.4.1 The Foreign Ministers, meeting in the framework of European political co-operation, hereby decide, on the occasion of the signing of the Single European Act, to adopt the provisions set out in the body of this text concerning the practical application of certain aspects of Title III of this Act. These provisions may be reviewed in accordance with the procedures in force within European political co-operation.

The Ministers confirm that the customary procedures which have been set up to ensure the practical working of European political co-operation, in particular in the Luxembourg (1970), Copenhagen (1973) and London (1981) reports and the Solemn Declaration on European Union (1983), and which are summarized in the 'Coutumier', remain in force, the following provisions being supplementary to them.

I–Relations between European political co-operation and the European Parliament

With a view to ensuring the close association of the European Parliament with European political co-operation contacts with the European Parliament shall take place as follows.

1. The Presidency shall regularly inform the European Parliament of foreign policy topics discussed in the context of European political co-operation.

2. The Presidency shall address the European Parliament at the start of its period in office and present its programme. At the end of this period, it shall present a report to the European Parliament on progress made.

3. Once a year, the Presidency shall send a written communication to the European Parliament on progress in the field of European political

co-operation and take part at ministerial level in the general European Parliament debate on foreign policy.

4. The Presidency-in-Office of European political co-operation and the members of the Political Affairs Committee of the European Parliament shall hold an informal colloquy four times a year to discuss the most important recent developments in European political co-operation.

In order to prepare these colloquies, the Political Committee shall draw the Minister's attention to the positions adopted by the European Parliament on foreign policy matters.

In order to make these discussions more fruitful, the Presidency and the Political Affairs Committee of the European Parliament shall communicate to each other in advance the main possible topics for discussion.

5. By joint agreement, special information sessions at ministerial level on specific European political co-operation topics may be organized as required.

6. The Presidency shall reply to parliamentary questions on European political co-operation activities and take part in European Parliament question time according to the approved customary procedures.

7. The Presidency shall ensure that the views of the European Parliament, as expressed in its resolutions, shall be duly taken into consideration in European political co-operation work.

It shall reply to resolutions on matters of major importance and general concern on which the European Parliament requests its comments.

8. The Presidency shall transmit to the European Parliament as soon as possible declarations adopted within the framework of European political co-operation.

II–Co-operation of Member States' missions and Commission delegations in third countries and international organizations

1. Member States' missions and Commission delegations shall intensify their co-operation in third countries and international organizations in the following areas:
(a) exchange of political and economic information;
(b) pooling of information on administrative and practical problems;
(c) mutual assistance in the material and practical sphere;
(d) communications;
(e) exchange of information and drawing up of joint plans in case of local crises;
(f) security measures;
(g) consular matters;
(h) health, particularly in the field of health and medical facilities;
(i) educational matters (schooling);
(j) information;
(k) cultural affairs;
(l) development aid. The relevant Council provisions should be noted here.

2. The Member States' Heads of Mission and the Commission's Representative in third countries shall meet regularly in order to co-ordinate their views and prepare joint reports, either at the request of the Political Committee or on their own initiative when the situation requires.

3. With a view to strengthening the co-operation of missions in third countries, this topic shall be examined periodically by the Political Committee on the basis of reports drawn up for this purpose by the missions.

4. The Member States shall examine the possibility of providing help and assistance in third countries to nationals of Member States which have no representation there.

III–European political co-operation Secretariat: responsibilities and organization

The Secretariat of European political co-operation shall act under the authority of the Presidency. It shall assist the Presidency in preparing and implementing European political co-operation activities and in administrative matters.

It shall assist the Presidency in ensuring the continuity of European political co-operation and its consistency with Community positions.

The Secretariat shall:

(a) assist the Presidency in the organization of European political co-operation meetings, including the preparation and circulation of documents and the drawing up of minutes;

(b) work with the European Correspondents Group in the preparation of conclusions and guidelines and in carrying out any other task entrusted to the Group by the Political Committee;

(c) assist the chairmen of working groups as regards procedures and precedents and the drafting of oral reports and studies;

(d) assist the Presidency in the preparation of texts to be published on behalf of the Member States, including replies to parliamentary questions and resolutions as defined in item 7, paragraph 2 of Chapter 1 on relations between European political co-operation and the European Parliament;

(e) maintain the European political co-operation archives and assist the Presidency in preparing the six-monthly compilation of European political co-operation texts;

(f) keep up to date the body of European political co-operation working practices;

(g) assist the Presidency, where appropriate, in contacts with third countries.

2. The Secretariat shall make the necessary arrangements to provide interpretation into all the official languages of the Community at meetings of Heads of State or Government as well as ministerial meetings. It shall ensure that all European political co-operation texts submitted to or adopted at these meetings are immediately translated into all the official Community languages.

3. The Secretariat shall be composed of five officials. Following on from the support team arrangement, the Presidency-in-Office of European political co-operation together with the two preceding and the two following Presidencies shall each second an official for a period covering five presidencies. The status of the officials of the Foreign Ministries on temporary secondment to the Secretariat shall be identical to that of members of the diplomatic missions in Brussels, to which they shall be administratively attached.

The Head of the Secretariat shall be appointed by the Foreign Ministers under arrangements to be agreed between them.

4. Matters concerning administrative staff, infrastructure, equipment and operating expenses will be the subject of a further decision.

IV–Venues for European political co-operation meetings

European political co-operation meetings shall normally be held at the seat of the Secretariat. Ministerial-level and Political Committee meetings may take place in the capital city of the Presidency.

V–Use of languages in European political co-operation

Use of languages shall be in accordance with the rules of the European Communities

For meetings of officials and Coreu communications, the current practice of European political co-operation will serve as a guide for the time being.

ELEVEN

Conclusions

The main aim of this book has been to provide a factual account of how Parliament deals with foreign affairs towards the end of the twentieth century. It has done so by describing both the formal and the informal ways in which Members of Parliament (including peers) become involved in foreign affairs issues and by looking more closely at some particular episodes. Given that legislation on foreign policy matters is infrequent and that Britain has no written constitution which bestows treaty or war-making powers on the legislature, it might appear that there is little to be said about Parliament's role in this area. Perhaps for this reason the subject has been neglected in scholarly accounts of Parliament. Yet considerable changes have taken place in the relationship between Britain and the external world over recent decades, and it is important to know if they have been reflected in the way Parliament behaves. This concluding chapter attempts an assessment of how matters stand and how well Parliament is prepared for the challenges ahead.

Chapter 2 on proceedings 'on the record' found that the proportion of House of Commons time devoted to foreign affairs (by our definition, those matters involving a representative of the FCO or one of its predecessors) has slightly declined since the 1940s and 1950s. In recent sessions it has varied between 4 and 8 per cent. This refers to time on the floor of the House and excludes the time spent on committee proceedings. In Chapter 5 the time devoted to foreign affairs by the House of Lords was found to be around 5 per cent on average, but the comparison could be misleading. The House of Lords spends a higher proportion of its time on debating legislation, and legislation rarely emanates from the

FCO. When the House puts legislation to one side and determines its own priorities for non-legislative debates, 'foreign affairs' accounts for some 12 per cent of its time.

The consistency of this share over several decades may be surprising. Crises seem to have made little impact on the proportion for each session, perhaps because they occur with an almost predictable regularity. When a Suez, Falklands or Kuwait crisis takes place some extra time is created by emergency sittings, and the rest is found by squeezing out other foreign affairs topics. The more typical and durable subjects such as Rhodesia in the 1960s and 1970s and Hong Kong in the 1980s are not normally allowed to upset the routine Westminster procedures. Even during the high drama and emotion of the Falklands War the House of Commons was regularly able to switch its attention back to domestic matters such as the Finance Bill and Northern Ireland. Whatever overseas problems may arise the Government still has its programme of legislation to get through, the annual cycle of Private Members' Bills continues, the same number of days is allocated to the Opposition, there are the same regular debates on the Budget, the armed services, the Defence Estimates, Wales, Scotland, the arts, the Consolidated Fund, and so on.

The factors which limit the amount of time which Parliament is able to spend on foreign affairs also tend to limit the number of Members of Parliament who are prepared to devote themselves to it. We shall return in due course to the question of whether the community of foreign affairs 'specialists' at Westminster is as large as it ought to be. For the moment it is enough to note that the opportunities to contribute to debates and other proceedings on foreign affairs are limited.

Though the time allotted to foreign affairs may not have changed very much, the subject matter has. Where once the British Empire overseas loomed large in the eyes of Parliament, now multifarious European Affairs have taken over. This is not to say that Europe was unimportant in the 1950s, or indeed in the 1930s. Neither, at the present time, have Britain's overseas dependencies quite vanished – the 'dust of empire', in the shape of Gibraltar, Hong Kong and the Falkland Islands, occupied Parliament a good deal in the 1980s – but the Empire is no longer the continuous responsibility that it was in the 1930s and 1940s. With the shift of geographical focus has come a psychological shift. As long as the Victorian Empire survived it was perceived as a generally passive arena for British actions. Even when things went wrong, the responsibility still lay with London. In the late twentieth century the outside world more often appears to be creating the events to which Britain must respond.

In referring to 'Parliament' we are including, of course, the House of Lords as well as the House of Commons, while recognizing that the elected Chamber is much the more influential. The House of Lords asserts itself from time to time over legislation, but has little sway over policy where no legislation is involved. Chapter 5 found the role of the House of Lords in foreign affairs as a whole to be of fairly marginal importance, despite its distinguished membership. There are exceptions to this. The value of work done by the House of Lords Select Committee on the European Communities is widely acknowledged, but it is only at the margin of our present subject, being concerned with the merits or otherwise of EC proposals and their implications for the UK. In the wider field of foreign affairs the expertise of the House of Lords depends to a large extent on the accidents of its composition. For example in recent years the House has shown more awareness of the problems of Antarctica than the House of Commons, but this reflects the knowledge and enthusiasm of a handful of peers. Otherwise, when the House of Lords has exerted an influence, for example in the matter of British nationality for Gibraltarians, it has been closely linked to a current of back-bench opinion in the House of Commons. In general there is no overwhelming evidence to suggest that the House of Lords has a foreign affairs voice distinctive from that of the House of Commons or that it is capable of exerting independent influence on the FCO.

However, although the House of Lords may not have a distinctive influence from that of the Commons, it is possible that it could complement the role of the lower House in a more deliberate way. In particular there could be a greater use of joint Select Committees. Since 1973 there has been a joint Select Committee on Statutory Instruments, which replaced the earlier separate committees that had existed in both Houses. A joint Select Committee also deals with Consolidation Bills. In 1973 the Maybray-King Committee in the Lords suggested a joint Select Committee to examine European Community legislation, but this pro-posal did not commend itself to MPs. In 1978 the House of Commons accepted a motion for the establishment of a special commission of inquiry to consist of eight Members of both Houses to investigate further the question of responsibility for the breach of oil sanctions against Rhodesia, as chronicled by the Bingham Inquiry, but the House of Lords rejected this proposal, and the whole subject was allowed to lapse following the Conservative election victory the following year. In 1966 a joint Select Committee inquired into the subject of theatre censorship, but since then although the House of Lords has frequently employed Select Committees in an *ad-hoc* way to examine proposals for legislation (for example Lord Byers's Foreign Boycotts Bill in 1978), or to inquire into specified subjects (for example the causes and implications of Britain's deficit in manufactured goods in 1984), no joint committees have been used. In 1980 when the Commons disbanded its Select Committee on Science and Technology, the Lords appointed such a committee.

It is worth considering the possibility that some of these might have been joint committees. The Lords can provide a level of expertise and experience, in some areas at least, unmatched by the Commons, while the lower House does have the possibility of exercising a political clout unattainable by the peers. Furthermore it would seem that the Lords has less of a problem than the Commons in securing members willing to serve on at least some Select Committees.

The small quantity of legislation linked to foreign affairs and sponsored by the FCO was mentioned by several of those interviewed for this book as a reason for the FCO being less in touch with the ways of Parliament than other departments in the period preceding the Falklands conflict. It seems to be the case that FCO ministers have less reason to attend the House regularly than their colleagues in domestic departments and of course they are frequently overseas. FCO officials also spend a large part of their career abroad and therefore have less opportunity to be involved in day-by-day parliamentary business. Since the Falklands episode this problem has been formally recognized and the FCO is making greater and more organized efforts to keep in touch, specifically by encouraging MPs to visit the department for routine discussions as well as briefing sessions before and after foreign trips. The FCO is also in regular contact with the staff of the Select Committee on Foreign Affairs.

Chapter 2 also runs through the great variety of procedural devices which may be employed to bring about debates on foreign affairs in the House of Commons. At first glance the procedural aspect may seem arcane by comparison with the subject matter and an observer might wonder whether it is of any significance that, for example, famine in Africa might be debated under the Estimates procedure, on an Opposition day or on a Government motion for the adjournment. The significance lies in the fact that the different procedures derive from differences in the way in which the subject of debate is determined. In this example the debate on famine in Africa would have been chosen by the Liaison Committee (the committee bringing together the back-bench chairmen of Select Committees) in the first case, by the Opposition front bench in the second (or, on certain days, by one of the minor parties) and by the Government in the third. Other procedures, also described in Chapter 2, give individual back-bench MPs the opportunity to choose the topic of debate. Time on the floor of the House is strictly rationed for most types of business and there are always many rival claims for its use. The effect of having a range of different procedural devices available is that time on the floor of the House is spread around different groups and individuals and no single interest can monopolize the Commons' foreign affairs agenda. This is not to say that every legitimate topic will find its way on to that agenda. Those of overwhelming importance usually do. Other matters, which may be of great urgency and importance to some MPs, are subject to the luck of the draw in ballots for Private Members' motions, adjournment debates (including those following a Consolidated

Fund Bill) and Oral Questions. If all else fails there is always the possibility of a business question (asking the Leader of the House to provide time for a debate, and making a point about its salience in passing) or an Early Day Motion.

It is a regular feature of the Question Session which follows the Thursday afternoon Business Statement by the Leader of the House that many MPs make requests for debates which the Leader is unable to satisfy. The Leader rarely refuses outright, but frequently suggests that the topic in question might suitably be aired in time other than that controlled by the Government. It has been common in the past for demands to be made for more foreign affairs debates in Government time. In some ways the subset of MPs with a particular interest in foreign affairs is just like all the other subsets in hoping for more parliamentary time. By the 1988–89 session, however, demand was growing not just for more time, but for a different kind of debate, focusing on a particular region of the world.

In the 1989–90 session the dramatic turn of events in Eastern Europe did indeed give rise to a series of debates confined to developments in that region, but at the time of writing it is not clear that there has been any longer-term shift in thinking on the desirability of more narrowly focused foreign affairs debates.

While foreign affairs debates are still relatively infrequent and foreign policy issues rarely arise directly from the consideration of legislation, the House of Commons does have at its disposal one specialized instrument entirely devoted to monitoring the FCO.

The Foreign Affairs Committee, which was set up in 1979 in succession to the Defence and Foreign Affairs sub-committee of the Expenditure Committee, does not feature very prominently in our case studies, except in respect of Gibraltar, the subject of an inquiry in 1981.[1] The FAC has not considered Libya other than in the context of diplomatic immunities under the Vienna Convention;[2] most of the committee were abroad in connection with another inquiry at the time of the US bombing raid on Tripoli. The committee had not looked at Chile, nor did it examine the INF Treaty until after it had been signed.[3]

The impact of any particular Select Committee report depends a great deal on its timing. The influence of the committee is probably at its highest when it is slightly ahead of the game, having prepared its evidence and reached some conclusions just as the issue crystallizes into political controversy and substantive debate in Parliament.

An example of this was the impact (in Canada not less than Britain) of the three reports produced by the committee in 1981 on the matter, very contentious in Canada, of the patriation of the Canadian Constitution.[4] Such occasions are rare, partly because of the long gestation period of most Select Committee reports.

The practice of the FAC since its inception has been to deliver two or three major reports to the House each session and a similar number of shorter ones. The timing is rarely perfect, but the committee was unusually well-prepared for the European revolutions of 1989, having completed a general inquiry on *Eastern Europe and the Soviet Union*[5] and embarked on a new inquiry into Western Europe integration.[6] Several members of the committee made well-informed contributions to the debates on these themes already mentioned. The committee was also very active and influential on the subject of Hong Kong in 1989 and 1990.

As with other departmental Select Committees, the Foreign Affairs Committee has acquired a certain informal status which is distinct from its formal work of reporting to the House of Commons. The chairman of the committee in particular, and sometimes the senior Opposition rep-resentative too, is in regular demand to be interviewed on radio and television as a person whose opinion on any foreign affairs issues is likely to be valuable. The chairman is presumed to have a 'direct line' to ministers and may also have considerable influence within his own party. Since 1987 both the chairman and the senior Opposition member of the Foreign Affairs Committee have been former Cabinet ministers (David Howell MP and Peter Shore MP). The status accorded to the chairman of the FAC by the broadcast media was particularly apparent during the early stages of the Gulf Crisis in August 1990. Parliament was in recess when Iraq invaded Kuwait on 2 August and was not to be recalled until early September. During August David Howell was repeatedly inter-viewed on radio and television and was at times the only back-bench MP whose views on the crisis reached the public at large.

Could the Foreign Affairs Committee have a greater impact? The impact of the committee at present may be measured in terms of the number and quality of its reports and also in terms of the individual contributions which members and (to a lesser extent) former members of the committee make towards deliberations of the whole House. The quality of reports is already high, given the limitations inherent in consensual reporting across party lines. The number of reports could, perhaps, be increased, but then the limitations inherent in the small size of the committee would begin to impose themselves. A substantially higher output would almost certainly require the committee to delegate more of its work to sub-committees, as is the practice of its two counterpart committees of the US Senate and House of Representatives.

The committee does have some experience of this. From 1979 to 1983 it operated a sub-committee on overseas aid. This sub-committee was not recreated after the 1983 General Election. One of the difficulties appears to have been a common problem in committee work: as long as a main committee insists on its right to determine the contents of all of the reports issued in its name the creation of a sub-committee causes more work, not less. If the Foreign Affairs Committee were to be greatly enlarged, on the US model, and a whole network of sub-committees established, the likelihood of friction between the main committee and a sub-committee might be reduced, but that would be to impose on the House of Commons a style of committee work to which it is not accustomed and to remove the Foreign Affairs Committee from the structure of near-identical departmental committees established in 1979.

Of the twenty chambers of the EC national Parliaments, all have Foreign Affairs Committees, with the exception of the House of Lords, and of the two Chambers of the Oireachtas, where the Seanad and the Dáil have joint committees on EC affairs and on Co-operation-with-developing Countries. The number of members of Foreign Affairs Committees is normally between twenty and forty. The exceptions are the smaller countries (eleven in Luxembourg, fifteen in the Netherlands Senate, seventeen in Denmark), and the larger countries (seventy-two in the French National Assembly and fifty-two in the French Senate, fifty in Greece, where the committee deals with both Foreign Affairs and Defence, and forty-nine in the Chamber of Deputies of Italy). The Foreign Affairs Committee of the House of Commons, whose eleven members match those of the equivalent committee of the Luxembourg Chamber, can by comparison to its peers in other national parliaments thus be said to be seriously under strength.

A modest increase in membership from the present figure of eleven could perhaps be justified on the grounds that the Foreign Affairs Committee represents a special case among departmental committees. Without necessarily creating a sub-committee the committee could, if it had a larger membership, decide to operate an informal system whereby some members take a more active part in one inquiry and a less active part in another. To some extent this already happens and it is rare for all eleven members of the committee to travel on a particular fact-finding mission abroad. A modest increase in membership could promote a degree of specialization within the committee and increase its output, assuming that increased staff and resources were also made available. It would also gradually expand the pool of past members of the committee in the House and therefore raise the general level of awareness of foreign affairs issues.

Chapter 3 looked at the treaty process, a corner-stone of parliamentary power over foreign relations in many states with written constitutions, but a rather obscure matter at Westminster. Until 1924 the House of Commons had no formal role in the treaty-making process, which was reserved as a prerogative matter. The establishment of the first Labour Government under the Prime Ministership of Ramsay MacDonald brought to the Foreign Office Arthur Ponsonby, who created the mechanism still used today whereby treaties requiring ratification are laid before Parliament for at least twenty-one days before ratification takes place. Our study of the current workings of the Ponsonby Rule demonstrates that it works effectively for treaties of major political significance which no Government would in any case be likely to conclude without being certain of its support in the House of Commons. The weakness of the present system is that there is a growing tendency for binding international agreements of lesser political significance to be concluded without provisions for ratification. These agreements are reported to Parliament only when they reach the Treaty series and are already in force. Even for treaties which are subject to ratification and are laid as Command Papers before the Government is fully bound by them, there is no formal scrutiny process and therefore no formal means of alerting MPs to their possible significance.

While there might be a logical case to be made for a formal change in the powers of Parliament in respect of treaties, such a change would disturb a deeply entrenched constitutional principle, namely that the ultimate responsibility for forming and maintaining legal as well as political relations between the UK and other states lies not with Parliament, but with ministers (who are, of course, usually Members of Parliament) acting under the Royal Prerogative and answerable to Parliament.

Some changes could be effected without constitutional upheaval. A small scrutiny committee on similar lines to the House of Commons Select Committee on European Legislation could sift draft treaties subject to ratification and make recommendations either to the whole House or else to departmental Select Committees that particular drafts be examined further. A slightly more radical change would be to include within the remit of such a committee all drafts of binding agreements whether or not they are subject to ratification and the existing Ponsonby Rule. As with the European Legislation Select Committee there could be arrangements for the normal mechanism to be overridden in cases of urgency. Whether or not the agreements not requiring ratification were included, the workload would not be heavy. When, in the past, the Foreign Affairs Committee of the French National Assembly had little else to do but scrutinize treaties it became known as a refuge for lazy deputies (*Le Monde*, 15 May 1987).

Chapter 4 delved into the less visible world of MPs' informal activities in the realm of foreign affairs. Here the line separating the 'monitoring' function of Parliament from direct parliamentary participation in international relations melts away. A group of MPs may travel to a foreign country under the auspices of the Inter-Parliamentary Union or at the invitation of some institution in the country concerned and make a political impact in a number of different ways. They might, for example, hold private discussions with local politicians and seek to influence them in a particular direction. They might make public statements while abroad designed to support, embarrass or otherwise bring pressure on the host government, for example over its human rights policy. The same group might form an impression that British diplomatic representation in the country in question is inadequate or under-resourced and make a point of reporting the situation on their return. Once back home they might report privately to an FCO minister or to FCO officials and to other members of their party, for example to its front-bench foreign affairs spokesmen. Some members of the group might then seek to use their experiences to contribute to proceedings on the record, through an adjournment debate perhaps, or an Oral Parliamentary Question. At any stage the group might have contact with other actors in international relations, for example with foreign embassies in London or with pressure groups such as the Anti-Apartheid Movement, Greenpeace, Peace Through Nato or Amnesty International.

The conclusion was reached in Chapter 4 that this semi-submerged world of parliamentary activity taking place away from the floor of the House of Commons and outside of the Foreign Affairs Committee is of growing significance. The amount of foreign travel undertaken by Members of Parliament seems to be increasing, as does the amount of organized lobbying by foreign embassies and private organizations interested in British foreign policy. Questions inevitably arise about the vulnerability of Members of Parliament to manipulation by special interests. The worry is not so much that corrupt or improper influence might be sought, but rather that MPs might be plied with and influenced by unbalanced and inaccurate information. That there is concern about some aspects of foreign affairs lobbying is demonstrated by the fact that in April 1989 the Select Committee on Members' Interests decided to take evidence on the nature and scale of the Bophuthatswana lobby, an organized campaign to persuade the British Government that it should recognize the independence of the Bophuthatswana territories in South Africa.[7]

The four case studies included in this book attempt a perspective different from that of the preceding chapters, by offering an analysis of Parliament at work on specific foreign policy issues. While in other chapters we have tried to describe procedures and processes with the help of examples, in the case studies we try to reintroduce the political context and ask questions about the influence of Parliament on matters affecting foreign policy. There are obvious methodological difficulties in this approach: the events described are very recent and our knowledge of them lacks the detail which may eventually come with the opening of the relevant archives and the publication of memoirs. A certain amount has been gleaned from interviews, but the main sources have been the official reports of Parliament itself. These are difficult to analyse. *Hansard* provides a coherent and somewhat sanitized version of speeches uttered in the two Chambers and in committee rooms, but it rarely conveys the atmosphere which can alter the sense of a remark. It does not give any indication, for example, of how many Members were present in the Chamber at a particular moment unless the fact is alluded to by one of the speakers. Some of the words uttered are carefully weighed, others not. Often there are but subtle hints at the political point which the speaker is trying to make. The context counts for a great deal.

We have not included a case study of the Falklands episode, despite the amount of parliamentary time and energy devoted to it in 1982–83. The theme is a big one which has received much attention already.[8] Allusions to the Falklands may be found at several points in this book and we hope that the more manageable case studies included here may throw some light on the Falklands too.

The nearest parallel to the Falklands issue, at least in its pre-1982 phase, is probably provided by Gibraltar (Chapter 6). Following the single issue through *Hansard* over a period of fifteen years, Christopher Hill found a record of near-continuous parliamentary interest in Gibraltar and a definite example of parliamentary influence on Government in the case of the decision to confer the full rights of UK citizenship on the Gibraltarians.

A surprisingly large number of individual MPs (133) became involved in the Gibraltar issue in the course of the period studied but this number conceals a much smaller hard core of long-term 'activists', most of whom were linked to an All-Party Gibraltar Group. The activists numbered around ten. The pre-1982 'Falklands lobby' in Parliament was much the same size. The Gibraltar lobby was characterized by its persistence and willingness to nag away at the Government of the day by means of Questions, EDMs and occasional adjournment debates. It may be difficult for a small group to maintain continuity across Parliaments, particularly if key activists are lost (e.g. Albert McQuarrie at the 1987 General Election), but the continuous involvement of back-benchers may exceed that of ministers and their civil servants, who rarely stay at the same desk for more than three years.

Hill's conclusion was that the Gibraltar issue, involving as it does a symbolic test of British values and commitment, was one on which parliamentary influence could be decisive. The call to prevent a 'sell-out' (assuming that the Government and the FCO, more interested in Spain than Gibraltar, might, left to their own diplomatic instincts, have compromised over the sovereignty of Gibraltar in the same way that they were prepared, before 1980, to compromise over the Falklands) appealed to MPs of all parties. There are few issues with quite the same chemistry as Gibraltar and the Falklands. Some of the same arguments were and are applicable to Hong Kong, but the scale is quite different. Not only is the population of Hong Kong much greater and the history of British involvement different, but also ministers and back-benchers have been acutely conscious that the political and military implications of a decision to defy China on behalf of Hong Kong placed the latter in a category quite distinct from Gibraltar and the Falkland Islands. Parliamentary interest in Hong Kong has been intense, but it has never crystallized into a single 'lobby' with a simple policy recommendation. In 1989–90 a parliamentary battle was to break out over the sensitive issue of British passports for Hong Kong people. Inevitably this exposed much deeper divisions in the House of Commons than had the corresponding debate over Gibraltar.

The case study of the Libyan raid presented in Chapter 7 is of a different nature. Here the focus was on a single unexpected event in which the UK was involved only indirectly (as the host country for the US Air Force planes which bombed Libya), but which raised important questions about UK relations with the USA and the uses to which the USA might put its military assets in the UK. The study finds that a large number of MPs asked questions, made interventions or spoke in the debates which took place in the days immediately following the raid. A total of eighty-eight MPs and forty-two peers expressed views or implied them by the slant of their Questions. The procedures proved sufficiently flexible for the business of both Houses to be altered at short notice and allowed many different views to be expressed. From the political point of view the House of Commons was by far the more important focus and the debate in the House of Lords was distinctly secondary. The issue was also debated in the European Parliament, but this fact seems to have had no discernible impact on the British Government. The political outcome was that the Commons endorsed the Prime Minister's decision, but in such a way as to suggest that there would be no open-ended commitment to respond in the same way in the future. To this extent the House of Commons might be said to have issued a warning to both the British and US Governments and to have exerted an influence over how such matters might be dealt with in the future.

The third case study (Chapter 8), on the handling of the INF Treaty negotiations, was also partly concerned with UK–US relations. In this case it is very difficult to detect anything which could be described as parliamentary influence on the executive. The negotiations on intermediate-range nuclear forces (INF) vitally affected the UK, because the US weapons concerned were partly based in the UK and the Soviet weapons concerned were partly aimed at the UK. Even had the threat been limited to continental Europe, UK interests would still have been deeply affected. The negotiations at Geneva did not involve the UK, but were between representatives of the USA and USSR only. The UK Government was kept informed through NATO consultation mechanisms, but not through direct participation. The only question for the House of Commons, for most of the period concerned, was whether or not to back the Government's decision, announced in 1979, to accept the

US missiles if negotiations to ban them on both sides did not succeed. With a few exceptions noted in the chapter the House of Commons divided on party lines on this issue. The Liberal and Social Democratic parties distinguished their position by calling for a dual-key arrangement to ensure a British veto on the use of the missiles, which the Government refused. Frequently the debates were emotional and acrimonious, but sometimes they reflected the finer nuances of the issue as well as the stark political choices.

There came a point in the negotiations, in the spring of 1987, when Parliament could have assumed a more prominent role had it not been for the General Election. In the Federal Republic of Germany the coalition Government had reservations about Gorbachev's double-zero offer. Some of its members would have preferred to retain some intermediate-range capacity with land-based nuclear missiles and remove short-range missiles on both sides instead. A similar opinion was held by some NATO commanders and was shared by some politicians in the UK. In most of the Western European countries affected parliaments were consulted before the Governments announced their decision. In the UK the Conservative Government announced its acceptance of 'double-zero' during the election campaign which had prevented a debate in Parliament. There is no reason to believe that Parliament would have withheld its endorsement in the circumstances.

The episode may serve as a reminder of the limitations of parliamentary influence in another sense. Parliament breaks for long summer recesses (from the end of July to mid-October) and is periodically dissolved for new elections. Emergency recalls of the House of Commons during the summer recess have been rare, if recalls for the sole purpose of dissolution are excluded. There have been only seven such occasions since 1945, of which five were caused by foreign crises (Korea in 1950, Suez in 1956, Berlin in 1961, Czechoslovakia and Nigeria in 1968, Kuwait in 1990).

The INF episode was played out in a House of Commons in which the governing party had successive large majorities and was united within itself on the broad principles of its nuclear defence policy. These circumstances have not always prevailed in the past. There was enough interest and knowledge of these matters displayed in the Commons in the 1980s to suggest that a Government with a small majority might have been in difficulty, unless its defence and arms control policy enjoyed bipartisan support.

Arms control negotiations are primarily the responsibility of the FCO (though clearly the MoD has a strong interest too), but do not at present fit easily into foreign affairs debates. Since the 1990s may well witness significant negotiations in which the UK is a direct participant (unlike INF) there might be a case for the Government to make a regular report to

Parliament and to hold an annual debate specifically on arms control, with ministers from the FCO and MoD taking part. Time for this could be found by bringing the format of the armed services debates into line with the division of ministerial responsibility in MoD. Thus in place of the present navy, army and air force debates there could be debates on defence procurement, the armed forces (personnel) and arms control, the last of these with FCO participation.

The final case study (Chapter 9), on Chile, looks at another kind of lobbying operation over a span of years. It differs from the Gibraltar question in that no great 'British' issue was at stake and there were, in effect, two lobbies operating, one linked to each side of a political conflict in a distant country. The situation is not dissimilar in this respect to many others (e.g. Nicaragua, Sri Lanka, Cyprus).

The Chile study shows how a great deal of lobbying effort by organizations outside of Parliament may produce only a small trickle of parliamentary activity on the record, but succeed none the less in keeping the issue under scrutiny and thereby limit the freedom of action of the Government. Without such scrutiny Governments might act no less responsibly in what they regard as the national interest, but they might also reach different conclusions as to the correct balance between ethical, commercial and diplomatic considerations. Compromises have frequently to be made. In the later 1980s, for example, the British Government was faced with a series of awkward decisions about its relations with Libya, Syria, Iran and Iraq in the light of actions taken by the Governments of those states. In each case ministers had to take into account the reaction that their decision was likely to receive from a sceptical House of Commons and in particular from those back-benchers known to have a continuous and well-informed interest in the Middle East.

The role of Parliament can be a positive one in this context if there are a sufficient number of well-informed back-benchers covering each area of the globe in which Britain has significant interests. There is no fixed number which could be regarded as 'sufficient'. On some occasions one or two respected voices might be sufficient to change the perception of fellow MPs, ministers, journalists and members of the public watching on television as to how a particular statement had been received. Our research has shown that the number of back-benchers making regular contributions to debates, questions and statements on foreign affairs is fairly large but the appearance is deceptive because many are interested in only one region or topic. In Chapter 4 Michael Lee identified a community of about 130 Members of the House of Commons in the 1983–87 Parliament who devoted a considerable proportion of their time to foreign affairs. This community could be subdivided in a number of different ways according to the nature of the involvement. Around one-third (40–45) would probably have regarded themselves as foreign affairs 'specialists'. The situation might be illustrated by a series of concentric circles in which only the inner circle represents those MPs with an interest in foreign policy as a whole. The outer circles would represent those MPs with deep, but geographically limited interests, and then those with only occasional and limited interest. It was the judgement of several of those who spoke to the Study Group that the number of MPs with sufficient interest and knowledge to see foreign policy in its broader interrelationships (that is not just from the point of view of a particular interest, however legitimate) is not large enough and may have diminished in recent years.

This judgement is based partly on the perception that there are now fewer MPs than there once were who have served in the armed forces abroad or, for example, in colonial administration. This may be misleading. A considerable number of younger MPs have worked abroad in business, diplomacy or teaching. There is also a sizeable set of ex-Members of the European Parliament (nineteen elected or re-elected in 1987). A more serious problem appears to be that few MPs seem to see much electoral mileage or career advantage in foreign affairs. Electoral mileage and career advantage are naturally connected. Domestic issues such as inflation, employment, local government, health, education and social security are seen to be the issues which win and lose elections and make or unmake parliamentary reputations.

Those perceptions in turn stem from the belief that the electorate is either not interested in 'abroad' or else cannot understand political arguments about the complex outside world and also that, even if the voters were more interested, it would be unwise to adopt a strongly partisan vote-seeking approach to foreign policy. There could, after all, be great dangers in exposing domestic political choices to manipulation by foreign governments. For one reason or the other it is unlikely that the salience of foreign affairs in the eyes of MPs will be raised by electoral considerations. It is more likely to be raised by the Europe Question and a growing sense of interdependence in the world as a whole.

There is some evidence that this may already be happening as more MPs are nudged towards an interest in international relations by their primary interest in trade, interest rates, immigration, drugs, terrorism, environment or whatever. There is an increasing awareness of the linkages between the UK and Europe East and West which has served to bring more MPs into the orbit of foreign affairs. Domestic issues may indeed win elections, but they can no longer be tackled exclusively on a national basis.

Chapter 10 looked at European Political Co-operation and its impact on the House of Commons. EPC is the formal name for the process of consultation and joint action by the foreign ministers of the European

Community 'Twelve' in respect of their political relations with the rest of the world. It is the germ of a common foreign policy and as such could eventually develop in such a way as to reduce the Parliament at Westminster to the status of a mere regional assembly with no more competence in foreign policy than the Landtag of Baden-Würtemburg or the Tasmanian House of Assembly. This development is still far from realization. The following Written Question and Answer appeared in *Hansard* on 9 November 1988:

European Community (Foreign Policy)

Mr Cran: To ask the Secretary of State for Foreign and Commonwealth Affairs if he will make a statement on the extent to which Britain's foreign policy remains independent of the other member states of the European Community.

Mr Eggar: Britain's foreign policy remains British. Within the framework of European political co-operation we have an obligation to inform and consult our European partners on matters of general interest. The ability of the Twelve to speak and act together is significant help in achieving British objectives.

(col 203W)

The Foreign Affairs Committee drew attention to the 'potential for the erosion of national competence' presented by the section on EPC in the Single European Act.[9] Returning to the same subject in the 1989–90 session the committee found that 'so long as EPC sticks strictly to the consensus approach we see no evidence to justify these fears'.[10] They noted the view of the Foreign Secretary that certain individual countries retained national policy interests in particular parts of the world which they were 'not prepared to put totally at the disposal of EPC'. The disagreement over South Africa at the EC Dublin Summit of February 1990 and the decision of the UK to lift unilaterally one of the sanctions agreed in EPC in September 1986 indicated that the UK was one such country. The Foreign Affairs Committee also noted that one of the effects of the Single European Act had been to enlarge the role of the European Parliament in EPC.[11] It also found some support in EC countries, especially Spain, for the further development of EPC to include a voting procedure instead of the present reliance on consensus and for other developments such as the greater involvement of the EC Commission in EPC and its extension into security matters. The committee concludes

All three proposals for change would clearly have major implications for the freedom of manoeuvre of British foreign policy and would involve a transfer of decision-making from the Westminster parliament to EC institutions. For the present, it is clear that interaction between EPC and the EC's own policies will continue to strengthen; and that the 'political' element in a whole range of other matters will increase, whether or not EPC is altered

institutionally, as shown by the fact that the distinctions between EPC and
EC are getting increasingly blurred.

(para 60)

Clearly the FAC is pointing here to a possible trend within the process of
European integration which the House of Commons as composed at
present might find most uncongenial. The committee declares itself
unconvinced about the priority being given in other European countries
to the 'deepening and accelerating' of EC integration.[12] We saw in
Chapter 2 that in the Commons debate of 22 February 1990 the minister
winding up detected a consensus in favour of a 'wider and looser' Europe
which would be incompatible with a tightly harmonized common foreign
policy.

Whatever the outcome of this European debate in the 1990s, Parliament
at Westminster will want to keep a careful check on EPC until such time as
it feels ready to give up its competence in foreign policy. Chapter 10
indicated that at present the House of Commons' awareness and scrutiny
of EPC is rather haphazard. The inclusion of EPC in periodic government
reports to the House on *forthcoming* summits, as recommended by the
Select Committee on Procedure in *The Scrutiny of European Legislation*
might help to remedy this.

Another possible remedy would be to broaden the terms of reference of
the existing Commons Committee on European legislation to cover
European Affairs in a wider definition, including EPC. On the European
Continent, most of the twenty Chambers of the national Parliaments of
the Community Member States have established a Committee on EC
Affairs. In fact, only the Bundestag, the Hellenic Parliament, the
Luxembourg Chamber of Deputies and the Belgian Senate have not done
so; in the Bundestag, the Europe Committee became in 1987 a sub-
committee of the Foreign Affairs Committee. The Italian Chamber of
Deputies has specifically charged its Foreign Affairs Committee with the
task of monitoring EC affairs. In France both Chambers have appointed
Delegations on EC affairs, which act *grosso modo* as committees. The House
of Commons Procedure Committee considered the creation of a new and
separate Select Committee on European Affairs in its aforementioned
report on *The Scrutiny of European Legislation*, but concluded that this
would not be feasible. In its reply to the report the Government accepted
this recommendation.[13]

We have looked at the strengths and weaknesses of the British
Parliament in relation to international relations and have found that the
constitutional limitations on its power in this field are matched by
limitations of interest and awareness, but that the procedures are
sufficiently flexible to allow a significant parliamentary input into most
foreign policy situations. If there is a major weakness it is perhaps that the

burden of delivering an informed and nuanced parliamentary response to a given situation rests on too small a corps of interested MPs. We did not set out to make recommendations and have discovered no simple recipes for reform, but we would suggest that an agenda for possible change should include the following items:

1 *A review of the provision of 'Government' time for foreign affairs debates*   Until recently most of this has consisted of general *tour d'horizon* debates. More of this time might usefully be allocated to specific regions or topics. Even in the absence of momentous developments occasional half-day debates on regions such as the Middle East or Southern Africa might be helpful.

2 *Opportunities for debating developments in arms control*   Arms control falls squarely between foreign affairs and defence and does not always receive the attention which it deserves. The time currently devoted to the three armed service debates is under-utilized at present and could be redistributed so as to include an annual debate on arms control.

3 *The size of the Foreign Affairs Committee*   A modest enlargement might enable the committee to cover more ground and have a greater impact on the House.

4 *Improvements in the scrutiny of European Political Co-operation*   These would concentrate on making Parliament more aware of developments in EPC and linking them to consideration of foreign affairs as a whole.

5 *A review of the working of the Ponsonby Rule*   This would aim to establish a more consistent mechanism for scrutiny of all significant external commitments entered into by the Government.

In a parliamentary democracy such as the UK aspires to be, all Government policy and decision-making has to be subject to parliamentary scrutiny which is carried out on behalf of the general public and in the light of public opinion. Parliamentary activity in the broadest sense (which may sometimes include influence exerted behind the scenes) serves to reflect the public view, and, in so far as it is conducted openly, may also influence that view.

Policies and decisions in the realm of foreign policy are no different, despite the British constitutional traditions which urge otherwise; foreign policy is conducted against the political background of what the public and hence Parliament want and will tolerate. This may not always be apparent in matters of detail, but when strategic choices have to be faced (e.g. to join the European Community or not) or when crises suddenly erupt (Suez, the Falkland Islands, Kuwait) Government decisions have to take account of parliamentary opinion and ministers are bound to ask themselves: how will the House of Commons react?

The quality and wisdom of that reaction is then the responsibility of the House of Commons itself. There is no magic which endows the House with wisdom. There are no substitutes for knowledge, experience and judgement. Without a lively and continuous awareness of the foreign dimension to public policy Parliament will not be in a position to meet the challenge.

Notes and references

1 Introduction

1 P. Richards (1967) *Parliament and Foreign Affairs*, London: George Allen & Unwin, p. 164.
2 C. Tugendhat and W. Wallace (1988) *Options for British Foreign Policy in the 1990s*, Chatham House papers, London: Royal Institute of International Affairs, pp. 118–99.
3 A. Ponsonby (1915) *Democracy and Diplomacy: A Plea for Popular Control of Foreign Policy*, London: Methuen.
4 F. Flournoy (1927) *Parliament and War*, London: P. S. King and Son.
5 W. Wallace (1976) *The Foreign Policy Process in Britain*, London: RIIA/George Allen & Unwin.
6 Sir George Clark (1956) *The Later Stuarts 1660–1714*, 2nd edn, Oxford: Clarendon Press, p. 13.
7 Cmnd. 8787; HC Deb, 25–26 January 1983, cols 789–870, 920–1,000; HL Deb, 25 January 1983, cols 136–247.
8 C. von Clausewitz (1833) *On War*, translated and edited by M. Howard and P. Paret (1976), Princeton: Princeton University Press, p. 87.
9 See for example the adjournment debate of 26 April 1990, HC Deb, col 619.
10 *The Scrutiny of European Legislation*, Fourth Report, House of Commons Select Committee on Procedure, HC 622 of 1988–89, Cm 1081.
11 *The Review Committee on Overseas Representation*, (The Duncan Committee report) Cmnd 4107, July 1969.
12 The Sachsenhausen case was one of the first to be investigated by the newly-created Parliamentary commissioner (or ombudsman) in 1967. It concerned the way in which the Foreign Office had administered compensation made available under the Anglo-German Agreement of 1964 to UK

victims of Nazi persecution. A group of former inmates of the Sachsenhausen concentration camp claimed to have been unfairly denied compensation by the Foreign Office. The case had been raised in Parliament, but to no avail until the Parliamentary Commissioner's report was debated early in 1968, whereupon the Foreign Secretary agreed to make more money available. The affair seemed to demonstrate that the Foreign Office was out of touch with the House of Commons. An account of the case may be found in E.C.S. Wade and A. W. Bradley (1985) *Constitutional and Administrative Law*, 10th edn, London: Longman, p. 726.

13 C. J. Boulton (ed.) (1989) *Erskine May's Treatise on the Law, Privileges, Proceedings and Usages of Parliament*, 21st edn, London: Butterworths, p. 215.
14 G. Drewry (ed.) (1989) *The New Select Committees: A Study of the 1979 Reforms*, 2nd edn, Oxford: Clarendon Press.

2 Proceedings on the record: the floor of the House, the Foreign Affairs Committee and other committees

1 P. Richards (1967) *Parliament and Foreign Affairs*, London: George Allen & Unwin.
2 HC Deb, 27 July 1989, col 859W.
3 Fourth Report, House of Commons Select Committee on Procedure, 1989, HC 622 of 1988–89.
4 Govt Response to the Procedure Committee's Fourth Report of Session 1988–89: Cm 1081.
5 HC Deb, 12 January 1989, col 996.
6 HC Deb, 27 April 1989, col 1099.
7 HC Deb, 22 February 1990, col 1087.
8 HC Deb, 22 February 1990, col 1163.
9 J. A. G. Griffith and M. Ryle (eds) (1989) *Parliament: Functions, Practice and Procedure*, London: Sweet & Maxwell, p. 350.
10 Griffith and Ryle, op. cit., p. 358.
11 An account of the development of Foreign Office Questions up to the mid-1960s is given in Richards, op. cit., pp. 82–5.
12 Griffith and Ryle, op. cit., p. 382.
13 For example G. Drewry (ed.) (1989) *The New Select Committees: A Study of the 1979 Reforms*, 2nd edn, Oxford: Clarendon Press. Chapter 9 discusses in detail the work of the Foreign Affairs Committee 1979–83.
14 Third Report, House of Commons Foreign Affairs Committee, HC 11 of 1984–85.
15 Minutes of Evidence from the House of Commons Foreign Affairs Committee, Session 1985–86, HC 69-v.
16 See for example the meetings and visits listed in the Second Special Report, House of Commons Foreign Affairs Committee, HC 21 of 1988–89.
17 Fourth Report, House of Commons Select Committee on Procedure, HC 622 of 1988–89; see also First Special Report from the Select Committee on European Legislation, HC 512 of 1989–90.

3 Parliament and treaties

1 Lord Gore-Booth (ed.) (1979) *Satow's Guide to Diplomatic Practice*, 5th edn, London: Longman, pp. 239–69.
2 For a recent survey of parliaments and the treaty-making power see *Constitutional and Parliamentary Information*, 1st series no. 145 (1986, 1st quarter).
3 HC Deb, vol 171, cols 2003, 2005.
4 C. J. Boulton (ed.) (1989) *Erskine May's Treatise on the Law, Privileges, Proceedings and Usages of Parliament*, 21st edn, London: Butterworths, p. 215.
5 P. Richards (1967) *Parliament and Foreign Affairs*, London: George Allen & Unwin, pp. 43–4.
6 HC Deb, vol 171, cols 2003–4.
7 I. Brownlie (1990) *Principles of International Law*, 4th edn, Oxford: Clarendon Press, p. 607.
8 HC Deb, 9 December 1985, col 623.
9 Second Report, House of Commons Select Committee on Defence, HC 233/130 of 1986–87, v.
10 HC Deb, vol 54, cols 918–24.
11 HC Deb, vol 108, cols 481–6.
12 This arose in June 1989 with the extension of the International Coffee Agreement. Because of the summer recess the Government anticipated that it would not be able to observe the normal twenty-one day procedure. It therefore placed copies of the draft resolution in the Commons Library and explained the reason in a Written Parliamentary Answer (HC Deb, 30 June 1989, col 578W).
13 HC Deb, 16 March 1953, col 166W.
14 Comments of M Jean-Marie Daillet, reported in *Le Monde*, 15 May 1987.
15 HC Deb, 21 October 1986, col 853W.
16 P. S. Rundquist (1988) 'Treaties and executive agreements: evolving practices', *CRS Review*, January, 14.

4 Behind the scenes in the House of Commons

1 *Guardian*, 26 February 1990, quoting Oleg Gordievsky on the previous evening's BBC TV's *Panorama*.
2 The author wishes to thank Dr Cliff Grantham and Professor Colin Seymour for their allowing him to see an advance text of their chapter on political consultants, in M. Rush (ed.) (1990) *Parliament and Pressure Politics*, Oxford: Clarendon Press.
3 British–American Group (1989) *Report of Executive Committee 1988–9*, London: British American Group, p. 12.
4 D. Healey (1989) *Time of My Life*, London: Michael Joseph, p. 195.
5 S. Crosland (1982) *Tony Crosland*, London: Jonathan Cape, pp. 323–4.
6 The Annual Report of the British group of the Inter-Parliamentary Union (1982) London: British Group of the Inter-Parliamentary Union.

7 BBC Radio 4, *The Week in Parliament*, 10 February 1990.
8 Interview with Capt Peter Shaw RN, Secretary of the IPU British group, 9 December 1989.
9 J. Douglas (1979) *Parliament's Voice Abroad*, England: Pertlands Publications.
10 Information from CIIR.
11 *Observer*, 21 January 1990.
12 Interview with Mr Jeremy Corbyn MP on 8 December 1989.
13 The lists of visits and funding were prepared from the *Registers of Members' Interests* for the 1983–87 Parliament (HC 249 of 1983–84; HC 197 of 1984–85; HC 240 of 1985–86; HC 155 of 1986–87) and from the annual reports of the British branches of the CPA, IPU and BAG for the same period. The names of those chosen to attend the North Atlantic Assembly and the COE/WEU were taken from *Hansard*.
14 The case of John Browne MP led to a great deal of journalistic comment, e.g. ITV *World in Action*, 15 January 1990; *Independent on Sunday*, 25 February 1990; *Guardian*, 7 March 1990.
15 Ian Findlay gave evidence to the Select Committee on Members' Interests: see HC 44-viii of 1988–89.
16 Andrew Rawnsley's column in the *Guardian* sometimes takes up the theme of Members' interests, e.g. his comments on John Carlisle MP on 13 February 1990.
17 The identification of the forty-nine most active MPs during the 1983–87 Parliament was by an analysis of the figures made available through POLIS, the computer data base that serves Parliament. Suggestions to categorize the types of activists are made on pp. 69–70.
18 Labour MPs blamed the increasing cost of answering Parliamentary Questions on the increasing number of parliamentary consultants: see for example Adam Sage's report in the *Independent*, 1 April 1990.
19 U. Kitzinger (1973) *Diplomacy and Persuasion*, London: Thames and Hudson, pp. 197ff.
20 The *Guardian* (20 April 1990, p. 6) carried a report by Sarah Boseley on the career of George Galloway MP who had been the general secretary of War on Want.
21 *The Review Committee on Overseas Representation* (Sir Val Duncan) (Cmnd 4107, July 1969) benefited from the research interests of Andrew Shonfield.
22 The *Independent* (5 March 1990) published a list of MPs who had not spoken during the last session; this contained a number who had been active in the promotion of overseas interests.
23 W. Preston, jr, and others (1989) *Hope and Folly: The United States and UNESCO 1945–1985*, Minneapolis: University of Minnesota Press, has an appendix (pp. 338–49) which is an account by Gough Whitlam, the former Prime Minister of Australia, of the campaign to get the UK out of Unesco.
24 The All-Party Latin America Group took credit for contributions to the Consolidated Fund debate: see HC Deb, 28 July 1988, cols 708–28; HC Deb, 28 July 1989, cols 1311–29.
25 Michael Marshall MP in his speech to the IPU noted that it had kept open contact between Britain and Guatemala during the twenty-three years when diplomatic relations had been suspended: see *Summary Records of the LXXIXth*

Inter-Parliamentary Conference, Guatemala City, 15 April 1988, p. 138. See also HC Deb, 4 May 1988, cols 466–7W.

26 See Peter Fry's evidence to the Select Committee on Members' Interests, HC 44-viii, p. 215.

5 The House of Lords and foreign affairs

1 On the House of Lords generally see M. A. J. Wheeler-Booth (1989) 'The Lords', in J. A. G. Griffith and M. Ryle (eds) *Parliament: Functions, Practice and Procedure*, London: Sweet & Maxwell; D. R. Shell (1988) *The House of Lords*, London: Philip Allan.

2 Lord Carrington (1988) *Reflect on Things Past: The Memoirs of Lord Carrington*, London: Collins, p. 280.

3 Lord Franks (Chairman) (1983) *Falkland Islands Review: The Report of a Committee of Privy Councillors*, Cmnd 8787, London: HMSO.

4 Carrington, op. cit., p. 370.

5 On Lord Goronwy-Roberts's appointment see Lord Callaghan (1987) *Time and Chance*, London: Collins, p. 294.

6 Baroness Ewart-Biggs (1988) *Lady in the Lords*, London: Weidenfeld & Nicolson, especially at pp. 79, 131.

7 HL Deb, 10 June 1988, col 1609.

8 HL Deb, 16 May 1986, col 1438.

9 HL Deb, 10 June 1988, col 1654.

10 Franks Report, op. cit., Annex F; see also HC Deb, 2 December 1980, cols 195–204.

11 Franks Report, op. cit., para 90.

12 HL Deb, 7 October 1981, cols 146–59.

13 HL Deb, 17 December 1973, cols 42–3.

14 HC Deb, 12 December 1989, cols 880–922; HL Deb, 4 December 1989, cols 604–79.

15 HL Deb, 4 June 1990, cols 1080–208.

16 Private interview with the late Lord Spens.

17 T. Blackstone and W. Plowden (1988) *Inside the Think Tank: Advising the Cabinet 1971–1983*, London: Heinemann, p. 168.

6 Case Study I: Gibraltar and the House of Commons 1977–88

1 These figures have been compiled on the basis of data collected by Dr Pamela Beshoff, whose research assistance in connection with this chapter has been invaluable. The time-span was chosen so as to cover at least a decade, and to commence once the immediate post-Franco concerns had begun to abate. The period ends before the controversy over the SAS shootings of March 1988 had had a chance to distort the figures seriously. The number of *PQs* includes

supplementaries of all kinds; ministerial *replies* are counted as one when they pertain to the same subject and involve repetition; *statements* involved more discussion but were rarer occurrences.

2 See HC Deb, 6th series, vol 123, 30 November 1987, cols 588–9, where Robert Adley MP criticized the Gibraltarians for holding up a possible compromise on European airfares.

3 See p. 88 and HL Deb, 5th series, vol 423, 22 July 1981, cols 241–78.

4 In, for example, the debate of 28 November 1984: HC Deb, 6th series, vol 68, col 928.

5 HC Deb, 6th series, vol 129, 7 March 1988, cols 21–6.

6 HC Deb, 5th series, vol 995, 10 December 1980, cols 1046–52.

7 HC Deb, 6th series, vol 138, 28 July 1988, cols 708–28. See also R. Graham (1988) 'Latin America fails to lure the UK', *Financial Times*, 23 August.

8 *Gibraltar: The Situation of Gibraltar and UK Relations with Spain*, Seventh Report, House of Commons Foreign Affairs Committee, HC 166 of 198–81.

9 ibid., para 207.

10 ibid., para 64.

11 ibid., para 34.

7 Case study II: the Libyan raid

1 T. Zimmermann (1987) 'The American bombing of Libya', *Survival*, May–June, 206, pp. 195–214.

2 *Debates of the European Parliament*, Proceedings from 14–18 April 1986, 158.

3 For a discussion of the strains which this episode put on European Political Co-operation see the case study of the Libyan crisis in A. Pardalis (1987) 'European Political Cooperation and the United States', *Journal of Common Market Studies*, XXV, June, 4, pp. 271–94.

8 Case study III: the INF Treaty

1 L. Freedman (1988) *The Price of Peace*, London: Macmillan, p. 180.

2 L. Freedman (1980) *Britain and Nuclear Weapons*, London: Macmillan, p. 123.

3 J. Haslam (1989) *The Soviet Union and the Politics of Nuclear Weapons in Europe, 1969–87*, London: Macmillan and Birmingham University, p. 113.

4 ibid., p. 123.

5 J. Cartwright MP and J. Critchley MP (1984) *Cruise, Pershing and SS-20: The Search for Consensus: Nuclear Weapons in Europe*, London: North Atlantic Assembly and Brasseys, p. 118.

6 ibid., p. 117. See also C. Marsh and C. Fraser (eds) (1989) *Public Opinion and Nuclear Weapons*, London: Brasseys, p. 127.

7 Cartwright and Critchley, op. cit., p. 118.

8 Haslam, op. cit., p.177.

9 'Double-zero' was debated in the Bundestag on 7 May 1987. For an account of

the political debate in the FRG see S. Peters (1989) 'The Germans and the INF Treaty', *Arms Control*, 10, 1, May, pp. 21–42.

10 *Strategic Nuclear Weapons Policy*, Fourth Report, House of Commons Select Committee on Defence, HC 36 of 1980–81.

11 *The Political Impact of the Process of Arms Control and Disarmament*, Third Report, House of Commons Foreign Affairs Committee, HC 280 of 1987–88.

9 Case study IV: Chile

1 J. Timerman (1987) *Chile: Death in the South*, Harmondsworth: Penguin, p. 8.
2 HC Deb, 28 November 1973, cols 462–583.
3 Both received Written Answers.
4 HC Deb, 17 January 1980, cols 1872 ff.
5 Source: private interview.
6 HC Deb, 15 December 1989, col 13177.
7 A Labour front-bencher estimated that about one letter a day was sent to the party by individuals on Chile, and that isolated constituents might also write to their local MP (source: private interview).
8 Source: private interview.
9 Source: private interview.
10 The help of the FCO, Chilean Embassy in London, the Chilean Campaign for Human Rights and George Foulkes MP in preparing this chapter are gratefully acknowledged.

10 European Political Co-operation

1 *European Political Co-operation*, Official Publications Office of the EC, Luxembourg, 1988.
2 Single European Act, Title III, Article 30 (1).
3 Second Report of the Foreign Ministers to the Heads of State of the EC Member States, July 1973, Part I.
4 Second Report, op. cit., Part II, final paragraphs.
5 *European Political Co-operation*, 3rd edn, published by the Press and Information Office of the Federal Government, Bonn, 1978, point 10.
6 ibid., point 12.
7 Report on European Political Co-operation and the role of the European Parliament (Document 1–335/81); rapporteur on behalf of the Political Affairs Committee: Lady Elles. Resolution adopted on 9 July 1981.
8 Third Report on EPC, London, 1981 Supplement 3/81 to the Bulletin of the European Communities, published by the Commission.
9 See note 7.
10 Solemn Declaration on European Union, Bulletin of the EC, no 6–1983, Section 6. The Greek Government made declarations in the minutes with reference to the development of EPC; the Danish Government made reservations with

reference to EPC, wider influence for Parliament, greater economic and judicial co-operation, and a review of the Declaration by 1988.

11 Single European Act, Title III, para 6(a) and (b). See Supplement 2/86 to Bulletin of the EC, published by the Commission.

12 ibid., para 4.

13 Decision adopted by the Foreign Ministers on EPC, Bulletin of the EC, no 2–1986, point 3.4.1.

14 ibid., part I, para 4.

15 *The Impact of the EP on Community Policies*, Research and Documentation Paper (Action Taken Series no 3), November 1988, published by the Directorate General for Research, EP, Luxembourg.

16 *The Operation of the Single European Act*, Second Report, House of Commons Foreign Affairs Committee, HC 82 of 1989–90, evidence.

17 Extract from *Bulletin of the European Communities*, no. 2, 1986, Luxembourg: Office for Official Publications of the European Communities, pp. 115–6.

11 Conclusions

1 *Gibraltar: The Situation of Gibraltar and UK Relations with Spain*, Seventh Report, House of Commons Foreign Affairs Committee, HC 166 of 1980–81.

2 *The Abuse of Diplomatic Immunities and Privileges*, First Report, House of Commons Foreign Affairs Committee, HC 127 of 1984–85.

3 *The Political Impact of the Process of Arms Control and Disarmament*, Third Report, House of Commons Foreign Affairs Committee, HC 280 of 1987–88.

4 *The British North America Acts: The Role of Parliament*, First Report and Supplementary Report, House of Commons Foreign Affairs Committee, HC 42 and HC 295 of 1980–81; Third Report on the *British North America Acts: The Role of Parliament*, First Report, House of Commons Foreign Affairs Committee, HC 128 of 1981–82.

5 *Eastern Europe and the Soviet Union*, First Report, House of Commons Foreign Affairs Committee, HC 16 of 1988–89.

6 Reported as *The Operation of the Single European Act*, Second Report, House of Commons Foreign Affairs Committee, HC 82 of 1989–90.

7 The evidence appears in HC 44-viii of 1988–89. The growth in the organized lobbying of Parliament is described in another study carried out under the auspices of the Study of Parliament Group: M. Rush (ed.) (1990) *Parliament and Pressure Politics*, Oxford: Clarendon Press.

8 Lord Franks (Chairman) (1983) *Falkland Islands Review: The Report of a Committee of Privy Councillors*, Cmnd 8787, London: HMSO; T. Dalyell (1982) *One Man's Falklands*, London: Cecil Woolf. W. Little (1984) 'The Falklands Affair: a review of the literature', *Political Studies*, XXXII, 2, June; pp. 296–310. C. Christie (1984) 'The British Left and the Falklands War', *Political Quarterly* 55, July–September; pp. 288–307. M. Charlton (1989) *The Little Platoon: Diplomacy and the Falklands Dispute*, Oxford: Blackwell. G. M. Dillon (1989) *The Falklands: Politics and War*, Basingstoke and London: Macmillan.

9 *The Single European Act*, Third Report, House of Commons Foreign Affairs Committee, HC 442 of 1985–86, paras 54–5.

10 *The Operation of the Single European Act*, Second Report, House of Commons Foreign Affairs Committee, HC 82 of 1989–90, para 28.
11 ibid., para 31b.
12 ibid., para 69.
13 *The Scrutiny of European Legislation*, Fourth Report, House of Commons Select Committee on Procedure, HC 622 of 1988–89, Cm 1081.

Index

United States—*cont'd*
  CIA, 54, 127, 138
  Congress, 30, 37–8, 40, 48, 54, 148
  Embassy in London, 56, 70
  INF negotiations, 114–17
  Middle East Policy, 154–5
  relations with European
    Community, 142, 148, 155
USSR, 19, 29, 30, 47, 165
  INF negotiations, 114–17, 120
  KGB, 50
  Supreme Soviet, 47, 68

Van Straubenzee, William, 96
Van den Broek, Hans, 109–10
Venice Declaration, 153–5
Vickers, Baroness, 87
Votes and Proceedings, 42

Wakeham, John, 17–18
Waldegrave, William, 19
Wall, Pat (1933–90), 133
Wall, Patrick (1916–), 96, 106

Walters, Dennis, 26, 55, 106
War Crimes, 89–90
Western European Union, 19, 55, 57,
  66, 69–70, 106
West Indies Act, 89
Whitehead, Phillip, 129
Whitelaw, Lord (William), 107–8
Whitney, Ray, 134
Wilson, Lord (Harold), 58, 82
Winnick, David, 106, 130
Woodhouse, Christopher, 129
World Health Organization, 43
World Peace Council, 62
Wray, Jimmy, 132
Wyatt, Lord (Woodrow), 76, 78

York, Archbishop of (John Habgood),
  108
Young, David, 96
Young, Baroness, 83, 85, 107, 109

Zimbabwe, *see* Rhodesia